Dassel-Cokato Jr. Sr. High School
Library Media Center

As part of a continuing series sponsored by The Foundation of The Dramatists Guild, Inc., these ten plays were produced in association with Circle Repertory Company in the Young Playwrights Festival, April 27 through May 16, 1982, at Circle Repertory Company, New York, New York. Young Playwrights Festival: Gerald Chapman, Artistic Director; Peggy Hansen, Managing Director. Circle Repertory Company: Marshall W. Mason, Artistic Director; Richard Frankel, Managing Director; B. Rodney Marriott, Literary Manager.

THE YOUNG PLAYWRIGHTS FESTIVAL

Ten plays written by

ADAM L. BERGER	JULIET GARSON	STEPHEN GUTWILLIG
JENNIFER A. LITT	KENNETH LONERGAN	SHOSHANA MARCHAND
JOHN McNAMARA	PETER MURPHY	LYNNETTE M. SERRANO
	ANNE PIERSON WIESE	

Directed by

GERALD CHAPMAN ARTHUR LAURENTS MARSHALL W. MASON
ELINOR RENFIELD CAROLE ROTHMAN

With

KATE ANTHONY	JONATHAN BOLT	TIMOTHY BUSFIELD	LUCY DEAKINS
WANDA DE JESUS	TRISH HAWKINS	DAVID LABIOSA	BRUCE McCARTY
ALBA OMS	BURKE PEARSON	JAMES PICKENS, JR.	ZAINA RIVERA
KAREN SEDERHOLM		TED SOD	

| *Sets by* | *Costumes by* | *Lighting by* |
| JOHN LEE BEATTY | ANN ROTH | DENNIS PARICHY |

Sound by

CHUCK LONDON MEDIA
Stewart Werner

Original Music by

LOUIS ROSEN
(It's Time for a Change)

DAVID VALENTIN
(The Bronx Zoo)

Production Stage Manager

JODY BOESE

Stage Manager

KATE STEWART

The Foundation of The Dramatists Guild Board of Directors:

JULES FEIFFER	MURRAY HORWITZ	MARY RODGERS
HERBERT GARDNER	DAVID E. LeVINE	STEPHEN SONDHEIM
RUTH GOETZ	TERRENCE McNALLY	PETER STONE
JOHN GUARE	EVE MERRIAM	RICHARD WESLEY
SHELDON HARNICK		

Cast List for the 1982 YOUNG PLAYWRIGHTS FESTIVAL Staged Readings:

SHEILA ALLEN	MARY CAROL JOHNSON	RICHARD PATELMO
JOCELYN BENFORD	OLEG KARENSKY	ERIC SCHIFF
NEIL BENSON	KEN KLIBAN	DENNIS SCULLY
JOE BREEN	RON MARASCO	KAREN SEDERHOLM
JEFFREY FRANK	CHARLOTTE MOORE	CLAUDE SEEMAN
ROB GOMES	CHRIS MURRAY	SAM SOKOLOW
KEITH GORDON	CHRIS NICKERSON	BERNARD TELSEY
GARDINER HARRIS	CYNTHIA NIXON	MARK WEINTRAUB
MICHAEL HIGGINS	SARAH JESSICA PARKER	MARTY ZONE

Avon Books are available at special quantity discounts for bulk purchases for sales promotions, premiums, fund raising or educational use. Special books, or book excerpts, can also be created to fit specific needs.

For details write or telephone the office of the Director of Special Markets, Avon Books, 959 8th Avenue, New York, New York 10019, 212-262-3361.

THE YOUNG PLAYWRIGHTS FESTIVAL COLLECTION

Ten Plays by Young Playwrights Between the Ages of Eight and Eighteen

Compiled and Edited by
The Foundation of The
Dramatists Guild, Inc.

Preface by
STEPHEN SONDHEIM
Introduction by
GERALD CHAPMAN

A BARD BOOK/PUBLISHED BY AVON BOOKS

THE YOUNG PLAYWRIGHTS FESTIVAL COLLECTION is an original publication of Avon Books. This work has never before appeared in book form.

These plays are protected by Copyright and may not be performed or otherwise presented without the author's written permission. All inquiries should be directed to the playwright in care of The Foundation of The Dramatists Guild, Inc., 234 West 44th Street, New York, New York 10036

PREFACE Copyright © 1983 by The Foundation of The Dramatists Guild, Inc. Reprinted by permission.
INTRODUCTION Copyright © 1983 by The Foundation of The Dramatists Guild, Inc. Reprinted by permission.

The following plays are reprinted by permission of their respective playwrights:
IT'S TIME FOR A CHANGE Copyright © 1982 by Adam L. Berger
SO WHAT ARE WE GONNA DO NOW? Copyright © 1982 by Juliet Garson
THE BRONX ZOO Copyright © 1982 by Lynnette M. Serrano
THE RENNINGS CHILDREN Copyright © 1982 by Kenneth Lonergan
PRESENT TENSE Copyright © 1982 by John McNamara
COLEMAN, S.D. Copyright © 1982 by Anne Pierson Wiese
EPIPHANY Copyright © 1982 by Jennifer A. Litt
BLUFFING Copyright © 1982 by Peter Nicholson Murphy
IN THE WAY Copyright © 1982 by Stephen Gutwillig
HALF FARE Copyright © 1982 by Shoshana Marchand

AVON BOOKS
A division of
The Hearst Corporation
959 Eighth Avenue
New York, New York 10019

Published by arrangement with The Foundation of The Dramatists Guild, Inc.
Library of Congress Catalog Card Number: 82-90928
ISBN: 0-380-83642-4

All rights reserved, which includes the right to reproduce this book or portions thereof in any form whatsoever except as provided by the U. S. Copyright Law. For information address The Foundation of The Dramatists Guild, Inc.

First Bard Printing, May, 1983

BARD TRADEMARK REG. U. S. PAT. OFF. AND IN OTHER COUNTRIES, MARCA REGISTRADA, HECHO EN U. S. A.

Printed in the U. S. A.

OP   10 9 8 7 6 5 4 3 2 1

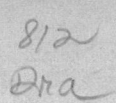

TABLE OF CONTENTS

PREFACE *by Stephen Sondheim*	vi
INTRODUCTION *by Gerald Chapman*	1
IT'S TIME FOR A CHANGE *by Adam L. Berger*	11
SO WHAT ARE WE GONNA DO NOW? *by Juliet Garson*	23
THE BRONX ZOO *by Lynnette M. Serrano*	35
THE RENNINGS CHILDREN *by Kenneth Lonergan*	73
PRESENT TENSE *by John McNamara*	103
COLEMAN, S.D. *by Anne Pierson Wiese*	123
EPIPHANY *by Jennifer A. Litt*	145
BLUFFING *by Peter Murphy*	221
IN THE WAY *by Stephen Gutwillig*	231
HALF FARE *by Shoshana Marchand*	247
BIOGRAPHIES OF CONTRIBUTING AUTHORS	261

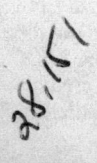

PREFACE

The notion of the Festival first arose in 1977. I had been president of The Dramatists Guild for four years and a subscriber to the London Sunday *Observer* for fifteen. Each year I would read in that paper's magazine section an announcement of the entry rules for the forthcoming annual Young Writers' Play Competition: a competition open to anyone in Great Britain under the age of eighteen, the winning plays to be professionally performed during a two-week period in the spring at the Royal Court Theatre. Each year I'd think, "Why don't we have something like that over here?" and each year I'd answer, "Because it's too difficult to organize, because who knows how to deal with Boards of Education, because no theatre group would be interested, because etc.,..." and do nothing about it. But in the mid-Seventies we were expanding our cultural wings at the Guild and the time suddenly seemed appropriate, so I slammed my gavel down at a council meeting one day, convinced everybody what a wonderful idea such a competition would be and appointed a committee to get it going consisting of Jules Feiffer, who'd had dealings with the New York City schools, Mary Rodgers, who'd written numerous children's books and songs, and myself, to keep convincing everybody what a wonderful idea it would be.

We immediately held a press conference to announce the project, complete with the usual paraphernalia (coffee, pastry, photographer). Alvin Klein, the theatre critic for WNYC, came. Only Alvin Klein came. Jules, Mary and I together with the Guild's executive director David LeVine and a gentleman from the New York City Board of Education (a substitute for the higher-up who cancelled at the last moment) stood in the large, empty, elegant conference room at the Guild and answered his questions (two, I believe). There were long periods of silence, the pastry melted, the stacks of informational flyers, painstakingly prepared, went unthumbed, and we decided the competition was a good idea whose time had not yet come. It was too difficult to organize, no one knew how to deal with the Board of Education, no theatre group was interested, etc.

The notion probably would have remained dormant if I hadn't found myself in London two years later while the Festival at the Royal Court was actually taking place. It was my first opportunity to see what I had only read about for so many years, and it was an experience so moving and exhilarating that I returned to the council with renewed vigor. I wrote to Robert Cushman, the *Observer*'s theatre critic, to find out exactly how the event was organized, and asked Ruth Goetz, a council-member who lived in London at the time, to do some detective work at the Court. She came up with the key to it all: a fellow named Gerald Chapman. I went to England to meet him; and in 1980 he came to work for the Guild and created the program which resulted, among other things, in this book.

Gerald's galvanic intensity and experienced confidence caught fire. The committee was expanded to include Ruth, Eve Merriam, and Murray Horwitz. Council members and other Guild playwrights began accompanying Gerald to his workshops in the schools. We made a liaison with Circle Rep. There was the raising of money, an endeavor theatre writers are all too familiar with but seldom have to do entirely themselves. For these and sundry administrative matters, we hired Peggy Hansen. Shortly thereafter, we were lucky enough to get the invaluable advice and support of Leonard Fleischer, the senior advisor for the arts program of Exxon.

Our highest hopes were realized. The first American Young Playwrights Festival was as moving and exhilarating as the Royal Court's and even more encouraging: in their best years, the Court had received between three and four hundred manuscripts, and these from all over England. Our competition was publicized only in New York and a few scattered outlying districts, yet we received over seven hundred from thirty-five states. I had always assumed that the literacy level of Britain's young people was higher than ours. I was wrong.

As I write, we're planning the second Festival. It would be nice to think that it would be an annual event here, as it is in London. That will take time, money and more Gerald Chapmans. With some luck and a lot of commitment, we can have them all. And when the practicalities become discouraging, we can take heart in the fact that there are hundreds of young writers around who have not yet been totally persuaded that television sit-coms and formless movies and their innumerable (though often numbered) spin-offs represent the state of the narrative art—as the plays in this volume happily prove.

Stephen Sondheim
August 28, 1982

INTRODUCTION

This anthology consists of ten plays written by young people between the ages of eight and eighteen. What they all have in common is that they have shared the platform of a professional stage: seven of them received full-scale productions and three received staged readings as part of the first Young Playwrights Festival. This Festival, at the Circle Repertory Company, New York, in April–May 1982, was sponsored by The Foundation of The Dramatists Guild, and is an annual event focusing on the best work written by young people in the United States. The plays are produced at the highest possible professional standards at a theatre with a recognized national reputation.

The ten plays in this volume were selected from seven hundred thirty-two scripts, submitted from thirty-five states. The only limitation was that of age: writers had to be eighteen or under. We received plays written by six-year-olds, three-act musicals complete with scores, two-page skits, scripts with no dialogue (two such plays consisted entirely of diagrams), puppet-plays (with some of the puppets enclosed in the envelope), pastiches of Agatha Christie thrillers or Beckettian nihilism, agit-prop, melodrama, television soap-opera, and a great deal of what one might call social-realist drama with titles like *A Family Problem in the Chicago Suburbs*. The most obvious fact that emerged from this astonishing variety was the absence of the fantastical, of fantasy for its own sake. Very few scripts told a fairy tale or followed the model of some children's literature and much children's theatre. The plays we received depicted the known world, often one that was distorted or stereotyped by media images of reality, or by archaic notions of theatre (such as characters with double-barreled names sitting in armchairs and trying to sound profound). The good plays were those which depicted the world the writer knew well, a reality which could be presented to the audience with clarity and honesty because it had been experienced. The best plays were able to go one step further and present this reality at one remove from the author: slightly distanced, with a point of view that cast it in some relief, and therefore allowed the audience to judge it not so much against the author's private concerns but the audience's own awareness of the world. This widening of the terms of reference from the private act of creation to the public act of performance is the distinctive quality of the art of theatre; it is what gives it its power, and it is the way the crucial ingredient of empathy is achieved. The different ways in which this process happens define both the stance of a play and what one may call the voice of the writer. In the case of the writers represented in the Young Playwrights Festival it was particularly interesting to observe how the difference in age between an eight-year-old and an eighteen-year-old encompassed more emotional territory than any equivalent period later in life.

Adam Berger's voice, in *It's Time for a Change*, expresses a universal fear of failure in the very particular tale of an eight-year-old's humiliation in front of his classmates in the competitive world of school sports and the gymnasium. The way the play's hero, Kirk, copes with his anxiety is to fulfill in fantasy what he knows he can do in reality: cross-country skiing; except this time it will be in the gym, not on the ski slopes. The commitment to fantasy happens at the moment when Kirk wonders if the teacher will mind if the gym floor is covered with snow, and his father replies, "That's a risk we'll have to take." That line was always greeted with a roar of approving laughter and applause by adults in the audience because they recognized the way the father was being drawn into the child's fantasy. This identification helped the audience itself to accept the fantasy, not simply as a childlike diversion, but as a genuine human need. This was a bold and deftly engineered piece of drama by an eight-year-old playwright who knew exactly the effect he wanted, and who, in rehearsal, took notes on the production and could succinctly point out where improvements had to be made.

Juliet Garson's *So What Are We Gonna Do Now?* also uses fantasy as a distancing device to help us understand the world of two pubescent girls growing up on the violent, male-chauvinist streets of New York. Driven out of the house by hostile or uncomprehending parents (the home scenes poke fun at the crass lack of communication between two generations) the two girls have to survive by their wits, each threatening encounter pointedly forcing them to construct an increasingly unreal role. The finale takes this to its hilarious and logical conclusion when these two twelve-year-olds impersonate prostitutes bent on murdering their clients. The burlesque style does not obscure the awful irony of young girls who are forced to compromise their dignity in order to avenge themselves on their destructive environment.

The Bronx Zoo, by Lynnette Serrano, shares a similar voice of protest about a neighborhood that is especially violent to women. In this play, however, the perspective is far from comic. The central act of appalling violence, which happens offstage, impels the play to its abrupt and shocking denouement, but it is a violence that is insistently foreshadowed from the prologue onwards. As with a Greek tragedy or medieval morality play, the audience can guess the main outline of events, and is invited not so much to see what happens but how and why it occurs. While taking the risk of portraying the cliché of crime in a minority neighborhood, the play tries to provoke an audience to question rather than passively accept an all too familiar scenario. And in performance the play indeed evoked strongly differing responses.

A similarly divided reception greeted *The Rennings Children*, by Kenneth Lonergan, the most elusive of the ten plays. Set in a mental hospital, the play is less about why Paul Rennings is confined to an institution than about his love-hate relationship with his sister who visits him. Mary brings no solace from the outside world and eventually contributes to a further breakdown of her brother's fragile sense of stability. Ironically, Paul appears at one stage to be happier than his sister. But his confinement is never sentimentalized; in two memorable scenes, first with a fellow patient and second when he describes his recurring nightmare, Paul's real situation is agonizingly portrayed. More than the others in this book, this play is susceptible to the nuances of interpretation in performance, for beyond the impressive fluency of the writing is the elusive relationship between brother and sister, a relationship charged with an intangible tension that could almost be incestuous in its passion.

Present Tense, by John McNamara, is a comedy about another young man's self-doubt. Unlike the fantasy in *It's Time for a Change*, which fulfills a little boy's dream to succeed in gym, the fantasy which obsesses Norm only serves to torment him further and drive him to a paroxysm of insecurity. In this case it is his inability to believe that his girl friend really likes him which triggers a series of fantasy sequences in which he imagines her conspiring with the school jock to bring about Norm's sexual humiliation. At one point the play changes tack by portraying Norm, once again in fantasy, trying to enjoy the favors of someone he thinks is a "dumb blonde," but even this encounter ends in rejection. Norm's comment "I can't even have fun in my imagination" exactly defines the guilty pleasures of adolescent sexual feelings.

In *Coleman, S.D.*, Anne Wiese also investigates the contrast between adolescent fantasies and reality, and in particular how these may be limited by class differences. This play is about a classic love-triangle between three adolescents whose friendship, nurtured in the pastoral and carefree atmosphere of summer vacations, is abruptly shattered by one of the girl's becoming pregnant. Hope (a significant name) intends to marry Terry and set up housekeeping, even though this means abandoning their mutual dream of going to college. But Terry remains infatuated with Laurel, who differs from her working-class, provincial friends in her sophisticated, urban, middle-class aspirations. Laurel pours scorn on what she considers Hope's sentimentalized faith in the values of a stable home; and while Hope busies herself with the preparations for her marriage the following day, Laurel and Terry finally declare their love for each other. The ending carefully balances Terry's love for Laurel (and the spirit of arrogant independence she represents) against the sad reality of a working-class couple who find that they cannot afford their teenage dreams anymore.

A very different kind of love-triangle is to be found in *Epiphany*, by Jennifer Litt. Set in an exclusive English school, part of the celebrated Public School system, this play is the most literary and seemingly far removed of the ten in this book.* It deals with a homosexual affair between two boys, and how it is changed by the appearance of a beautiful girl,

---

*In England the term "Public School" actually refers to a private school. Many of these schools were established over a hundred years ago; some were even founded by monarchs in the sixteenth century.

the sister of a new boy at the school. The play contrasts the down-to-earth ordinariness and self-assurance of the love between Richard and Perry with the brittle, rarefied relationship between Richard and Georgina. Even the way the two sets of couples kiss each other is carefully contrasted: the one relaxed and warm, the other frantic and impassioned. But Jennifer Litt's coup de théâtre is to set the whole story in 1912! The differences between the three teenagers are thrown into high relief as we observe an adult world of stiff conventionality and brutality. The cruelty and snobbery of the school system reflect the upper-class reality into which these young people are growing, and to which their ill-fated first love is vulnerable; and it is a reality that will shortly become murderous with the onset of the Great War.

Bluffing, by Peter Murphy, offers a very different perspective on the theme of friendship. This short play makes fun of six men who calmly play poker while surreptitiously and treacherously performing character assassinations behind each other's backs. The game metaphor informs the whole piece, and the blatant cruelty with which this exclusively male group of friends operates is a neat satire on the exclusively male operations of other groups, who play different games, such as some politicians or the Mafia. The inspiration for the play came from Peter Murphy's own experience with his friends, and the distancing device he used was simply to double the ages of the original characters.

The theme of death, whether of the body or of a dream or illusion, is common in the plays young people write. Stephen Gutwillig's *In the Way* investigates the effect of a woman's death on her surviving husband and son. The bereavement redefines the parent-child relationship, releasing long suppressed frustrations and feelings of guilt and anger. On the day of the funeral father and son try to care for each other in ways that do not betray the memory of the woman they loved so very differently. What is "in the way" of this mutual support is not just the piano (a potent symbol of the dead mother) but the recrimination that has festered, like pus in a wound, through the duration of the woman's long and painful illness, and the sacrifices that her condition demanded.

Half Fare, by Shoshana Marchand, also focuses on a parent-child relationship which has gone wrong. In this case the absent mother is divorced, and the father and daughter are left to stake out their emotional territory in the claustrophobic atmosphere of a one-bedroom apartment. Claudia's sexual precociousness is used not simply as a device to embarrass her middle-aged father, but as the springboard into the main theme of the play—her insecurity. She yearns for a discipline, a set of rules and objectives against which she can measure standards of conduct, ways of living. But George finds this anathema, refusing to be stereotyped as a father-figure and fearful of closing off options which he wishes Claudia to experience. Each clings to a fantasy: Claudia, to one of a strong, directive father she can at once love and rebel against; George, to a set of counter-cultural values which provide the necessary alternative to an acquisitive and rapacious society. Each feels betrayed by the other's failure to prove his or her case. In a final desperate attempt to engage her father's elemental feelings of parental possessiveness Claudia threatens to walk out. More than the other plays in this collection, the powerful ending to *Half Fare* indicts an older generation for its weakness and vacillation.

Why have plays by young people not been presented in professional theatres before? Partly because playwriting is rarely taught in schools. The only way a play can be judged is through performance, but this requires some form of drama training on the part of a teacher. It is significant that more than half the authors in the Festival attended schools which have active drama programs. Where there is no such program it is very difficult for teachers to understand that the verbal wit in the playground and the dialect of the streets, the capacity to survive through quick repartee or clownish behavior—these things which many children possess—are the very stuff of drama. They are far removed from the sometimes forbidding requirements of syntax and spelling which are demanded of more formal written work. Instead, the main requirement for playwriting is a vivid awareness of the life around you and inside you, and this awareness, as we find in these plays, is direct and often uncompromising in its voice. School authorities will not necessarily sympathize with this awareness, or at least with the way it is expressed, and that is a further reason why playwriting is not widely taught: it is too risky to take seriously. A common escape route is for the playwriting course never to find its way to the school stage but to end up continually within the confines of a pupil's folder. It is fair to add that children are acutely aware of the status of

Introduction

their creativity, and a play which they write will be worth more to them if it can live on a stage rather than remain dead on the page.

A common handicap for young people who do write plays is that they see very little theatre in comparison to television and cinema, or musical events. Theatre-going is often limited to metropolitan areas. It is also sometimes perceived as having a social cachet which may put people off. In many cases it is simply too expensive for parents to take children, or for teenagers to go on their own. Ironically, the plays which children enjoy most tend not to be shows written specially for them but rather the smash-hit musical. It is as if they sense that children's theatre in this country is considered to be, and treated as, second-rate. Their delight at a Broadway-style show partly consists of an awareness of how special and alien the experience is for them: they are entering unfamiliar, even awe-inspiring territory, especially if the building is a gloriously old-fashioned-looking playhouse. But these precious experiences remain isolated events for most young people: they may reinforce the notion that the theatre is too specialized or exclusive an art for them to enjoy, that it somehow does not belong to them, when in fact the opposite is the case.

The invitation to pretend, which underlies the world of theatre, is irresistible, and children accept it instinctively from the moment they learn to play. Creative dramatics is arguably the most accessible of the arts, and its use in schools in countries all over the world has proved beyond any doubt that it can be enjoyed by any child, irrespective of academic ability. Most children love acting, and it is the natural way to introduce them to playwriting. In one of the playwriting workshops which the Festival has conducted in schools throughout the New York City area I observed a dyslexic nine-year-old painstakingly writing his play for no other reason than because he wanted to play the main part. Yet with all this devotion and sense of fun, with all this inherent passion for dramatizing on the part of children, the professional theatre has so far largely ignored the opportunities which they offer, and has largely ignored its responsibilities to young artists and young audiences. The Young Playwrights Festival, with its emphasis on professional productions, not only stretched out a hand to children but also issued a clarion call to the theatre community, a call which celebrated the legitimate arrival of some new and unfamiliar artists. Quite apart from the merits of the plays themselves, the fuller participation of young people in professional theatre, which the Festival symbolized, helps to widen the base of what is considered valid, and this can only be for the good. It is as if a new spring were located and allowed to mingle with and refresh the main stream.

It is obviously too early to judge the effect of this project on the professional theatre as a whole, but one or two observations can be made. The Festival mounted full productions of apparently unfinished work by authors who had not yet "lived and suffered," and who had not, therefore, supposedly earned themselves the right to be called artists. If people assume that children cannot understand the world around them, the plays in this book prove them wrong. It is, indeed, often the case that even very young children have the knack of penetrating to the core of an issue, of asking the most pertinent questions. And sometimes this knack is embarrassing or even infuriating. Such a quality is one of the hallmarks of a good dramatist: the theatre is at its most healthy when it has the guts to say what it pleases. There are many forces which threaten the theatre's ability to remain provocative, which mute a writer's individual voice by imposing standards of propriety or aesthetic convention. But time and again, especially in the theatre, which is potentially the most embarrassing of all the arts because it is the most public, artists push back the boundaries of what it is possible to see, hear and understand. The Festival's invitation to young dramatists is simply another indication of the theatre's inordinate capacity to allow people to say what they please.

The Young Playwrights Festival took seriously the work of artists who would usually have been considered unformed and immature. Rewrites took place, but not at the expense of the primacy of the author's voice, because in this instance the author was a legitimate partner whose investment in the show was never diminished by his or her collaborators. A shift in power relationships occurred which ensured that the young authors could indeed consider the theatre to belong to them: the platform was *theirs* and nobody else's. The latent power of the stage to move and disrupt with the opinions and passions of an otherwise silent or ignored constituency was the single most radical effect that the Festival could promote, and it was the reason for the electricity that galvanized the audience nightly. For what the Festival discovered was that the best young authors do not conform to a predetermined aesthetic. They write untamed, for themselves. They have not yet learnt the sleight of hand which veils the provocation or disguises the truth; their utterance is direct, at times fearless. They are learning their craft boldly, by testing their image of the world in the crucible of performance. They have not yet had to encounter fully the limitations on the art with which their adult counterparts struggle.

Perhaps playwrights are more often un-made than made. The *New York Times* critic hinted at this when, commenting on *So What Are We Gonna Do Now?* and *It's Time for a Change,* he quipped, "If they were written by adult dramatists, one might say 'Miss Garson and Mr. Berger have regained the spontaneity and imagination of their earlier work.'" Other reviewers also commented, quite without irony, on how much older playwrights could learn from the Festival authors.* My own feeling is that the Festival cut the Gordian knot which ties adult writers into a system that is occasionally crammed with limitations, conventions and assumptions about how to become a produced playwright. To present the work of ten young writers with complete professionalism was, in itself, a provocation to the accepted way of doing things.

The Festival redefines how writers are perceived by honoring their creativity and taking seriously their points of view, however old they are. It asserts Eric Gill's famous dictum, "An artist is not a special kind of person: everyone is a special kind of artist," by inviting for the first time the full participation of children in an art which encourages them to think about life in a different way, an art which teaches them to use their imagination more rigorously and responsibly than does television. It proposes an alternative structure to children's theatre as a way of making the theatre real and alive for children, a place of their own. Especially between the ages of ten and fourteen, children are acutely aware of injustice and the way adult society smudges the line between truth and mendacity: the phrase that is often on their lips is "it's not fair." So there is the added value of allowing this unvarnished view of the world to be expressed in the public arena, a view which can provoke us to think more accurately about how we conduct our lives. Fun-

---

*The *Village Voice* remarked "Berger has what any writer past puberty must sweat blood to recover—his writing is utterly candid."

damentally, the Festival reminds us that we can only encourage the future health of an art if we take seriously our present obligations to the young. By investing in what young artists have to say about what it means to be human today we have a chance to fashion what it may mean to be human tomorrow.

> Gerald Chapman
> August, 1982

IT'S TIME FOR A CHANGE

by Adam L. Berger

CHARACTERS

MRS. SWELL
KIRK SWELL, eight years old

The boys and girls in Kirk's gym class:

ALLAN
BEN
SALLY
BRUCE
JIM
SUSAN
AMANDA

MR. FEND
MR. SWELL

Scene 1

The kitchen of the Swell apartment. MRS. SWELL *is removing groceries from shopping bag as* KIRK *enters.*

KIRK: Hi Ma.
MRS. SWELL: Hi Kirk.
KIRK: Any mail for me?
MRS. SWELL: No. Anything wrong?
KIRK: Mom, I'm no good in gym.
MRS. SWELL: What makes you say that?
KIRK: The boys tease me.
MRS. SWELL: Why Kirk?
KIRK: I'm not good at running.
MRS. SWELL: Anything else?
KIRK: Yes, I'm not good at throwing or catching.
MRS. SWELL: Why don't you practice?
KIRK: Because I don't have enough time.
MRS. SWELL: What do you have to do?
KIRK: I have too much math.
MRS. SWELL: Why don't you practice now and do your homework later?
KIRK: Because there's a special science show I have to watch on television tonight.
MRS. SWELL: Why don't you have your friend record it on his Betamax?
KIRK: Because I have to hand in a report on the show tomorrow.
MRS. SWELL: Well then why don't you talk to Dad about it when he gets home?
KIRK: All right.
[*The phone rings.*]
MRS. SWELL: Hello. Oh, hi dear. How are you? Oh, well, that's okay...sure...Kirk and I will start without you and if

you're late I'll save it. Bye. [*To* KIRK] Dad's got a new supply of goods to sort through to see what needs to be tested. He may not be home 'til late.

KIRK: I don't like it, but I won't argue.

[*Lights dim.*]

Scene 2

Outside the gym—the students are waiting for the teacher to open the doors.

ALLAN: Boy, can you believe the questions on that science test?

BEN: I got a ninety-eight on that test.

ALLAN: What? I only got a fifty-two.

BEN: I studied hard.

[ALLAN *and* BEN *start doing push-ups while* BRUCE *and* JIM *are looking at baseball cards,* AMANDA *and* SUSAN *are gossiping.* KIRK *enters, bends over to tie his shoe.* SALLY *enters and leapfrogs over* KIRK.]

SALLY: Ta-da. Gym is my favorite class.

KIRK: Gym is . . . okay.

ALLAN: I'm the best in the class. I can run the fastest, I can kick the farthest and I can play baseball the best.

KIRK: I'm probably the worst.

ALLAN: That's a fact.

SALLY: What do you mean "probably"?

BRUCE: You make me look like a pro.

[*Enter* MR. FEND.]

MR. FEND: Okay, it's time for class to begin.

[*The kids enter through the gym doors.*]

MR. FEND: Go to your spots and sit down. Okay, before we start I've got a couple of announcements I'd like to make. Mr. DiNuncio, the principal, is coming in next week to observe and I want to show him we've got the best gym class in the school. Okay, everybody up! At ease! Best position. Jumping jacks and: one . . . two . . . three . . . four . . . one . . . two . . . three . . . four. Now, running in place. Okay, now push-ups: one . . . two . . . three . . . four . . . five.

It's Time For A Change

[*During this* MR. FEND *walks over to* KIRK, *who is unable to do even one push-up.* MR. FEND *helps* KIRK *to do his five push-ups. When he is finished the kids make comments and laugh at* KIRK.]

MR. FEND: Oh, you think that's funny? Well then, everybody, five more push-ups.

[*The rest of the class does five more push-ups, with more comments from the kids, including* BEN: Kirk-face.]

MR. FEND: Okay, today we'll start with a race from one end of the gym to another. Two lines of four. Okay, on your mark, get set—[*Whistle*]

[*They race in slow motion.*]

ALLAN: I'm first.

JIM: I'm second.

SALLY: I'm third, but I was almost second.

SUSAN: I guess I'm last.

MR. FEND: That's okay, you'll try again tomorrow, Susan. All right, Allan is the winner. Line up for the second race. On your mark, get set—[*Whistle*]

[*Second slow motion race*]

BEN: I'm first.

AMANDA: I'm second.

BRUCE: I'm third.

[*Everyone looks at* KIRK.]

KIRK: I'm last again.

ALLAN: I wouldn't brag about it if I were you, Kirk.

MR. FEND: Ben's the winner. Now we're going to shoot some lay-ups. Form two lines of four and don't forget to focus before you let the ball spring.

[*They shoot lay-ups,* KIRK *is the last to shoot.*]

BRUCE: If Kirk makes a basket, we'll have a perfect record.

[KIRK *dribbles in but misses.*]

BRUCE: I'll get the ball.

MR. FEND: Okay, Kirk, let's see how you do in a game of basketball. Let's choose up teams. Allan and Ben are captains. Ben, you choose first.

[*They choose: Team A:* ALLAN, SALLY, JIM *and* KIRK. *Team B:* BEN, AMANDA, SUSAN *and* BRUCE.]

ALLAN: [*To* KIRK, *when he is the only one unchosen*] Don't you foul up.

MR. FEND: Ben, you chose first so Allan's team gets the ball, so huddle up.

[*Each team huddles. They break and assume positions except for* KIRK, *who is lost.*]

KIRK: Where do I go?

SALLY: You play forward, down there. Don't you know anything, Kirk?

[MR. FEND *throws the ball to* ALLAN, *then whistles. There are four plays: 1)*SALLY *scores; 2)*BRUCE *scores; 3)*KIRK *gets the ball, but travels.*]

MR. FEND: [*Blows whistle*] Traveling, Kirk. Your team loses the ball.

[*4)* AMANDA *gets the ball and scores.*]

MR. FEND: Ben's team is the winner.

SALLY: That's not fair. We only had three people.

BEN: You did not, you had four.

JIM: But we had Kirk, and he hardly counts.

ALLAN: Kirk, it's all your fault that we lost.

AMANDA: And I had my best day.

SALLY: You were terrible, Kirk.

MR. FEND: That's all for today.

JIM: Thanks for messing up my pass.

SALLY: Yeah, thanks a lot, Kirk.

BRUCE: Thanks for leaving me wide open.

BEN: Where are you going, Kirk-face?

KIRK: To change my clothes.

[KIRK *picks up his bag and exits. The others follow. Lights dim.*]

Scene 3

Waiting at the bus stop.

AMANDA: My mother bought me a new dress. It's blue with red and white stripes.

SALLY: My mother bought me a new blazer *and* a new dress.

AMANDA: Well, my parents are taking me to dinner and I'm wearing my new dress.

BRUCE: Tomorrow's math test is going to be hard. I'm glad I've been studying all along.

JIM: The math test is going to be hard, but the social studies will be even harder. I hate that woman.

BEN: I'll trade you a Reggie Jackson for a Rich Gossage.

ALLAN: No way.

[*After* KIRK *has entered* ALLAN *grabs* KIRK's *cap and a game of keep-away ensues until* SUSAN *gets the cap and returns it.*]

BEN: Allan, why don't we finish that sports quiz we started yesterday?

ALLAN: Okay. That's a great idea.

KIRK: . . . I don't think so.

SALLY: I think we should, so you're outvoted.

ALLAN: Okay. I'll ask the questions. Name three Yankee pitchers.

KIRK: Brian Kingman, Reggie Jackson, and Johnny Bench.

SALLY: Wrong. You don't even know three Yankee pitchers! I do! Ron Guidry, Tommy John, and Rich Gossage.

ALLAN: Next question. Who had the most home runs in the 1980 season, and how many did he have?

BEN: Mike Schmidt. He had forty-eight.

KIRK: I thought he had fifty.

ALL: Wrong.

ALLAN: Next question. Who had the most stolen bases in 1980 and how many did he have?

KIRK: Bump Wills, and he had seventy-nine.

ALLAN: You're absolutely—

ALL: Wrong!

ALLAN: It was Ricky Henderson. He had one hundred.

SALLY: You don't know anything, Kirk.

[KIRK *exits. The others follow as lights dim.*]

Scene 4

The Swell kitchen. MRS. SWELL *is having coffee and reading the paper.*

KIRK: [*Entering*] I'm home.
MRS. SWELL: Hi, Kirk.
KIRK: Any mail for me?
MRS. SWELL: No. Dad's coming home early. He'll be here any minute. He has to test out a new product. We'll be in living heaven if the sales are high.
[MR. SWELL *enters*.]
MR. SWELL: Hi Kirk. Hi dear. Any mail for me?
[*She hands mail to him.*]
KIRK: Hi Dad, what did you bring home today?
MR. SWELL: The latest model of the computer-controlled, model 8, safety 3X, solarized, high technology, instant mini snow-maker!!!
KIRK: Wow!
MRS. SWELL: Sounds like a winner to me.
MR. SWELL: How was school today?
KIRK: I did well on my spelling test.
MR. SWELL: That's good.
KIRK: I did well on my math quiz.
MR. SWELL: That's good.
KIRK: I asked some smart questions in history.
MR. SWELL: That's good.
KIRK: But I was horrible in gym.
MR. SWELL: That's bad.
KIRK: I've got to talk to you about something, Dad.
MRS. SWELL: Well, I've got to finish my newspaper so if you two are going to be talking in here, I'll go to my room and read.
[*She exits.*]
KIRK: Dad, I don't know anything about sports and I don't play them well.
MR. SWELL: Well don't forget you're good at cross-country skiing and that's a sport.
KIRK: I guess so, but we don't do that in gym.
MR. SWELL: I guess you're right on that count.
KIRK: I have an idea! Early tomorrow morning you bring the mini snow-maker to school and put some snow on the gym floor. Then when we have gym class, I'll show everyone how well I can ski and you'll be testing your product all at once.
MR. SWELL: I think that's a great idea!
KIRK: What if the gym teacher doesn't like it?

It's Time For A Change 19

MR. SWELL: That's a risk we'll have to take.
KIRK: It would be neat to have a race.
MR. SWELL: Let's get moving. We've got a big day ahead of us.
[*They exit as lights dim.*]

Scene 5

Outside the gym.

ALLAN: I hope we play basketball again but with different teams so that my team doesn't have Kirk.
BEN: I hope we have the same teams so that Kirk won't be on my team.
SALLY: Wherever Kirk is I bet I'll beat him.
AMANDA: I hope we play soccer today.
JIM: I'm going to run in the New York marathon this year.
BRUCE: Whoopy-doo.
JIM: Did you see the new issue of *Runner's World* about warming up?
BRUCE: All that stretching takes as much time as running.
[MR. FEND *enters.*]
MR. FEND: All right. It's time for class to begin.
ALLAN: Are we going to play basketball today?
MR. FEND: We'll see.
SUSAN: Mr. Fend, are you married?
MR. FEND: Now, why do you want to know that?
SUSAN: Well, Sally wants to know.
SALLY: Do you have a girl friend?
MR. FEND: Now, that's none of your business. Let's go.
[*They go through the gym doors. Snow falls in the gym as they enter.*]
AMANDA: It's a winter wonderland.
SALLY: How did this happen?
BRUCE: Look at all the skis and poles and boots.
ALLAN: Holy-moly.
BEN: This is a joke.

JIM: Are the skis for us?
SUSAN: There are just enough.
MR. FEND: Who did this?
KIRK: I did. And I brought in the skis, the poles, the boots, and the snow. Could we ski, if it's okay with you?
ALLAN: Can we please, Mr. Fend?
[*Everyone ad-libs agreement.*]
MR. FEND: All right.
[*Conceding, throwing up his hands*]
KIRK: Everybody find a pair of skis, poles, and boots and I'll show you what to do. Everybody take off your shoes and put on your boots.
[*They take off their shoes and begin miming putting on the boots.*]
MR. FEND: Some of you kids didn't wash your socks like I told you to.
[*Several ad-libs*]
KIRK: Does everybody have their boots on? Now for the skis. Put your toes into the binding, put the three holes on the three prongs, push down on the latch and then let go.
ALLAN: Like this?
KIRK: No, don't you know anything? Now, pick up your poles, push on the poles one at a time and move forward on your skis.
SALLY: I know what to do, Kirk.
BRUCE: Shut up, Sally, this is interesting.
ALLAN: I bet I can cross-country ski better than anyone else in class.
MR. FEND: Oh yeah?
ALLAN: Yeah.
MR. FEND: Then let's have a race to find out. Who wants to race in the first line? Jim, Amanda, Sally, and Susan. Everybody else against the wall.
JIM: I wonder if these are the same muscles you use for running.
BRUCE: Will you stop talking about running.
AMANDA: I like this, I can't wait to try.
SALLY: As soon as I get good at one sport, I have to learn another one.
SUSAN: Gee, Kirk, these skis feel great.
MR. FEND: Kirk, before we race, why don't you demonstrate so we can all watch and learn.
[KIRK *demonstrates.*]

MR. FEND: Well, that's fine, Kirk. Now, let's start a race. First line, on your mark, get set, go.
[*They race.* SUSAN *wins.*]
MR. FEND: Susan is the winner. Second line, on your mark, get set, go.
[*They race.* KIRK *wins.*]
KIRK: I'm first for once.
BRUCE: I'm second.
ALLAN and BEN: [*They fall.*] We tied for last.
MR. FEND: [*Picking up* BEN *and* ALLAN] Okay all-stars, I'll give you a hand. Now let's have a play-off with Susan and Kirk from one end of the gym to the other and back again. On your mark, get set, go.
[*They race.* KIRK *wins.*]
MR. FEND: Looks like Kirk is the best skier in the class.
SALLY: Wait. Wait. Wait. Give me a week, I can beat him.
ALLAN: I don't believe I lost that race to you Kirk.
BEN: Kirk, you actually proved you were good at something.
ALLAN: I guess you're right, Ben.
KIRK: Well, gym's getting better.
[KIRK *does a circuit of the stage as lights dim.*]

SO WHAT ARE WE GONNA DO NOW?

by Juliet Garson

CHARACTERS

JENNIFER, eleven or twelve (pre-teen), middle-class New York City background.
PATRICIA, Jennifer's mother. Probably sophisticated, single working parent.
MARY, Teresa's mother, with immigrant accent. About fifty-five years old.
TERESA, Jennifer's friend, eleven or twelve (pre-teen), working-class Ukranian background.
FIRST MAN, young Puerto Rican.
SECOND MAN, older black, not a wino but getting there.
JOHN, Teresa's father, also old and immigrant.
THIRD MAN, middle-aged white, chubby, balding.
POLICE OFFICER, white young man. Blond, blue-eyed. A little dumb maybe but very kind and honest and trying to do the right thing.

SETTING: *The play takes place on a Sunday in New York City. There are three locations which are all on stage throughout the play. On the left side is* JENNIFER's *living room which just needs a good coffee table. On the right side is* TERESA's *bedroom which she shares with her mother. All that is needed is a chair and a cheap dressing table with mirror. The walls and dressing table are cluttered with* TERESA's *posters of movie stars and her makeup and* MARY's *statues of Jesus. The middle of the stage is a city park. All that is needed is a park bench and maybe a fake pigeon.*

ACT I

Scene 1

JENNIFER's *living room.* JENNIFER *is clearly sitting on the coffee table.*

PATRICIA: [*Entering*] Jenny, stop sitting on the coffee table.
JENNIFER: I'm not sitting on the coffee table.
PATRICIA: Jennifer, you're sitting there on the coffee table telling me you're not sitting on the coffee table.
JENNIFER: But I'm not! I swear!
PATRICIA: Jennifer, get off the coffee table!
[JENNIFER *stands up quickly and heads for the door.*]
Where are you going?
JENNIFER: I'm going someplace where they believe me! I am going to Washington Square Park and buying pot from those black guys with the wacky braids. And then, since I have no money, I'm going to pay each and every one of them by giving them a blow job!
PATRICIA: Jennifer!
JENNIFER: You can't stop me now! There's no way you can stop me! You drove me to do this! You're the one who's always hocking me to China! You don't care about me at all. Not at all! You'd let a cup of coffee sit on your table before you'd let me, your own daughter!
PATRICIA: Jenny get out! Just go!

[JENNIFER *runs out slamming door.* PATRICIA *rolls her eyes to heaven. Blackout*—JENNIFER's *house. Lights up*—TERESA's *house.*]

Scene 2

TERESA's *bedroom.* TERESA *is brushing on blush in front of the mirror while her mother sits in the chair watching her.*

MARY: Teresa, you put makeup too much. Is enough.
  [TERESA *is ignoring her mother.*]
  Where you go?
TERESA: [*Sarcastically*] Confession.
MARY: You lie! You go see Jeneef!
TERESA: [*Mimicking*] Yes, I lie, I see Jeneef!
  [MARY *scolds in Ukranian; she is hurt by* TERESA's *mimicking.*]
  Mom! If you're gonna talk to me in that language don't talk! Okay!? Just don't talk!
MARY: Go Teresa! Go, no comeback! Go! Go!
  [TERESA *walks out. Blackout*—TERESA's *house. Lights up—park*]

Scene 3

JENNIFER *is sitting on bench waiting for* TERESA. FIRST MAN, *the young Puerto Rican, comes up to her.*

FIRST MAN: Hey, how ya doin' babe? [JENNIFER *looks straight*

So What Are We Gonna Do Now? 27

ahead, ignoring him.] What's ya name? [JENNIFER *is still ignoring him.*] You don't want to talk to me? [JENNIFER *looks straight ahead, ignoring.*] Ya very pretty, ya know. Ya look Italian. You Italian? [*No reaction from* JENNIFER] Irish? [*Still no reaction*] Jew? [*No reaction*] Come on, tell me, what are you?

JENNIFER: [*Faces him and says seriously—*] I'm black.

FIRST MAN: Aw get outa here, you ain't black.

JENNIFER: Yes, I am.

FIRST MAN: You serious?

JENNIFER: Yes.

FIRST MAN: Come on, you kiddin' me.

JENNIFER: No, I'm not kidding. I'm black and I'm proud. Anything wrong with that?

FIRST MAN: No, that's all right, it's cool, it's really cool. Well, uh, see you 'roun.

[FIRST MAN *walks away muttering. He is convinced that* JENNIFER'S *crazy.* TERESA *comes up to* JENNIFER.]

TERESA: [*Joining* JENNIFER *on bench*] So what do you wanna do?

JENNIFER: Do you have any money?

TERESA: No.

JENNIFER: Well, I guess we're stuck with hanging around in the park.

[*Enter the* SECOND MAN]

SECOND MAN: Hey little girls! [*They freeze, determined to ignore him.*] Come here little girls. [*They continue to ignore him.*] Little girls, I got somethin' to show you.

TERESA: On the count of three.

[*They count and on "three" run to* TERESA'S *house. As they get off the bench to run, the lights go out and only the spotlight is on them. They go to* TERESA'S *house.* TERESA *is opening the door with her key. Her father springs up at her. The spotlight remains on the girls outside the house and the lights go up in* TERESA'S *house.*]

FATHER: Teresa! Mary say you been bad.

TERESA: Dad, it's none of your business.

MARY: She was bad! She shame her mother! She shame!

FATHER: [*In a rage*] No my business!? I kill you! You shame you mother no my business?! Get out a here! I kill you, you brat! No my business! I kill—

[TERESA *slams door from outside. Blackout in* TERESA'*s house.*]

JENNIFER: My house.

[*The girls run to* JENNIFER'*s house with the spotlight on them. They reach* JENNIFER'*s house. She rings the bell. They wait awhile.*]

TERESA: Don't you have your key?

JENNIFER: No, I left in such a rage this morning that I ran out without it. Now, you know whose fault this is, it's my mother's. If she's gonna drive me out of the house, she should at least have the courtesy to drive me out into a decent neighborhood. I mean, gosh, how can she expect me to grow up to be a normal human being, let alone an honest one, when look at the atmosphere she's set up for me. She's given me a choice, live in a house of distrust or go out into the streets of slime. The streets where scum drips from every man's mouth. [*Imitating various types of perverts*] "Hey, babe you know, ya beautiful." [*For this next type she puts her hand down near her you-know-what to make it look like a guy who's holding* his *you-know-what which is something they often do while they're speaking.*] "Five more years little girl. Hey little girls, come 'ere I got somethin' ta show you. Hey little girl, you evuh suck dick befo'? Jou want to come to my house? I take jou to da movies and buy jou candy." I swear! I can't go anywhere without hearing that junk! I can't walk on my block after dark without a car slowing down and following me. Stopping when I stop to tie my shoes. Because they think I'm a hooker! Me! A hooker! It makes me so upset. It makes me feel like *I'm* the disgusting one! Why should I feel disgusting because of their diseased minds?! I can't play in the park, I can't walk on my block, I CAN'T LIVE IN THIS WORLD ANY MORE! Wait a minute. I should be able to live in this world. *They're* the ones who shouldn't be able to! They want prostitutes! Prostitutes they'll get— and *DEATH!*

TERESA: What?!?!?!?!!!

JENNIFER: [*Really excited about her plan and making it seem all perfectly logical*] We'll dress up like prostitutes and every time a guy comes to pick us up, we'll take him to a deserted alley and kill him and before you know it, there won't be a sleaze left in Manhattan.

TERESA: Jennifer, I think killing people is a little bit drastic.
JENNIFER: I agree but we have to do this for the good of ourselves and all harassed young ladies.

[*Blackout.*]

ACT II

Scene 1

The light comes up dimly, because it's dark, on the two girls, who are dressed up as prostitutes; seductive music might be a good special effect.

JENNIFER: Did you bring the knife?
TERESA: Yes.
JENNIFER: Good.
TERESA: Maybe we'd better not do this. I mean, we have no idea what prostitutes do. [*Correcting herself*] I mean, I know what they do. But like what's the procedure? How does the conversation go? I mean, if a guy comes up to us who's a professional sleaze he'll know by how our procedure goes that we're not real professional prostitutes.
JENNIFER: You're right. I'm very worried too, but we have to do it, for the good of the cause.
[THIRD MAN *waddles over toward them. He takes a piece of paper out of his pocket and reads it out loud.*]
THIRD MAN: Okay, step one, take the tunnel to the West Side Highway and get off at Bethune Street. I did that. Step two, park the car and find a prostitute. I did that. Step three, ask him or her, "How much?" I didn't do that yet. Okay, here goes: How much? [*The girls look at each other for an answer while* THIRD MAN *continues reading.*] Step four, bargain with them. [*He looks up from the paper.*] I have five dollars and I need thirty cents to ride the Path back home to New Jersey and I want to buy some peanut chews and that's thirty cents, so that's five dollars minus sixty cents, so that's four dollars and forty cents. Is that a good

So What Are We Gonna Do Now?

price? [*They look at each other for an answer.*] I'm sorry if that's not the going rate. It's just that I'm new at this. This is my first time and all I know is what's on this instruction sheet that my brother-in-law wrote up for me and— [*A sigh of relief from the girls*]

JENNIFER: Four-forty is fine. Don't you think so?

TERESA: Yes, four-forty is fine, but you have to take both of us. We work as a team.

THIRD MAN: Woo woo-woo.

JENNIFER: Now you just sit down on the sidewalk.

THIRD MAN: Sit down on the sidewalk? *That's* not on the paper.

TERESA: Don't ask questions, this is how it's done.

JENNIFER: Just relax and close your eyes.

THIRD MAN: It didn't say that on the pa—

TERESA: Don't ask questions, this is how it's done.

JENNIFER: All right sucker, now you're dead. [*The* THIRD MAN *opens his eyes startled.*]

THIRD MAN: Huh?

JENNIFER: [*Talking to* TERESA *with eyes fixed on* THIRD MAN] Give me the knife. [TERESA *confidently gives her the knife.* JENNIFER *looks at it, horrified.*]
A butter knife! Couldn't you at least have gotten a steak knife? This thing isn't sharp enough.

TERESA: Are you kidding? My dad would go bananas if he found out I left the house with a steak knife. He'd think I was trying to kill someone.

JENNIFER: What're we going to do?

TERESA: I don't know.

THIRD MAN: What's going on? How come it doesn't say anythin' about a knife on the paper? [*Suddenly very angry*] Are you playing a trick on me?!
[*All through this scene the girls should be frantically making up their stories off the top of their heads.*]

JENNIFER: Oh no, it's no trick, it's just—um—ah—

TERESA: It's just a ritual that's performed your first time and your brother-in-law didn't write it down because it's a secret.

THIRD MAN: [*He's calm now.*] That sounds sensible. [*He thinks about it for a second and then gets angry again.*] Wait a minute. Why'd you call me a dead sucker for? You girls tryin' a kill me?

TERESA: Well you see, that's part of the ritual. You see— um— ah—

JENNIFER: You see, the person is seated on the sidewalk and the prostitutes have to— figuratively speaking of course— kill all the purity in him and let only the corruptness of his soul survive. Isn't that right?

TERESA: Right.

JENNIFER: And we use a butter knife as a symbol of death because butter comes from cows and the cowboys killed the Indians. Isn't that right?

TERESA: Right.

JENNIFER: And— um—

TERESA: Jennifer! A cop! What do we do? He'll see the knife.

JENNIFER: [*To* THIRD MAN] Um— hold this knife. It's part of the ritual. [*To* OFFICER] Officer, arrest this man, he has a knife and he threatened us with death if we didn't dump our clothes in the river and wear these slutty clothes that he gave us. And he's been speaking obscenity to my sister here and she's really upset. Isn't that right?

TERESA: Yes, I'm really upset. Boo-hoo-hoo. He's a bad man, he's making me cry. Boo-hoo.

OFFICER: Come with me, sir. Perhaps you girls should come too.

JENNIFER: Oh no, we can't go with you. You see, I have to stay with my sister. You see, she was born with part of her brain missing and she can't cry and walk at the same time.

OFFICER: All right then, I'll carry her.

[*He picks her up.*]

JENNIFER: Put her down right this second! You can't carry her. You see, she has this other part of her brain that's missing, so that if someone picks her up she'll think that she's flying.

TERESA: Weeeh! I'm flying!

JENNIFER: See? And then her brain goes totally berserk and she won't know what's going on and she'll get total amnesia.

TERESA: Who am I? Where am I? What am I doing in this gorgeous hunk's arms?

[OFFICER *puts her down.*]

OFFICER: Well I'll call a doctor.

JENNIFER: There's no time for that now! Look he's getting away!

[*He isn't really trying to get away.*]

OFFICER: Come back here you.

[*Turns to face* THIRD MAN]

So What Are We Gonna Do Now?

THIRD MAN: I wasn't going anywhere. Hey! She stopped crying.
TERESA: Waaaaah!!!!
JENNIFER: That's right! Play innocent and put the blame on this poor child.
OFFICER: He's right. She did stop crying. Young lady, are you deceiving me?
JENNIFER: You think I'm deceiving you? You don't trust me? You should never distrust a child. It makes the child lose all self-confidence! I feel so terrible about myself now without your confidence that I'm beginning to lose parts of my brain too. I can't talk and breathe at the same time! I'm flying!!! Who am I? Waaaah!
TERESA: Waaaah!
OFFICER: [*Feeling guilty, embarrassed and terrible, accusing the* THIRD MAN] See what you've done.
THIRD MAN: I'm not the one that didn't believe her.
OFFICER: Shut up and come with me.
   [*Upset* OFFICER *leaves with* THIRD MAN. *The* OFFICER *is leading him like a criminal.*]
TERESA: This was a good idea Jennifer. It was so fun.
JENNIFER: Fun? Who cares about fun? We've failed. All we've done is make that cop feel awful and put that pervert in jail for *one* night.
TERESA: Face it Jennifer. There's no way we can get rid of these creeps. We'll just have to live with them.
JENNIFER: Speaking of creeps! My mom! I gotta get home!
TERESA: Oh Jesus, you're right! See ya Monday at school—bye!
   [*The girls race home in opposite directions.*]

Scene 2

Spotlights out in park. Lights up in TERESA's *and* JENNIFER's *house. From now on, if people in one house are talking, the people in the other house freeze until it's their turn to talk.*

MARY: Where you go? Is ten o'clawk. You no can come home at ten o'clawk. Look at your clothings.

PATRICIA: Where have you been? It's after ten o'clock. Look at the way you're dressed!
TERESA: This is America, Mom. I can dress any way I want and I can come home any time I want.
JENNIFER: Why? Don't you trust my taste in clothes? Don't you trust me enough to let me come home when I want?
[MARY *scolds in Ukranian.*]
PATRICIA: Frankly, I don't trust a girl who comes home after ten looking like that.
TERESA: Good-bye Mom!
JENNIFER: Good-bye Mom!
MARY: Where you go?
PATRICIA: Where do you think you're going?
JENNIFER: I'm going somewhere where they trust me!
TERESA: I'm going somewhere where they speak English!
BOTH GIRLS: Just remember, you drove me out of the house!
[*Both doors slam. Blackout. Lights come up in park.*]
TERESA: So what are we gonna do now?
JENNIFER: There really are different parts of the brain, right? There's a part for seeing, a part for hearing, and a part for being a sleaze, right?
TERESA: I guess so.
JENNIFER: So listen, we'll dress up like doctors, stand under the West Side Highway—
TERESA: And in the park—
JENNIFER: And everywhere that the sleazes are. *Then* we'll tell them all that they have V.D.
TERESA: Great!
JENNIFER: And that we'll have to operate on them.
TERESA: Then we will operate on them.
JENNIFER: Only instead of getting rid of V.D., we'll remove the sleazy part of their brains. Before you know it, there won't be a sleaze left in Manhattan. Just nice normal people with parts of their brains missing.
TERESA: Oh boy! . . . But Jennifer, we're not doctors. How are we gonna operate on them?
JENNIFER: Well, we have a butter knife.
[TERESA *gives* JENNIFER *a skeptical look.*]
TERESA: [*Shrugs*]
So what are we gonna do now?
[JENNIFER *snaps her fingers or does something to show that she has another idea. Blackout.*]

THE BRONX ZOO

by Lynnette M. Serrano

CHARACTERS

JUNITO DIAZ, seventeen
EVIE MEDINA
ROSA
MIKE
RAMON
SANTO
BUM
LOUIE
LUCY DIAZ, mother of Junito, Angel and Clara
ANGEL DIAZ, twenty-four
CLARA DIAZ, eight years old
TONYA MEDINA, Evie's mother
FIRST GIRL
SECOND GIRL
DOCTOR

Author's Note

(The meaning behind THE BRONX ZOO)

Many people ask me about the significance of my title selection and I say to them, that's where I'm from. Of course they look at me strangely until I explain to them, that I was born in the "Land of Broken Promises." For many, it is a cursed niche of the Bronx that provokes fear; for those who built their lives here, it is the only place for survival. In short, *The Bronx Zoo* is my way of saying: my people are tired of being treated like animals and caged into the many roles society puts us in.

Prologue

Silence. A mugger runs across the stage, takes out money from a purse, then throws the bag off the stage. A spotlight fixes on him and he acknowledges the audience. It's JUNITO. *He is wearing a ski-mask.*

MUGGER: Wow, I look at all you fine young men out there and see myself... Sure I had dreams too... I was gonna save the world from itself... but I guess someone else is gonna have to do it... I asked for help, but you did not lend a hand. So, why should you get mad when I take what I want?... You call me sucio... You refuse to walk next to me 'cause you're scared of where I'm from... [*Addresses someone in the audience*] Hey you, look at me... [*Takes out a knife*] Are you afraid? Is this the only language you understand? [*Flicks the knife; it's a comb—passes it through his hair*] I'm not here to justify what I'm doing... I stopped doin' that one a long time ago... but this is where I am confined, and here you either join us or you don't; there are no in-betweens.

ACT I

Scene 1

TIME: *Friday, April 3, 1981; 6:00 p.m.*
PLACE: *East 147th Street, St. Anne's Avenue in the South Bronx.*

The lights fix on a large mural on the upper-back part of the stage. The faces in the painting are hollow and dark, depicting the lives of the people. Wild Latin music begins to play in the background. As the lights go up, five people are on stage. ROSA, MIKE, and RAMON are talking endlessly about playing the numbers. ROSA takes out a "Big Red" betting-sheet and shows the other two. SANTO, the fourth person, is leaning against a rail and drinking beer out of a paper bag. The fifth person, an elderly BUM, is standing by a light-post mumbling to himself. LOUIE enters carrying a large radio and greets everyone. At the corner, JUNITO and EVIE enter and engage in a fierce argument. At this point the music begins to fade. LOUIE crosses them, exchanges a look with EVIE, then exits. MIKE leaves also.

JUNITO: Listen woman, didn't I say I'd call you last night? Where in the name of Je—
EVIE: Please Nito, don't create a scene.
JUNITO: That's exactly what I'm gonna do.
EVIE: Well, that's what you're gonna get if you don't stop it.
JUNITO: Threaten me . . . go ahead!!
  [EVIE *clenches her fist.* JUNITO *backs down.* ROSA *and* RAMON *linger on for a while, then exit.* SANTO *leaves also. The* BUM *moves up to the rail outside of* EVIE'S *apartment where* SANTO *was. It begins to rain and thunder.*]
JUNITO: Where the hell were you?
EVIE: Don't be raising your voice at me. I hate that shit.
JUNITO: At this point I don't care what you hate or not.

[*The* BUM *reaches out his hand.* EVIE *reaches into her change purse and gives him a coin.*]

EVIE: Listen Mr. Diaz, you ain't my husband to be telling me what to do.

JUNITO: Jus' 'cause I ain't your husband, doesn't mean you have to be rapping to every guy you see.

[*Suggests the* BUM]

EVIE: I don't believe you... How dare you say that to me? Hey, listen, if I wanna go to... fuckin' Forty-Second Street and sell myself, I'll do it. [*Points between her legs*] Por que esta, esta es mia.

JUNITO: Go to Forty-Second Street... Earn a buck. If you're fuckin' around, you might as well get paid for it. You're a bitch anyway.

EVIE: Bitch?!... Maricon!!

JUNITO: You want to see my maricon?!

EVIE: Save yourself the humiliation.

[*Silence*]

JUNITO: You know something lady?! You're so into yourself that you can't bear to part with that cold love you got in there.

[*Touches her chest roughly*]

EVIE: [*Moving back*] What does all of this have to do with now?

JUNITO: Well, if you would've been home last night, I would've told you.

EVIE: Are you fuckin' stupid or what?... I told you I'd be at Julia's house, and you've got her number too.

JUNITO: Jesus Christ... I forgot. Hey baby, I'm really very sorry.

EVIE: Sorry?!... Listen you poor excuse for a man, I'm sick and tired of your jealousy fits, and I don't want to see you or your stupid Puerto Rican ass again!!

JUNITO: But Evie—

EVIE: Get away from me, Nito!!

JUNITO: I said I was sorry.

[*Taking out her keys, Evie quickly opens her front door.*]

EVIE: [*Turning around*] You should grow up Junito.

[*The door slams in* JUNITO'*s face. He observes the* BUM *as he walks to his place at the light-post, turns, then leaves. When* JUNITO *is sure that he is alone, he takes out a pen and pad, and begins to write. A short musical interlude introduces the change in scene. The tune is light and jazzy, and almost comical.*]

Scene 2

TIME: *Friday, April 3, 1981; 6:30 p.m.*
PLACE: *The living room of the Diaz family.*
The room is shabbily decorated with religious articles as well as small reminders of the past. There is a worn-out sofa-bed to the left side of the room. Next to it, is a table holding a tiny white elephant and a telephone. A rocking chair is just outside of the French doors leading into the boys' bedroom. On it are clothes left over from the morning laundry. To the right side of the room is a door leading to the kitchen. Next to the door is a large dresser used as a mantle to hold candles, and pictures and statues of saints. There is also an ominous picture of the dead father on it and a small television set.
As the scene opens, LUCY, JUNITO's *mother, is on the phone.*

LUCY: No pude ir... Tenía que quedarme con la nena... ¡Ay que loca!... No, no,... así fue... I heard that chair rose up and hit against the wall. Esa espiritista es buenísima.
[ANGEL *enters with a broom, puts it to the side, then begins to fold the clothes. He then looks at his mother, and turns off a small transistor radio she brought in with her.* LUCY *continues to speak on the phone.*]
LUCY: Well, Carmen was there... Yeah, you know how she is... She told me que la espiritista told Dolores about her two cortejos.
ANGEL: ¿Quién es?
LUCY: Sandra.
ANGEL: Ask her what came out for Brooklyn. I have a lot riding on the hostage number, 444.
LUCY: Oye. What came out for Brooklyn?... [*To* ANGEL] 234 escalera.
ANGEL: Shit! Ten bucks down the drain!

[ANGEL *takes out his books from the dresser, and sits in the recliner.*]

LUCY: Yeah, he lost again... Well anyway, what was I saying?
[LUCY *sits at the edge of the sofa.*]
¿Oh, sabes quienes son verdad?! You mean you don't know?!
[LUCY *screams and throws herself back in the sofa.* ANGEL *looks at her alarmed.*]

ANGEL: Ma, I'm expecting a call.

LUCY: Shh... [*Returning to her conversation*] Bueno, you know that guy who works in the candy store?... The one in Courtlandt... He has brown kinky hair... Yeah that's him.

ANGEL: Not Johnny?!

LUCY: ¡No joda, Angel!... Yeah, I know... I'm sorry... Oh, what was I saying? Yeah, yeah... that's right. Carmen said—

ANGEL: Ma, I need the phone!!

LUCY: ¡Callate ya, Angel!... [*Returns to the conversation*] That's right... Carmen said that Dolores was turning red and—

ANGEL: And te va pisar la lengua.

LUCY: Excuse me, Sandra. [*Covers the receiver*] ¡Me vas a dejar hablar o que, carajo! [*Returns to the conversation*] It's Angel, parece que le pica el culo.

ANGEL: ¡Ay Dios mio!! ¡La lengua del Bronx!!

LUCY: Listen negra, I'll call you back later. Angel's bitchin'.
[LUCY *hangs up the phone loudly.*]

ANGEL: [*Teasing her*] Why'd you hang up?

LUCY: You know why!

ANGEL: Well ma, it says here in my psychology book that people who gossip have nothing better to do and lack confidence in themselves.

LUCY: Let me sit down. I feel a lecture coming on. [*Sits*] Okay Freud?!

ANGEL: You're making fun of me again, aren't you?

LUCY: No. Not at all. I just feel that your life isn't all that perfect for you to be telling others how to live theirs.

ANGEL: Oh really?... And how long have you been having these delusions?

LUCY: Seriously, Angel... You worry me sometimes.

ANGEL: Worry you?... Come on, ma! You talk on the phone for hours with women who have police records about chairs flying in the air, and you're worried about me?

LUCY: Police records?
ANGEL: Yeah. Didn't you know Sandra was arrested for shoplifting last week?
LUCY: Well, well, well, Sandra's back to her old tricks. [*Goes to the phone*] Wait till I tell Carmen!!
ANGEL: You're gonna tell Carmen?
LUCY: Well, of course. This is too juicy to keep to myself. [*Lucy dials the number.*]
ANGEL: I thought so... My dear Mrs. Diaz, you are a victim of that incurable disease called bullshititis.
[LUCY *dials.*]
LUCY: Meaning?... Oh, Carmen!
ANGEL: I lied.
LUCY: Shit!

[*Slams down the receiver.* LUCY *begins to chase* ANGEL *around the room. He sticks out his tongue at her, grabs a sheet which is lying on the couch, and throws it at her.* ANGEL *teases her.*]

ANGEL: Oh Carmen help me... I got bullshititis... What should I do? Go to a doctor or the espiritista?

[LUCY *throws the sheet over* ANGEL *as he settles down in the recliner.*]

ANGEL: Well, good-bye Carmen. I'm gonna call Sandra now!
[*The door springs open;* JUNITO *enters. Silence.* LUCY *turns around suddenly angered.*]
LUCY: Where were you?

[JUNITO *throws himself on the couch, tossing* ANGEL'*s books on the floor.* ANGEL *gives a sigh, then picks them up.*]

LUCY: Answer me!
JUNITO: At work.
LUCY: Don't lie to me! Where were you?!
JUNITO: [*Biting his nails*] I told you.
LUCY: [*Slapping his hand away from his mouth*] Listen, you'd better stop lying. Mr. Rivera called.
JUNITO: Shit!

[JUNITO *gets up and heads for his room. The phone rings. He and* ANGEL *race for it.*]

ANGEL: It's for me.
JUNITO: [*Grabbing the phone*] Hello?...
[*He hands it over to* ANGEL. JUNITO *walks over to the recliner, then turns on the television set.* LUCY *follows him.*]
LUCY: Why weren't you at work today?!

JUNITO: [*Mumbles*] I went to the old block.
LUCY: I can't hear you!
JUNITO: [*Louder*] I went to the old block!
LUCY: ¡Mira que tiene cojones!! Didn't I tell you not to go down there?!
JUNITO: I know, but—
LUCY: But nothing. I told you not to go in there!!
ANGEL: Shh!!
JUNITO: Jesus ma... Will you stop being so overprotective! I'm seventeen years old already!!
ANGEL: [*Covering the receiver*] Ma, Nito, could you please go into the other room?
JUNITO: Would you be terribly offended if I said no?
LUCY: Leave your brother alone. This call's important to him.
JUNITO: Ask me if I care?
LUCY: I know you don't care. You know why you don't care, because your life lacks direction. You should be like your brother. He's not afraid to make things happen for himself. He's a winner, and you're a—
JUNITO: Say it ma... a loser, right? Well, let me tell you something ma, I have plans too!
LUCY: But you'll never make it writing songs... You've got to sweat a little bit too—
[JUNITO *turns up the television set full blast.*]
ANGEL: Please be quiet!!
[LUCY *leaves, going into the kitchen.*]
JUNITO: Sure winner, I'll be quiet!! How's that for quiet!! Is that quiet enough for you!!!
ANGEL: What?... I can't hear you... Yes... yes... I'm really very sorry... Thanks. [ANGEL *hangs up the phone and screams.*] You fuckin' little punk!! Turn off that shit right now!!
[LUCY *comes in, and turns off the set.*]
LUCY: Shh! Abajo vive gente!
JUNITO: [*To* ANGEL] ¡Pendejo!
[ANGEL *clenches his fist.* LUCY *puts it down.*]
LUCY: Come on, Angel. Don't do anything stupid.
JUNITO: Anything stupid? How can your little darling do anything stupid?!
ANGEL: I'm warning you, cabrón!
LUCY: Angel please—

The Bronx Zoo

JUNITO: Please what? Please don't fight with this little nothing, right?!

ANGEL: For heaven's sake Nito, you're almost a man and look at the way you're acting.

JUNITO: What do you suggest, Einstein, that I act more like you? I mean, you are perfect. Except for the fact that you're gay and a momma's boy, you're practically another Jesus Christ, aren't you?!

ANGEL: You're gonna make me forget that we're brothers, and when this happens, I'm gonna stick my foot straight up your ass!!

[JUNITO *finds* ANGEL's *book on the side of the recliner, and begins to look at it.*]

JUNITO: Is this yours?! [*He rips out a page.*] It's a very interesting book.

[ANGEL *grabs* JUNITO's *hands just as he begins ripping another page. The two brothers begin to fight right on the recliner. At first* JUNITO *is in the recliner, but he overpowers* ANGEL *in such a way that* ANGEL *is thrown on the seat.* LUCY *begins to shout at them both, but they continue to fight throwing kicks and punches at each other.*]

LUCY: Stop it!! ¡Ay Dios mio!! I've mothered two animals instead of two sons!! Stop it!!

[LUCY *begins to strike them very wildly. In all the confusion,* JUNITO *accidently hits her back. After this, a creepy sort of silence enters the room.* JUNITO *angrily goes into his room and slams the door.* ANGEL *tries to help* LUCY *from the floor.*]

ANGEL: I'm sorry ma.

LUCY: Get off me . . . I've mothered animales!! ¡Animales!!

[*Little* CLARA *enters as* ANGEL *sits back down on the recliner. Seeing her mother on her knees, she kneels down next to her.*]

CLARA: [*Making a cross, then closing her eyes*] What are we praying for?

ANGEL: Come on baby. [*Attempts to pick up* CLARA] Let's leave mommy alone. She's very sad.

CLARA: [*Resisting* ANGEL's *grip*] Mami, why are you sad? [*Strokes* LUCY's *hair gently*]

LUCY: [*Gets up and takes* CLARA *by the hands*] I'm okay mamita. Are you hungry?

CLARA: Yeah.

[LUCY *walks to the door of the kitchen, then turns to* CLARA.]
LUCY: ¡Ay shit! No hay manteca.
CLARA: Why don't you send Junito to get some?
LUCY: He won't go.
CLARA: Is that why you're so sad?
LUCY: Yeah, but it doesn't matter now. I have my guardian angel to protect me.
CLARA: Who's that?
LUCY: [*Picking her up*] You baby.
CLARA: That's funny.
LUCY: Why cielito?
CLARA: I dreamed I was an angel with pretty white wings last night.

[LUCY *exchanges a look with* ANGEL, *before putting* CLARA *down on the rocking chair.*]

CLARA: What number is that in your Bible?
LUCY: Bible?
CLARA: Yeah, that book of numbers you bet with. Angel calls that "La Santa Biblia."
LUCY: Well, that's just your brother's idea of a joke.
CLARA: Could've fooled me.

[CLARA *closes her eyes, for a moment, then after a pause, looks at* LUCY.]

CLARA: Is papi in heaven?
LUCY: Yes, I told you that a long time ago.

[JUNITO *enters the room.*]

LUCY: Why do you ask?
CLARA: I've just been thinking about him, that's all.

[CLARA *notices* JUNITO'S *presence in the room, runs, then jumps into his arms.*]

CLARA: Nito!!

[JUNITO *holds* CLARA, *then addresses his mother.*]

JUNITO: You okay ma?
LUCY: Yeah.

[JUNITO *goes into his room carrying* CLARA. LUCY *gets up and takes a few steps.* ANGEL *goes to her knowing that she is in need of comfort.*]

ANGEL: It's okay ma, it was only her dream.
LUCY: I don't think so... You remember the day Clara was born?
ANGEL: Ay mami, that has nothing to do with her dream.
LUCY: Yes it does. Your father died that day.

ANGEL: I know, but what does that have to do with now and Clara.
LUCY: She's been having too many dreams about death lately... Don't you see? Your father is trying to tell us something!
ANGEL: Ma, yo no creo en eso.
LUCY: I know what I'm saying and no kind of psychology is gonna change what's in my heart... never Angel.
[LUCY *looks deeply into* ANGEL's *eyes as the lights fade.*]

Scene 3

TIME: *Saturday, April 4, 1981; 7:00 a.m.*
PLACE: *The living room of the Diaz family.*

The room is dark and eerie. A slow solicitous tune accompanies the creaking rocking chair, as well as the swaying kitchen door. All of a sudden, the door violently shuts, but the chair stays rocking at a moderate pace.
LUCY, *who is sleeping on the couch with* CLARA, *gets up to stop the rocking of the chair.* CLARA *wakes up also.*

CLARA: Mommy?
LUCY: Estoy aquí.
CLARA: What are you doing?
LUCY: I'm trying to keep this rocking chair still.
CLARA: Why didn't papi stop it?
LUCY: ¿Papi? Ay nena, you've been dreaming.
CLARA: No ma, it was real.
LUCY: Dreams have that effect on people, baby.
CLARA: Ma, I know I saw him... He even spoke to me.
LUCY: Nena, papi's in heaven con los angelitos.
CLARA: Well, he was here... He sat in that rocking chair watching you sleep. He wanted to touch you.
LUCY: Negra—
CLARA: Ma, please believe me... He even told me about the

day he was killed... my birthday.
LUCY: Clara, who told you?
CLARA: Pa.
LUCY: Cielo, papi can't say anything. Papi is dead.
CLARA: Well, he was alive last night.
LUCY: In your dreams.
CLARA: No ma... He actually spoke to me... He said that the day I was born was the happiest day in his life... He had taken the day off from the garage... bought a bouquet of flowers and a box of cigars. As he headed to the old block, two boys tried to rob him. When he fought back... one of them pulled out a gun—
LUCY: I know the rest.
CLARA: He came to tell me that one of us is gonna suffer.
LUCY: Why are you telling me this? Why, Clara?
CLARA: Papi just said—
LUCY: [*Slaps her across the face*] I don't want to hear any more... Not about your dreams... not about your father...
[*The two boys stumble into the room.* ANGEL *has on a sleeveless undershirt and pajama bottoms, and* JUNITO *is wearing jockey-shorts.* LUCY *is still carrying on.*]
LUCY: Do you hear me?
CLARA: But ma—
LUCY: ¿Me quieres volver loca? ¡Pues no, mija!
ANGEL: ¡Calmate! ¿Que pasó?
[JUNITO *goes to* CLARA *and notices the slap mark.*]
JUNITO: Are you crazy? [*Taking* CLARA *and carrying her out*] Vente baby, I love you.
ANGEL: Tell me... What happened?
LUCY: She saw him.
ANGEL: Who?
LUCY: Your father.
ANGEL: [*Sighs gently*] She's a child ma... All she saw was her own imagination coming to life. I'm sure she made the whole thing up.
LUCY: Then how did she know?
ANGEL: Know what?
LUCY: That your father was killed the day she was born.
ANGEL: [*Searching for answers*] Well... well she probably heard us talking yesterday. You know how she picks up everything.

LUCY: I know, but Clara knew the whole story.
ANGEL: Clara's a pretty smart kid who's capable of almost anything. She probably read your diary.
LUCY: But it's in Spanish.
ANGEL: Clara isn't exactly Japanese, you know?
LUCY: [*Looking at* ANGEL *suspiciously*] She doesn't read Spanish... Although I know someone who does.
ANGEL: I plead the fifth, Perry Mason.
LUCY: I'm gonna kill you!
[ANGEL *takes a pillow and hits her over the head with it.*]
ANGEL: You'll never get me alive!
[LUCY *takes the other pillow and hits him in the groin.*]
ANGEL: That was a low blow!
LUCY: You deserve it, nosy!
ANGEL: So you have a thing for the butcher... No wonder we've been up to our necks in hamburger meat.
LUCY: You little devil.
ANGEL: Oh no, you named me Angel, remember?
LUCY: I should've named you Elmo!
ANGEL: You know something lady? You're retarded.
LUCY: I take after my children.
ANGEL: Not this one.
LUCY: Especially this one.
ANGEL: Tell your boy friend that your children want to eat chuletas tonight.
LUCY: Shut up! ¡Bandido!
[*She hits him over the head with the pillow.*]
ANGEL: [*Makes two circles around his eyes*] You wouldn't hit a guy with glasses would you?
[LUCY *hits him anyway, but* ANGEL *pulls her down on the bed. The two of them lie on the bed trying to catch their breaths.*]
ANGEL: You're a sadist.
LUCY: I do try.
ANGEL: [*Innocently*] Ma, I didn't know you had a thing for men with gold teeth.
LUCY: Will you stop that?... You're sick... Did you really read my diary.
ANGEL: Only the juicy parts.
LUCY: ¡Desgraciado!
ANGEL: Not me... Yo soy un angel.

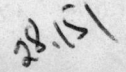

LUCY: You are my angel.
ANGEL: [*Kissing her on the forehead*] That's sweet.
LUCY: You're not at all like the other two.
ANGEL: You think so?
LUCY: I do, really ... There are times when I lie awake at night thinking about how Junito and Clara are gonna turn out, but I never worry about you ... You're a worker ... You love education.
ANGEL: Do you think I'll make it? It's an awful big world out there.
LUCY: Are you doubting yourself? That's not like you.
ANGEL: I know ma, but I can't help it ... I can't help thinking about all those millions of other people who want to go into the medical field. It's when I think of them, that I wonder whether I'm good enough.
LUCY: Of course you are, but you have to realize that no matter where you go, there will always be someone a little bit better than you.
ANGEL: The question is, how do I stand up high above the rest.
LUCY: By believing in yourself and by never giving up.

[LUCY *gets up and heads to the kitchen.*]

ANGEL: [*Jokingly*] With advice like that, how can I ever go wrong?

[LUCY *gives him a wink before going into the kitchen.* ANGEL *stays and fixes the sofa-bed.* JUNITO *and* CLARA *are standing in the boys' room near the French doors.* JUNITO *is fixing* CLARA's *hair, as she begins to hum.*]

JUNITO: Stop it.
CLARA: Why?
JUNITO: You're disturbing me ... Where did you hear that?

[*The rocking chair in the living room begins to sway furiously.*]

CLARA: I don't remember.
JUNITO: That's spooky.
CLARA: Why?
JUNITO: Papi used to sing it to me.

[*The rocking chair stops rocking when* LUCY *comes into the living room and sits down on the recliner.* CLARA *enters with* JUNITO. *She looks at her mother, then looks away.*]

LUCY: Don't worry baby, I'm not gonna hurt you.
JUNITO: Then why did you smack her?
ANGEL: Come on man, I'll explain it to you later. [*Hands him*

the pillows] Help me with these, okay?
[ANGEL *and* JUNITO *exit.* CLARA *walks up to* LUCY.]
CLARA: Why are you afraid of papi?
LUCY: I'm not afraid.
CLARA: He told me you were because he's a spirit.
[LUCY *holds her face in her hands and begins to weep.*]
CLARA: [*Grabs her wrists*] Papi's alive now, isn't he?
LUCY: I don't know.
CLARA: Ma, he held my hand and it was cold.
LUCY: Please baby, no more stories.
CLARA: I just can't forget about him.
LUCY: I'm not asking you to forget him, just to let go a little. He's not part of our world anymore.
CLARA: But he's a part of mine.
[CLARA *leaves angrily and bumps into* JUNITO *as he enters the room.*]
JUNITO: What's up with her?
LUCY: She said she saw your father.
JUNITO: Ma, why don't you take her to a psychiatrist. Está un poco loca.
LUCY: I don't think she is. It goes beyond that.
JUNITO: You can believe in dead people and spirits all you want, as for me . . . [*Grabs his jacket*] I'm gonna do some livin'.
LUCY: Where are you goin'?
JUNITO: To see Evie.
LUCY: I told you, I don't want you going down there.
JUNITO: I have to see Evie or I'll go crazy. Besides what can happen to me so early in the day? [*Kisses* LUCY] Bye, ma.
LUCY: Wait!
[LUCY *goes to the dresser, lifts up the small television set and removes three dollar bills.*]
LUCY: Before you go . . . Get me a "Big Red" and play the 317 combo and the 666.
JUNITO: Ooo . . . You're loaded.
LUCY: Yeah I hit the number last night . . . God's good to me, Nito. Whenever he sees that my children are hungry, he always lets me win a couple of bucks back.
JUNITO: Then I suggest you play something else besides the devil number.
LUCY: Hurry up, Nito . . . They stop taking the morning bets in fifteen minutes.
JUNITO: Bendición.

LUCY: Dios te vendiga.
[LUCY *turns on her transistor radio to a Spanish station, which signals the change to the next scene.*]

Scene 4

TIME: *Saturday, April 4, 1981; 10 a.m.*
PLACE: *La Banca, which is a gambling ring within a candy store.*

There are benches on the left side of the place as well as betting-sheets taped to the wall. There is a large bullet-proof booth with two people seated behind it taking bets.
As the scene begins, the BUM *is talking to himself, and gradually begins to lean against* TONYA. ROSA, *one of the two people behind the booth, is filing her fingernails.* MIKE, *the other person, is counting the money.*

BUM: He called me up the other day... [*Mumbles*] He should've been here by now... I drew the blueprint already... [*Turns to* TONYA] I hate all these complications... I have to make a note of it... [*Looks into his bag, takes out an old pad and a blunt pencil*] That building should've been started a week ago... [*Acknowledges a bit of information from the pad*] Oh shit... oil embargo... That has to be next on the agenda—
TONYA: Ooo... the four is coming. I can feel it.
ROSA: Bueno, you gonna play?
TONYA: Yeah... I'm just waiting for Evie to pass by and give me some money.
MIKE: [*Under his breath*] She never comes in here.
TONYA: I know.
MIKE: Is she too good or something?
TONYA: As a matter of fact, yes.
ROSA: That's tellin' him, Tonya!... How is Evie anyway?... I haven't seen her in days.
TONYA: Pues, lo más bien... She's just doing a little overtime.

They make her work hard in Wall Street... She wants to get me out of this stinkin' city.

ROSA: In love with Manhattan?

TONYA: No sé.

MIKE: Maybe she's waitin' for the kid to take her away from this evil kingdom.

BUM: Bad kingdom... [*Mumbles, then writes something down on his pad*] I'm tellin' my congressman about this!

TONYA: ¡Que gracioso!... I don't know what it is, but something has changed Evie, something good. She would never waste her time like you, Mike. Diosito has been good to her.

MIKE: Baloney! There's no God in here!

BUM: He's in Washington!... [*Mumbles*] Damnit! He should have been here by now!

[*Pretends to look at his imaginary watch*]

TONYA: ¡Callese ya!

[*The* BUM *turns around facing the door.* SANTO *enters a little drunk. He bumps into the* BUM *on the way in.*]

TONYA: Santo, prestame un pesito.

SANTO: Mira nena... No soy millonario.

TONYA: Pero tienes para emborracharte.

SANTO: So what? I work for my money.

TONYA: Selling chiba to little kids? That's not work... That's murder.

SANTO: ¿Y tu eres una santa?... Didn't you blow your rent money on this last week?!

TONYA: Aw, shut up, Santo!

SANTO: When was the last time your kids had their heads on straight?... You know I met your daughter the other day—

TONYA: ¡Que mentira! Jus' 'cause she wouldn't go out with you.

TONYA: Que mentira! Jus' 'cause she wouldn't go out with you.

SANTO: Tell your daughter that. She's the one advertising.

TONYA: Why don't you go sober out?... I think the sun's beginning to affect you.

ROSA: Good for you, Tonya.

[SANTO *feels intimidated by* ROSA's *remark, but makes one final attempt to make* TONYA *look bad.*]

SANTO: Thank your daughter for a lovely evening... I think that will be enough.

[SANTO *throws a dollar bill on the floor.* SANTO *turns to leave and bumps into the* BUM *on his way out.*]

SANTO: Move out the way!

[TONYA *stays staring at the dollar. When the door slams, she screams.*]

TONYA: ¡Hijo de la gran puta!... I hope your fuckin' prick falls off!

[*The* BUM *claps.* RAMON, *the owner of La Banca, enters. He takes out a big roll of bills, counts it, then puts it back into his pocket. He sees the* BUM.]

RAMON: Hey you!... Get the hell out of here! You're stinkin' up the place!

[*The* BUM *gets up slowly, looks at him, then exits.* LOUIE *enters. He sees the dollar on the floor and goes to pick it up.* TONYA *puts her foot on it.*]

RAMON: [*To* MIKE] Hey kid, I'll collect the rest of my money later. Before you leave today, make sure the books are straight. I don't want any stupid mistakes this time.

[LOUIE *walks up to the booth, places his bet then leaves.*]

MIKE: Okay boss.

RAMON: Mira Rosa... lock up at six.

ROSA: Why so early?

RAMON: The cops are makin' their rounds today... [*Laughs*] I'm not givin' them the satisfaction of breakin' us up.

[RAMON *begins to walk out. He notices the dollar bill on the floor and picks it up.*]

RAMON: [*To* TONYA] Es tuyo?

TONYA: [*Grabs it out of his hands*] Si.

[RAMON *exits and two little girls enter.*]

FIRST GIRL: [*To* ROSA] Ma, can I have a dollar?

ROSA: What for?

FIRST GIRL: We wanna munch out.

ROSA: I don't have a dollar.

SECOND GIRL: Then give us a food stamp.

[ROSA *opens the door for the first girl, and the other gets on the bench and begins to draw on the bet-sheets.* JUNITO *enters.*]

JUNITO: Mike, is there time?

MIKE: Yeah.

JUNITO: Hi Tonya.

[TONYA *places her bet.*]

JUNITO: Is Evie at home?

TONYA: I don't know.

JUNITO: Bye Mike... See ya later, Tonya.
TONYA: Bye Nito.
  [JUNITO *exits*. MIKE *looks up and sees the* SECOND GIRL *drawing on the bet-sheets.* TONYA *sits.*]
MIKE: [*To the* SECOND GIRL] Hey stop that!
SECOND GIRL: For God's sake, these stupid papers don't help nobody.
MIKE: Watch your mouth. Want me to tell your mother on you?
SECOND GIRL: [*Mocking him*] You want me to tell yours on you?
  [*The* FIRST GIRL *reenters.*]
FIRST GIRL: Let's get out of here... Bendición, ma.
ROSA: You better be home when I get there tonight.
SECOND GIRL: Don't worry... I'll take care of her.
FIRST GIRL: Asshole. You ain't my keeper.
ROSA: Hey! Watch your mouth... and get the fuck out of here!

Scene 5

TIME: *Saturday, April 4, 1981; noon.*
PLACE: *East 147th Street, St. Anne's Avenue in the South Bronx (the old block).*

EVIE is roller skating to disco music at the opening of this scene. JUNITO *watches* EVIE *for a while before addressing her. When she sees him, she turns around, and begins taking off her roller skates.*

JUNITO: Come on Evie, don't do this to me.
EVIE: Listen little man... I've taken enough shit from you... I love you... but I'm getting tired of your attitude... so just get away from me Nito.
JUNITO: [*Coming closer*] Evie, you know I didn't mean any of the shit I said.
EVIE: Nito you know how hard I work. The last thing I needed was an argument in the street.
JUNITO: God, I said I was sorry... Will you please look at me?
EVIE: Nope.

JUNITO: [*Lifts her chin*] Please?
EVIE: What do you want from me Nito?
JUNITO: I just want you to forgive me, baby. That's all!
EVIE: Never.
   [JUNITO *kisses her on the cheek.*]
JUNITO: Will you at least think about it?
EVIE: Maybe.
   [JUNITO *gives her a long lingering kiss.*]
JUNITO: Am I forgiven?
EVIE: So? ... What did you do?
JUNITO: That's better.
   [EVIE *notices the scratch on his neck.*]
EVIE: How did you get that?
JUNITO: I had another fight with Angel.
EVIE: Again? ... Boy, you're in a fighting mood lately.
JUNITO: Want me to leave?
EVIE: Nah come on, Nito.
JUNITO: The last thing I need is for someone else to get on my case.
EVIE: Somebody's gonna have to push you ... When are you gonna realize that to move ahead, you need your mind, not these. [*Kisses his fists*]
JUNITO: You're beginning to sound like him.
EVIE: There you have it ... We're both right.
JUNITO: Not really.
EVIE: You know what's wrong with you—
JUNITO: There's something wrong with me?
EVIE: Yeah! You try so hard to be Angel's opposite that you're hurtin' yourself.
JUNITO: I can't help it.
EVIE: Yes you can! You have to believe in yourself. That's all!
JUNITO: Evie—
EVIE: I know, shut up right?
JUNITO: Right.
EVIE: I'm sorry, but I won't shut up!
JUNITO: Look Evie. I have nothin' to give the world. Angel's the smart one, remember?
EVIE: And you're not? Let me tell you something, the only reason why you're not God's answer to ... Willie Colon, is because you don't want to be.
JUNITO: [*Laughing*] I'm not Willie Colon.

The Bronx Zoo

EVIE: Are you gonna let your talent go to waste?
JUNITO: What talent?
EVIE: Your song-writing.
JUNITO: Come on Evie... That stuff is garbage. I'm never gonna make it writing junk like that.
EVIE: What do you mean junk?... Remember that last song you wrote for me...[Sings] Keep me warm inside... Love me tenderly—
JUNITO: Shh!
EVIE: Nito, that song brought tears to my mother's eyes.
JUNITO: What ya do? Sing it to her?
EVIE: Yeah.
JUNITO: That's embarrassing.
EVIE: But it's such a beautiful song.
JUNITO: I'm just not used to sharing my stuff with everybody.
EVIE: Will you at least try?

[JUNITO *takes* EVIE *by the hand and holds her close.*]

JUNITO: Can I tell you a secret?
EVIE: What baby?
JUNITO: I'm a little scared of what people might think of me... but I'll do it for you.
EVIE: Don't do it for me. Do it for yourself.

[JUNITO *begins to kiss her.*]

JUNITO: You make everything sound so right.
EVIE: That's 'cause I love you.

[As JUNITO *and* EVIE *lock in a warm embrace,* LOUIE *sneaks up behind them.*]

LOUIE: [*Grabbing* JUNITO *by the waist*] Hey Nito.

[JUNITO *turns around as* LOUIE *pinches* EVIE *on the rear end.* JUNITO *doesn't notice* LOUIE *doing this.*]

LOUIE: Hey Evie.
EVIE: Hi Louie.
JUNITO: Where's the kid?
LOUIE: Johnny had to baby-sit his sister's kids.

[*He lights a joint and offers* JUNITO *some.* JUNITO *tries to take it, but* EVIE *pushes his hand away.*]

JUNITO: What, again?
LOUIE: Yep.
JUNITO: Damn, that chick's a regular baby factory.
EVIE: Oye... Why you say that?
LOUIE: You know what's gonna happen, right? She's gonna go

dancin' with some guy she'll meet at a bar, take him home, screw her black ass off, then voilà, another kid.

EVIE: How do you know?

[JUNITO *puts on* EVIE'*s Walkman and as he bends to turn it on,* LOUIE *begins dropping hints about being with Evie.*]

LOUIE: Come on Evie... That chick doesn't care about herself... She's like the one I was with last week... [*Caresses her cheek*] ¡Mano, bien caliente! You should check her out, Junito.

JUNITO: No thank you... I don't go for your scraps!

EVIE: I don't believe I'm hearing this!... You mean you guys actually pass your ladies around like joints?... Lou, what if that girl got pregnant?

LOUIE: That would be too bad, wouldn't it? Imagine me, a father, Evie?!

EVIE: You mean you wouldn't even try to support the baby?

[LOUIE *looks at her uncomfortably.*]

LOUIE: Look Evie, chances are if she does get pregnant, I won't be the father.

JUNITO: Ooo... You're a cold mother-fucker!

LOUIE: What can I say?! Life's a bitch?!

EVIE: Well, your interpretation of life lacks maturity... How dare you stand there all happy, while destroying that girl's reputation?!

LOUIE: Ain't my fault... I wasn't her first.

JUNITO: This is better than the Duran-Leonard fight.

LOUIE: You know? That chick is so low she sleeps with her guy's best friend... He's so in love with the bitch, he doesn't even know what's goin' on.

EVIE: Maybe she does love him, and only went to you out of pity.

LOUIE: Nope. I'm sure it was lust.

[EVIE *picks up her roller skates and goes inside her apartment building, first kissing* JUNITO. JUNITO *tries to go after her, but* LOUIE *holds him back.*]

JUNITO: Hey! Where are you going? Come on Evie, man!

LOUIE: Let her go... You know how girls are... You know, me and the guys are thinking of goin' to Loco Joey's on Friday.

JUNITO: Rippin' off stereos, again?

LOUIE: You don't have to come if you don't want to... I mean just 'cause you got a job and all... pumping gas, some job.

The Bronx Zoo

JUNITO: Look I wanna start over, okay.
LOUIE: You know... You're beginning to sound like your brother...
[LOUIE *turns to leave.*]
If you change your mind. You know where to find me.
JUNITO: Yeah... right.
[*When* LOUIE *leaves,* JUNITO *sits at the edge of the sidewalk/stage and takes out his pad and pen. The music begins to play in the background, and he begins to sing:*]
Lonely in the rain,
I've been seeking dreams I may not find again.
In all these years of happiness,
I'd never walked alone
Until I was lonely,
Lonely in the rain
Goin' home...
Lonely in the rain—

It seems like life
Has thrown me a curve,
I've been through times that
I don't even deserve,
But I'm free to walk through the rain—
And I'm free to love again—

I don't like Mondays,
Or cloudy skies,
But I walk to hide
These tears in my eyes.

'Cause I'm lonely—
In the rain...
Walking through the rain...
Hoping through the rain...
Dreaming through the rain—
Without you...

Scene 6

TIME: *Saturday, April 4, 1981; 5:00 p.m.*
PLACE: *The living room of the Diaz family.*

LUCY *and* CLARA *are seated on the floor playing cards.* ANGEL *is seated on the couch reading a magazine. The phone rings,* ANGEL *answers it.*

ANGEL: Hello?...Mr. Hunter?...Yes this is Mr. Diaz. [CLARA *mimicks him*] Oh that...That was just my brother's idea of a joke...I know...No sir, it wasn't very funny.
LUCY: [*Teasing him*] Ay que fino.
ANGEL: [*Shaking a fist at her*] Really?...Oh I'm looking forward to it...It's going to be a pleasure working for you...Yes sir.
LUCY: You got it?!
ANGEL: [*Covering the receiver*] Yeah!...Oh I will Mr. Hunter! [ANGEL *hangs up the phone gingerly, then jumps in the air.*]
ANGEL: I got the fuckin' job!!!
LUCY: I'm so proud of you!
ANGEL: [*To* CLARA] Aren't you gonna congratulate me?
CLARA: [*Sarcastically*] Congratulations.
ANGEL: Aren't you happy for me?
CLARA: Yeah, but I'm not surprised. That's why I'm not excited.
ANGEL: What do you mean by that?
CLARA: Well, you always get what you want.
ANGEL: Not always.
CLARA: More than me and Nito.
ANGEL: [*To* LUCY] For once I feel guilty about being the first. [*To* CLARA] Baby...Don't you see that everything I have I had to sweat for. It's not as if I snapped my fingers and had the whole world in my pocket.
CLARA: You never had to sweat for ma's love.

LUCY: Neither did you.
CLARA: But Nito did.
LUCY: Why do you say that, negra?
CLARA: You'll get mad.
LUCY: No I won't. I promise.
CLARA: You're afraid of Nito, 'cause he reminds you of papi.
ANGEL: Sweetie, I know you want to believe that papi is around, but he isn't... You're scaring mami with all these stories.
CLARA: They aren't stories.
ANGEL: Sometimes when people try to wish hard for something to happen, they begin to imagine that it's real. I know you only want to hear your truth—
CLARA: What do you mean my...
ANGEL: But you've got to listen to me... When papi died, ma almost did too. She couldn't accept it at first, so she tried to hurt herself.
CLARA: Did you, ma?
[LUCY *nods*.]
ANGEL: Now hearing all those stories about the day papi died, is bringing back those unhappy feelings.
CLARA: I'm sorry ma.
LUCY: You didn't know... But what you said about Junito is true. He does remind me of your father... There are times when he walks through that door that I feel like saying, "How was work today, Enrique?" But then I look at him and realize your father is gone forever. Coño, they are so alike... Like when I argue with Nito, he always has to have the last word. Como tu padre. They have that don't-bother-me walk, and sweet, wonderful laugh... I really do love your brother, but it's that—
ANGEL: That what, ma?
LUCY: I'm afraid if I love him too much, God might take him away from me.
ANGEL: No ma. That won't ever happen.
LUCY: Oh Angel, don't you see that I've made Nito an outsider?
ANGEL: Ma, this is a beginning for all of us... for Nito too. I really think that the two of you should talk things out.
LUCY: More of that psychology stuff? How am I gonna tell my own son I was afraid to love him? He won't know what the hell I'm talking about.
ANGEL: I think you underestimate Nito too much... He's so

bright. Even at times when he's impossible to reach, he sticks to his feelings...Ma?

LUCY: What?

ANGEL: I really feel that you're afraid that Nito might not love you...That's it, isn't it?

LUCY: Yes.

[*Five seconds elapse.* JUNITO *enters, and sits down on the recliner.* LUCY *goes to him.*]

LUCY: What's wrong?

JUNITO: Nothing.

LUCY: [*Feels his forehead*] Well, you don't have a fever. Want to tell me what it is?

JUNITO: You wouldn't understand.

ANGEL: Give her a chance.

JUNITO: Is there anything in this place that isn't your business?

ANGEL: Let me leave.

LUCY: Stay, Angel, please.

JUNITO: Ma...I've been thinkin' a lot about the future. You know...having a career...getting married...having kids...I don't want to end up being another stereotype.

LUCY: Looks like you've been doing a lot of soul searching.

JUNITO: Yep...No more hanging out with nobodies or selling hot radios from Loco Joey's. I have to do it for Evie. I want to prove something to you. I want you to see that what I write are more than pathetic love-songs.

LUCY: I'm sorry I said that to you.

JUNITO: That's okay. It gives me a bigger drive...But still, how do I tell Evie that I love her?

LUCY: By showing her...Oye, no more of those scenes in the street.

JUNITO: I still don't know what happened to me that day.

ANGEL: Love's what happened to you...seventeen isn't easy kiddo.

JUNITO: I bet you never had any problems.

ANGEL: Oh yes I did...I had a girl...very much like Evie, but I gave up on her when I wanted to continue my studies. All she ever wanted was someone to take her out to dinner and parties. She thought I was a walkin' wallet.

LUCY: Don't remind me.

ANGEL: ¿Verdad? Ma remembers.

LUCY: That girl was wild!

ANGEL: No she wasn't.

LUCY: She wore purple platform-shoes.
ANGEL: No she didn't.
JUNITO: Are you saying this girl was a hooker?
LUCY: Hooker? [*Laughs, looks at* ANGEL, *then becomes serious*] Of course not... She just wasn't as... clean... as Evie.
JUNITO: Evie's the greatest, isn't she?
 [CLARA *climbs on his lap.*]
CLARA: I love Evie.
JUNITO: So do I... [*Looks at* ANGEL] I'm really sorry for being such a bastard and ruining your chances for that job.
ANGEL: That's okay... considering that I got it anyway.
JUNITO: Really?... Man you sure can't lose.
 [*The two brothers hug despite the fact that* CLARA *is in the middle.*]
CLARA: Hey, I can't breathe.
 [JUNITO *hugs* CLARA *as* LUCY *watches them unite for the first time in a long time. She closes her eyes trying to keep the memory alive in her mind.*]
LUCY: It's gonna be hell letting go of you three.
CLARA, JUNITO and ANGEL: [*In unison*] ¡Bendito!
 [*Lights fade.*]

Scene 7

TIME: *Palm Sunday, April 5, 1982; noon.*
PLACE: *The living room of the Diaz family.*

The music which opens this scene is slow and gentle. Church bells are ringing in the background. ANGEL *is seated in the recliner studying.* CLARA *enters from the kitchen eating a sandwich, and turns on the television set.* JUNITO *follows* CLARA, *and adjusts the set. When the two of them sit down,* ANGEL *gets up and turns off the television set.*

JUNITO: Hey!!
ANGEL: I have to study.

[CLARA *looks at* ANGEL *for a long time, then at* JUNITO.]

CLARA: Forget it, okay?

[CLARA *gets up and heads for the boys' room, first sticking her tongue out at* ANGEL. ANGEL *sits back down on the recliner. When* JUNITO *is sure that* ANGEL *is absorbed in his book, he begins to crack his gum.*]

ANGEL: Will you stop it?!

JUNITO: Sorry.

[ANGEL *begins to read, but* JUNITO *continues to crack his gum.*]

ANGEL: What's up with you anyway?

JUNITO: Clara's birthday is coming up.

ANGEL: Aw shit! I forgot!

JUNITO: Every year she begs me to buy her a birthday cake, and every year I have to say no.

ANGEL: I hate ma's fuckin' ritual already!... First she'll lock herself in her room, say a few prayers, put on that goddamned lilac dress, then go to the spot in the old block where papi was killed.

JUNITO: And little Clara always misses out... I'm giving her a party.

ANGEL: I'd like to see you try it.

JUNITO: Well, ma's gonna have to live with it... Are you gonna help me or not?

ANGEL: Ma's not gonna like it.

JUNITO: Man, I knew you'd say that... Damn Angel, you're not a little kid anymore. You're twenty-four years old! Are you gonna let what ma thinks dominate your whole life?

ANGEL: Okay, okay.

JUNITO: Okay what?

ANGEL: I'll help you.

JUNITO: Great!... I'll get Clara... [*Calling*] Hey Clara.

CLARA: [*Entering*] What?

JUNITO: Where's ma?

CLARA: I don't know.

ANGEL: I think she went to see Carmen.

JUNITO: [*Sitting on the rocking chair*] Probably so... You know how she likes to get the news from the informadora.

CLARA: I don't like Carmen.

ANGEL: What she ever do to you?

CLARA: She pinches my cheeks as if I were a little baby.

JUNITO: [*Pinching her cheeks*] You mean like this?

ANGEL: Bendito.
CLARA: Stop it Nito...I'm gonna be almost a teenager soon.
[JUNITO *and* ANGEL *exchange a glance.*]
JUNITO: Well I could see how a lady of eight—
CLARA: Nine!
[JUNITO *takes* CLARA *and begins to swing her around the room.* CLARA *begins to squeal.*]
JUNITO: You're gonna be nine years old?!
ANGEL: Be careful with her!!
[JUNITO *finally plops down in the sofa with* CLARA.]
JUNITO: Remember when ma first brought her home?
[ANGEL *comes toward them.*]
ANGEL: Yeah...I swear I had never seen anything so small.
CLARA: Was I real little?
ANGEL: [*Exaggerates*] You were no bigger than my hand... [*Gives* JUNITO *a wink*] and when you slept, you'd curl up in a little ball at the corner of your crib so no one would be able to find you.
CLARA: Really?...[*Slaps him on the arm*] Liar!!
JUNITO: So now that you're almost a grown-up lady, what do you want for your birthday?
CLARA: A party?... Please!
JUNITO: What do you say big brother?
ANGEL: Let's give the little lady a party!!
CLARA: Yippee!
[CLARA *hugs her two brothers. The lights fade. The music for the next scene is harsh and loud.*]

Scene 8

TIME: *Good Friday, April 10, 1981; 11:30 a.m.*
PLACE: *The living room of the Diaz family.*

LUCY *is kneeling by her altar (on the dresser) praying.* CLARA *is leaning against the arm of the sofa waiting for* LUCY *to finish.* JUNITO *enters the room.* LUCY *makes the sign of the cross, gets up, then hugs* JUNITO. JUNITO *kisses her lightly on the cheek.* LUCY *then takes* CLARA, *and begins to walk out.* ANGEL *enters carrying a box of cake and a briefcase.*

JUNITO: Ma, we're gonna celebrate Clara's birthday today.
LUCY: Do you two know what day this is?
JUNITO: Yeah... This is the day we're celebrating Clara's birthday.
LUCY: Have you two lost your respect?... No parties in this apartment, ever!!
ANGEL: [*To* CLARA] Go get dressed baby...
   [CLARA *exits.*]
ANGEL: Ma... It's about time... Clara needs to grow up with other children... to laugh... to play... You've been punishing her for papi's death ever since she was born.
LUCY: Stop it! I don't want to hear any more... Sinverguenza ... For nine months of pain I carried you... Cleaned up your vomit... dirtied my hands with your shit!! Now you pay me back like Judas... You betray me the first chance you get.
ANGEL: I haven't betrayed you!!... But I refuse to let you destroy Clara's life... I'm sorry ma... things are gonna be different from now on. We're gonna have music... parties and cake. A big one just for Clara.
   [LUCY *tries to take the cake, but* JUNITO *snatches it just in time bringing with him a small serving tray.*]
JUNITO: Did you get the candles?
   [ANGEL *gives* JUNITO *the candles.* LUCY *goes over to the dresser and takes out a giant white candle.*]
LUCY: You guys want a party?!... You're gonna get a party!!
ANGEL: Ma, please!!
LUCY: Shut up!! Why are you doing this to me?!
ANGEL: Because Nito and I are both men... You can't shelter us from the goddamned world forever.
LUCY: No... no... You're still my babies.
ANGEL: No ma... Not anymore.
LUCY: For heaven's sake, why don't you two just drive a stake through my heart. It'll have the same effect!... ¡Ay Diosito! What did I do to deserve such sons? When they were hungry, didn't I feed them? When they were sick, didn't I take care of them?!
JUNITO: Stop it ma!
LUCY: I'm not talking to you... I'm talking to God.

[CLARA *enters in her communion dress.*]

CLARA: Is this okay? I don't have anything else.

JUNITO: That's beautiful, baby.

[*A knock is heard at the door.* LUCY *goes to answer it. It's* LOUIE.]

LOUIE: [*Entering briefly*] May I speak to you alone Mrs. Diaz?

LUCY: Okay.

[LUCY *and* LOUIE *exit.*]

JUNITO: [*To* ANGEL] I wonder what all that was about.

ANGEL: Don't know... Nito go get some matches.

[JUNITO *goes into the kitchen. The phone rings and* ANGEL *answers it.* CLARA *kneels down next to the cake and looks at it.*]

ANGEL: Yeah?... Oh, hello Carmen. No... I can't reach her at the moment...

JUNITO: [*Entering*] I'm gonna borrow some from next door.

ANGEL: [*To* JUNITO] Yeah...[JUNITO *exits.*] What?!! That can't be true!!... Calm down Carmen!! Okay... Ma's outside!! Shit I can't tell him that!! Let me get ma...[*Calling*] Mami!! Mami!!

[LUCY *walks in crying, and picks up the phone.*]

LUCY: Then it's true?! Oh God!! No!! I can't tell him yet. Is her mother with her now?... Okay...okay. I can't tell him. It'll kill him.

[LOUIE *enters and* ANGEL *calls him over.*]

ANGEL: How'd it happen? When?

LOUIE: Early this morning. They shoved a broken bottle up her—

ANGEL: Oh my God!

CLARA: What happened, Angel?!

ANGEL: Nothing baby. Go to the other room a little while while we talk.

[CLARA *exits.* LUCY *hangs up the phone very slowly and looks at* ANGEL. JUNITO *enters with the matches.*]

LOUIE: Bye... I have to go.

JUNITO: Yo man, why don't you stay. We're having a party.

LOUIE: I have to go.

[LOUIE *exits being escorted by* ANGEL *to the door.*]

JUNITO: Angel, I thought this was supposed to be a party. Where's Clara?

LUCY: Hijo...

JUNITO: [*Notices that her tone has changed*] ¿Qué te pasó?

LUCY: Hijo... What I have to say isn't easy, and loving you, mi corazon, doesn't make it easier. I want you to know that what God gives, he can sometimes take away.

JUNITO: What happened?... Please tell me.

LUCY: I can't... I can't.

JUNITO: Is it that bad... Are you sick?... You can tell me.

LUCY: You can ask me anything... but to hurt you by telling you this... Nito, I can't.

JUNITO: Please tell me... It'll be okay.

LUCY: Someone you love—

JUNITO: Evie?... It's not Evie ma?! [LUCY *nods*.] Oh my God!! Where is she?! Tell me what happened!!

[LUCY *looks down unable to tell him.* JUNITO *tries to run out, but* ANGEL *stands in his way.*]

JUNITO: Angel... tell me... What happened? I have to know... I'm gonna marry her... tell me please!!

ANGEL: Nito, she's okay now.

[CLARA *reenters the room and stays at a distance.*]

JUNITO: In the name of Christ, tell me!!

ANGEL: [*Breaks down*] I... can't.

[JUNITO *grabs him by the collar.*]

JUNITO: Tell me you fuck—

ANGEL: [*Crying*] She was raped.

JUNITO: [*Screaming*] No!!! Evie!!

[ANGEL *tries to hold* JUNITO *back, but he is too strong.* LUCY *helps* ANGEL, *frantically trying to calm him down.* CLARA, *who is terrified, begins to scream also.*]

CLARA: Nito no!!... Please!!

[*When* LUCY *and* ANGEL *bring* JUNITO *down,* CLARA *goes to him, and begins to weep against his shoulder. Then, the lights black out.*]

Scene 9

TIME: *Good Friday, April 10, 1981; 8:30 p.m.*
PLACE: *The waiting room of Lincoln Hospital.*

It is the night of EVIE'*s rape.* TONYA *is seated next to* ANGEL *and* LUCY. CLARA *is sleeping with her head on* LUCY'*s lap.* JUNITO *is sitting alone.* TONYA *is staring at a closed door.*

The Bronx Zoo

LUCY: I was telling Nito that maybe these things happen as an omen from God.

TONYA: I think it's just fate. Anyway, if my baby goes, I know God will take her by the hand—

LUCY: Tonya, what number is it when you dream about a dead person?

TONYA: Who?

LUCY: My husband Enrique.

TONYA: Ay Dios Santo...[*Makes the sign of the cross*] The number is 241, juegalo combinao.

LUCY: You think so?

TONYA: Yeah... How long have you been having these dreams?

LUCY: It's not me. It's Clara.

TONYA: Oh, that's awful.

LUCY: Why?

TONYA: They say that when a child dreams about the dead, tragedy soon occurs.

LUCY: Are you sure?

TONYA: Positive... Did she have any other dreams?

[*The* BUM *enters and sits down next to* ANGEL. *He has a head wound.*]

LUCY: No, but she did know the story of her father's death.

TONYA: ¡Ay Virgen Santa! [*Shows her arms*] Look, I'm getting goose bumps.

LUCY: Tonya, what should I do?

[CLARA *slowly awakens, then straightens up. She gives* JUNITO *a long glance.*]

TONYA: Light a candle every day at the church in Willis Avenue for Jesus.

LUCY: Why there?

TONYA: Because the priests there only make you pay a dime to light the candles, and the ones here make you pay a quarter. They say it's for the poor, but I know they use the extra money to buy Sangria... Also play the 241 for nine days.

LUCY: Will it work?

TONYA: Guaranteed.

[*Unable to take the smell of the* BUM, ANGEL *gets up.* CLARA *begins to hit her feet against the metal chair.*]

LUCY: Stop it.

CLARA: I wanna go home.

ANGEL: You can't go home until we decide to go home.

CLARA: Then I'll go home by myself.

ANGEL: Sure big woman, how you gonna get there?

CLARA: [*Getting up and walking away.*] I'll take the bus.
[ANGEL *sits her down harshly.*]
LUCY: Wake up! Can't you see the violence around us? Don't you care that what happened to Evie might happen to you? Clara, these are bad times... being locked up like animals is not for us... but it's all we have to protect ourselves from these sucios that are supposed to be our brothers and sisters. It used to be that I was able to leave the door open for your father when he came home from work... until they killed him. Aren't you afraid that one day we'll walk into the apartment and find it empty?
CLARA: I'm not afraid.
LUCY: ¿Oh sí? You know what you're saying, right? You're saying that your father's death at the hands of these punks doesn't mean a goddamned thing... Or that Evie's chances of living are shit? Don't you see? We aren't free anymore. Coño, don't you care?
CLARA: I do... but when *will* I be free?
LUCY: Some day, when I hit the number, we might be able to get the hell out of here. I'm just waiting for that one little combo to pull me through... We'll get a little house near the beach, so we can wake up to the smell of the ocean and go to sleep with the gentle song of the coqui.
JUNITO: Ma, quit filling her head with all this garbage about living somewhere else.
[CLARA *goes to him and he addresses her.*]
JUNITO: You're getting to be a big girl now, so let me tell you about this hell we're living in... You see, this is the Bronx Zoo. I'm an animal and you're an animal. Do you know what they do with animals in a place like this? They lock them up in jails, and in themselves, so they can't show that they're afraid.
[CLARA *sits on his lap.*]
CLARA: You're scaring me Nito.
JUNITO: I know baby... I get scared too at times. The thing that you've got to remember is that if you try to show your feeling too much, the people you hate, and even those you love [*Looks at* LUCY] will step all over you. People expect you to perform like seals in a zoo. We have to balance our emotions on the tip of our noses, and toss them about in such a way that people won't know what we're really feeling.

[CLARA *gets off* JUNITO's *lap when the doctor comes in.*]
DOCTOR: Medina—
[TONYA *gets up and he says something to her.* TONYA *stands there in shock. The* DOCTOR *leaves.*]
TONYA: [*Crying freely*] Se la llevó... [*To* LUCY] ¡Dios se la llevó!
[LUCY *reaches* TONYA *and hugs her as they both begin to weep.* ANGEL *sits* TONYA *down.* JUNITO *stares at her in disbelief.*]
JUNITO: She's dead?!... She's dead?!
[LUCY *goes to* JUNITO.]
LUCY: Hijo—
[JUNITO *jumps out of his chair.*]
JUNITO: No!... She's not dead... Ma, I didn't even get a chance to kiss her one last time... Ma, not even once... Nah, she ain't dead... She's playing a trick on us.
LUCY: Esta muerta.
JUNITO: No ma.
ANGEL: Nito, she's gone now.
JUNITO: Shut up man!!... I fuckin' hate you. You're just as bad as these fucks who did this to her!!... You see me hurtin' and you make me feel worse... Let me dream a few seconds longer... let me think that she's alive!... I want to fight like the animals do... I don't want to care any more.
[ANGEL *tries to stop him.*]
ANGEL: Nito—
JUNITO: Give your fuckin' mouth a rest!
[JUNITO *runs out.* ANGEL *looks at* LUCY *for some small sign of comfort.*]
LUCY: He's in too much pain.
[ANGEL *sits and* TONYA *turns to him.*]
TONYA: You know... She was the greatest gift God ever gave me. He let me borrow her for a while until I became sure of myself, but I can't lie to you... It weakens me. You know, her father never loved me, but Evie and I... We had each other. All I ask is that he put her in a special place.. [*Tries to get up*] Oh my God, I'm so weak.
[LUCY *takes* TONYA *outside.* ANGEL *stays to put* CLARA'S *jacket on.*]
CLARA: Just like papi said.
[*The lights black out. A fast, jazzy beat begins to play in the background.*]

Scene 10

TIME: *Saturday, April 11, 1981; 10:00 p.m.*
PLACE: *149th and Third Avenue in the South Bronx; outside Loco Joey's.*

JUNITO *and* LOUIE *are standing outside the store discussing whether to go in or not.*

LOUIE: We can't go in there now. There are too many people.
JUNITO: Fuck it, just give me the piece.
LOUIE: Are you sure you want to do this? I mean, you can save it for another day.
JUNITO: You're beginning to sound more like Angel every day.
  [LOUIE *hands* JUNITO *the gun while putting on his ski-mask.*]
LOUIE: Here ... but if that shit goes off, I don't know you.
  [JUNITO *puts on his ski-mask.* LOUIE *goes in as* JUNITO *stays looking at the gun. He also enters. Five seconds elapse before anything is heard. The next sounds are* JUNITO's *voice from inside the store.*]
JUNITO: Don't fuckin' move, or I'll blow your brains out!!
  [*Three seconds pass. A shot is heard. The two boys run out.* JUNITO *is in shock.*]
LOUIE: I fuckin' told you not to pull the trigger... I fuckin' told you... [*Screaming*] Come on, Nito man.
  [LOUIE *begins to pull him.*]
JUNITO: [*Crying*] No!!
LOUIE: Then fuck you man... I don't know you.
  [LOUIE *runs off as the lights fix on the mural, then the whole stage, and finally a spotlight of* JUNITO *holding the gun. Blackout*]

THE RENNINGS CHILDREN

by Kenneth Lonergan

CHARACTERS

PAUL RENNINGS
ATTENDANT
MARY JONES, Paul's sister
PARKINSON
DR. PIERCESON

The action takes place in an east coast mental institution.

Scene 1

TIME: *The present*
PLACE: *Visitors' room at a mental institution*
SETTING: *A table and two chairs, center stage. The rest of the stage is not furnished. On the table there is an ashtray full of cigarette butts. There are two glasses, empty, and a pitcher of water on the table. There is also a deck of cards. Standing at right is* PAUL RENNINGS, *and the* ATTENDANT. PAUL *is dressed in an inmate's uniform. He is a young man around twenty. The* ATTENDANT *is in his late twenties, dressed in a white uniform.*

PAUL: Come on, man, I don't want to wear this shit for my sister. It freaks her out. Just give me my clothes, please. Miss Markins has them. Please.
ATTENDANT: Hey, Paul, you know I can't do that.
PAUL: Of course you can do it. Just get me my clothes, please? I hate for my sister to see me wearing this thing. Tell Miss Markins. Tell Miss Markins, she'll let me. [*Pause*] She let me last time. Please?
ATTENDANT: All right, I'll ask her. Wait here.
PAUL: I'm going nowhere.
   [ATTENDANT *exits.* PAUL *wanders around the room. He lights a cigarette. He looks off after the* ATTENDANT.]
PAUL: I just want my clothes, you dumb asshole. I can't respect myself wearing these goddamned pajamas!
ATTENDANT: [*Entering, right*] What's the matter?
PAUL: What?
ATTENDANT: You shouted
PAUL: Misplaced aggression.
ATTENDANT: Here's your stuff.
   [*Throws clothes to* PAUL. PAUL *puts on his clothes. They consist of a gray T-shirt, a pair of old jeans, and some*

sneakers, which he leaves on the floor.]
ATTENDANT: I just saw your sister with Dr. Pierceson—
PAUL: Hey, man, you forgot my underwear.
ATTENDANT: She should be right in. [*Pause*] Hey, put on your shoes.
PAUL: Hey, what are you, my mother? Get off my back.
ATTENDANT: Put on your shoes, Paul.
PAUL: Where am I going?
ATTENDANT: Put on your shoes, Paul.
PAUL: [*Stooping to tie his shoes*]
Put on your shoes, Paul, put on your shoes, Paul...
[*Sings*]
Puttin on my shoes, baby
Puttin on my shoes
Johnson brought the news, baby
Johnson brought the news
Put on your fuckin' shoes, Paul
Put on your fuckin' shoes...
[ATTENDANT *exits.* PAUL *takes his shoes off and throws them against the wall.*]
PAUL: There are my goddamn shoes!
[*Pause.* ATTENDANT *enters with* MARY JONES. *She is a nice-looking young woman of twenty-five. She is dressed in a simple skirt and blouse, and looks slightly prim.* ATTENDANT *exits.*]
MARY: Hello, Paul.
PAUL: Hello, Mary.
[*Pause*]
MARY: Hello, Paul.
PAUL: Hello, Mary.
[*They laugh and embrace.*]
MARY: It's so good to see you!
PAUL: Can I offer you a little drink?
MARY: You're kidding.
PAUL: Nope, natural, wholesome tap-water, Mary. Goes great with bread. Want some?
MARY: No, thanks.
PAUL: You're really missing out, man...
[*Pause. They sit down.*]
MARY: So, how have they been treating you?
PAUL: Like a lunatic.
[*Pause*]

The Rennings Children

MARY: No, seriously, are they all right to you?
PAUL: Why, are you getting worried?
MARY: What?
PAUL: All I know is, man, they put too much saltpeter in the food.
MARY: They what?...
PAUL: Forget it. Sorry.
MARY: So... how are you feeling?
PAUL: I'm feeling fine, just fine. Top of the morning, as they say. Top of the morning to ya.
MARY: Stop that.
PAUL: Well, don't ask me that, Mary. You can't expect reason from a psychopath.
MARY: You're not a psychopath.
PAUL: I'm sorry. Forget it. [*Stubs out cigarette.*] My lungs must look a lot like my brains by now.
MARY: You know you shouldn't smoke.
PAUL: Why, cause I've got enough problems already?
MARY: Yes. You have more than enough problems already... When are you going to get out of here?
PAUL: That's up to them, not me.
MARY: It's up to you. Don't put it on them, that's ridiculous.
PAUL: It's up to them, man.
MARY: You're not even trying anymore.
PAUL: That's right, baby.
MARY: Well, don't say it like that. You know it's true.
PAUL: Okay, Mary. You go ahead. You tell me how that's true. You tell me how much I love being in here, baby, you go ahead.
MARY: Look, you can say that a million times, but it doesn't change anything. You don't care about anything anymore. Or anybody, for that matter.
PAUL: Fuck you, Mary. Don't tell me I don't care about anything. I care about some things.
MARY: Like what?
PAUL: I care about you.
MARY: Oh, do you?
PAUL: Don't get huffy, Mary. Of course I care about you. Would you like to know why?
MARY: Oh, sure.
PAUL: Because you're the only person in the whole goddamn family who's not too ashamed to come see me.

MARY: If it was just that they're ashamed, we'd be in good shape.
PAUL: I know.
[*Pause*]
MARY: [*Takes his hand*] Paul, I wish you'd get better and get out of here.
PAUL: So do I, man.
MARY: Then try.
PAUL: [*Taking his hand away*] I do try, goddamn it! I am trying. I just get so sick of all these lunatics! I mean, they act like they really know what they're doing, and how they really want to help you, and they're so full of shit... I'm trying, Mary, I'm really trying...
MARY: All right... I'm sorry.
PAUL: You don't have to be sorry. [*Pause*] I just need a little help, that's all.
MARY: You've got to help yourself.
PAUL: Well, that's pretty goddamn original, Mary. You sure are one to talk.
MARY: Would you please stop?
PAUL: I don't want to stop.
MARY: STOP!
PAUL: Why don't you stop, for Christ's sake? Why don't you— [*Falls back into his chair*] I'm stopping, I'm stopping. [*Pause*] So, how is everybody?
MARY: They're all wonderful.
PAUL: Did you tell mom I wanted to see her?
MARY: Yes.
PAUL: And what did she say?
MARY: She said, "Well! Isn't *that* a surprise!"
PAUL: What did you say?
MARY: I asked her if she was going to visit, or not.
PAUL: Yeah?
MARY: She got very angry and said, "What's wrong with you, Mary? Of course I will!"
PAUL: And that bitch still isn't here! Why the hell won't she come see me, what's her problem?
MARY: Paul...
[ATTENDANT *enters, right.*]
ATTENDANT: Everything all right, miss?
MARY: Yes, thank you.

The Rennings Children

[ATTENDANT *looks at* PAUL *for a moment, then exits.*]
MARY: If you don't start calming down, they won't let you have any more visitors.
PAUL: They let the goddamn guys in straitjackets have visitors. They always let you have visitors.
MARY: Nevertheless, I think that if you start trying to control your temper—
PAUL: I do try, Mary.
MARY: All right, all right...
   [*Long pause*]
PAUL: [*Rising*] Well, I think it's lunchtime...
MARY: [*Rising*] Okay.
   [*They cross toward the right exit.*]
MARY: I'll come see you next week.
PAUL: Good.
MARY: Take care.
   [*Kisses him*]
PAUL: Good-bye.
   [MARY *exits.* PAUL *lights a cigarette.* ATTENDANT *enters.*]
ATTENDANT: That was quick.
PAUL: I'm a fast talker.
ATTENDANT: Yeah, I know. Come on, it's lunchtime.
PAUL: I knew it.
   [PAUL *starts to exit; the* ATTENDANT *blocks his way.*]
ATTENDANT: Your clothes, Paul.
PAUL: Oh, come on, man!
ATTENDANT: Don't give me any shit. Put on your clothes.
   [PAUL *crosses to change his clothes as the lights fade out slowly.*]

Scene 2

TIME: *One week later*
PLACE: *The ward*
SETTING: *There are two cots placed center stage, with a small table in between them.* PAUL *is seated on one cot, and* PAR-

KINSON *is seated on the other. They are playing War.* PARKINSON *is a man in his late forties, unshaven, with wild brown hair. Both men wear inmate's greens.*

PARKINSON: Hey, Rennings.
PAUL: Yeah?
PARKINSON: You know what I got? [*Pause*] I got a joint—as big as my finger. And for a fiver I'll let you get in on a piece of the action.
PAUL: Where'd you get it?
PARKINSON: Got it from a friend of mine. My wife sends me a box of cigars on my birthday, and I told her to hollow out one of the cigars and stick the joint in there, see how it works? Johnson, he don't care. He lets me get my cigars. Di Nobili. I hate havanas, they burn a goddamn hole in my throat.
PAUL: What's your problem, man?
PARKINSON: What the problem is, is that all these poor neurotic psychopathic sickies are so goddamn zonked out on thorazine all the time, that even if they got better, no one would know it, so no one gets the hell out. They just stay here and rot. They rot!
PAUL: That's brilliant.
PARKINSON: You should talk, you bastard, you're allergic to it. [*Leans forward*] And I tell 'em I am, too. But I'm not.
PAUL: Shut your ugly trap.
PARKINSON: Hey, who put you in here, Rennings? Your sister? [*Pause*] Nice-lookin' girl, your sister. What say, you could introduce us maybe, next time she comes?
PAUL: You and my sister?
PARKINSON: Yeah? Why not? Somethin' wrong with me?
PAUL: No, nothin', Parkinson. I think my sister might just leave her husband for a guy who's so sick in the head he can't play nothing but War and Go Fish.
PARKINSON: Hey! You're a cruel guy.
PAUL: You think I'd fix my sister up with a lunatic like you? Get out of my face.
PARKINSON: I'm not in your face.
PAUL: [*Pushes him*] You are too in my goddamn face.
PARKINSON: I hope that wasn't an intentional shove, Rennings, I hope that a lot.

The Rennings Children

PAUL: I'll punch you in your ugly face if you don't shut up.

PARKINSON: Try it, you goddamn hippie freak!

PAUL: War!

PARKINSON: Ha!

[*They play out the War.* PAUL *wins.*]

PARKINSON: Shit!

PAUL: Some guys have it, some guys haven't. What's this? An ace! Amazing!

PARKINSON: You bastard, go ahead and gloat. Go ahead! I like it!

PAUL: I'm gloating, man, I am gloating. You're dead. I got all the aces now.

PARKINSON: You got all the aces? You got all the aces?

PAUL: Man, what'd I just say?

PARKINSON: But you don't have the brains, asshole; you ain't got it where it counts. [*Taps his forehead*] See, I got it up here. I know everything that's goin' on. [*Pause*] Listen, you wanna know what my wife is doing, right now?

PAUL: No.

PARKINSON: You wanna know?

PAUL: No.

[*Pause*]

PARKINSON: You wanna know?

PAUL: No, I don't want to know what your wife is doing! I don't give a crap for your wife!

[*Pause*]

PARKINSON: So, you wanna know?

PAUL: Shut up, and get off my back.

PARKINSON: Oh, now I'm on your back. Before I was in your face, now I'm on your back.

PAUL: [*Swipes the cards off the table*] Shut up, you fuckin' maniac! SHUT UP!

PARKINSON: All right, all right.

[*Pause*]

PAUL: Get the cards, man.

PARKINSON: [*Picking up the cards*] Now we have to start all over.

[PARKINSON *gathers up the cards, and divides the deck. They begin to play again. Pause.*]

PAUL: So, listen... What's your wife doing now?

PARKINSON: You really wanna know?

PAUL: Yeah, I really want to know.

PARKINSON: [*Leans forward*] She's on top of her desk, that's where she is.

PAUL: On top of her desk?

PARKINSON: Her boss's desk.

PAUL: Her boss's desk.

PARKINSON: And you wanna know what she's doin' there?

PAUL: I think I can guess.

PARKINSON: She's bangin' his filthy brains out!

PAUL: Wonderful.

PARKINSON: You wanna know how come I know?

PAUL: Sure.

PARKINSON: 'Cause they got a schedule. Every morning, nine o'clock sharp, blow-job.

PAUL: Great.

PARKINSON: Then at morning coffee break, she jerks him off, then at noon, he eats her out, just to keep her goin'. He's a pervert!

PAUL: You're sick, man...

PARKINSON: Then at two-thirty, every day, they do the job.

PAUL: How come you know all this stuff?

PARKINSON: 'Cause she sends me messages.

PAUL: She sends you messages?

PARKINSON: Yeah. At night. When I sleep. Tells me all about it.

PAUL: You're really off the fucking wall.

PARKINSON: Screw you, you bastard.

[*They play for a while.*]

PAUL & PARKINSON: War!

[*They play it out.*]

Double war!

[*They play it out.*]

[*Leaping to their feet*] Triple war! Triple war!

[PARKINSON *wins, and lets loose a loud cheer.*]

PAUL: Shit!

PARKINSON: Mine, all mine! King, queen, two queens! No problem. All mine!

[PARKINSON *starts arranging his cards.*]

PAUL: What are you doing?

PARKINSON: I'm makin' a power line.

PAUL: A what?

PARKINSON: A power line. [*Pause*] So, tell me, Rennings, how

The Rennings Children

come your foxy sister put you in here?
PAUL: I don't know, man.
PARKINSON: Bullshit!
PAUL: It is not!
PARKINSON: It is too, it's gotta be bullshit.
PAUL: All right, it's bullshit. I don't want to tell you.
PARKINSON: Well, that's different. Why didn't you say that in the first place?
[*Pause*]
PAUL: You really dig my sister?
PARKINSON: You kiddin'? Are you kiddin'? [*Pause*] Don't you hit me.
PAUL: I won't hit you... No, my sister's nice, and all, but she's a pain in the ass. I just wish she'd get off my back, that's all. She's always telling me I gotta do this or that, and get in better shape—what kind of shape is she in? She's always fighting with her husband, or mom, or whatever. She's always freaking out about something... Forget it...
PARKINSON: No, no, go ahead. I know what you're sayin'...
PAUL: You don't know what I'm saying. You don't even know what the hell I'm talking about.
PARKINSON: No, I do, I really do. My wife, she's exactly the same—
PAUL: Will you shut up already about your wife?
PARKINSON: No, listen, she's—
PAUL: Shut up! Get the hell out of my face!
PARKINSON: What is this with you and your goddamn face?
PAUL: [*Jumps up*] HEY, JOHNSON! HEY, JOHNSON! Get the hell in here, you lousy, good-for-nothing freak! JOHNSON!
[ATTENDANT *rushes in, out of breath.*]
ATTENDANT: What's the matter?
PAUL: Mr. Johnson, this man is insane.
ATTENDANT: Take it easy, Paul. Are you feeling all right, Mr. Parkinson?
PARKINSON: Fine. I'm just great. I'm playing cards with Attila the Hun, I'm great.
PAUL: Man, I'll kill you.
PARKINSON: Try it, long-hair!
[*They jump toward each other. The* ATTENDANT *steps in the way.*]
PAUL: One side, soldier, I'm a gonna kill that man.

ATTENDANT: Do I have to separate you guys like a couple of children?

PAUL: You're kidding.

ATTENDANT: I'm very serious, Paul. Now, I want you guys to shake hands.

PAUL: Listen, Johnson, I'm getting worried. Think you can hook me up, you know, with a little electro-shock action?

ATTENDANT: I'm warning you, Paul.

[*Pause*]

PAUL: Does this mean you won't take me dancing, now?

ATTENDANT: Keep it up, Paul. If you guys don't calm down, I'm calling Miss Markins. So do you guys want me to call Miss Markins?

PARKINSON: Dancing? You take him dancing?

PAUL: I don't want to go dancing with Miss Markins, I want to go with you. [*Pause*] I love you, Johnson. I've always loved you, ever since I saw you in that spotless white uniform, with your broad shoulders pressing against—

PARKINSON: You're both a couple of fairies!

PAUL: Hey, shut up, you.

ATTENDANT: All right, boys. This is your last warning.

[*He exits. Pause.* PAUL *and* PARKINSON *resume their game.*]

PARKINSON: You faggot.

PAUL: Oh, shit, man, why don't you just be quiet?

PARKINSON: Fuck you.

PAUL: War!

PARKINSON: I don't wanna play with you no more.

PAUL: Come on, man, I'm sorry.

PARKINSON: No wonder you're in the goddamn bin. You're nuts. You're a social menace.

[PARKINSON *throws down his cards and exits.*]

PAUL: Hey, Parkinson! Hey, man, come on . . . shit!

[*The lights fade out.*]

Scene 3

TIME: *Later that week*
PLACE: *The visitors' room*
SETTING: *The same as before.* PAUL *sits in the left-side chair, smoking a cigarette.* ATTENDANT *enters with* MARY.

ATTENDANT: Here's your sister, Paul.
  [*Exits*]
PAUL: Hey, Mary.
  [*They kiss, then sit.*]
PAUL: How you doin', Mary?
MARY: Okay, I guess.
PAUL: Okay, you guess? That doesn't sound too great.
MARY: Well, I'm not great.
PAUL: What's the matter?
MARY: Nothing. I don't want to bore you with the stupid little details of my stupid little life.
PAUL: That never stopped you before.
MARY: You're the one that needs to get going.
PAUL: How come you always want to talk about my problems but you never say nothing about yours anymore?
MARY: Because yours are much more interesting.
PAUL: Yeah, there are a lot of great guys in here.
MARY: I was just joking.
PAUL: I know. Sorry.
MARY: That's all right.
PAUL: No, but listen, man, what's wrong with your little life out there? Having problems with Mikey?
MARY: When am I not having problems with Michael?
PAUL: I don't know. What's he done now?
MARY: It's not just what he does... It's the whole thing...
PAUL: What whole thing?
MARY: You know, happily married at twenty-five, good solid career, joy, love, wifehood, womanhood... Little Mrs. Per-

fect... Soon I get a litter of Perfectettes. Michael just has no comprehension. I feel like I'm stranded... And you know, sometimes I just feel like saying, "Why bother?" I'm having troubles, but who really cares? It's like... Oh, forget it. I don't want to talk about it anyway. How are you?

PAUL: We're back to me again? Shit, that was fast.

MARY: You seem better than last week. You haven't attacked me yet.

PAUL: When did I ever attack you, Mary?

MARY: Well, you never actually attacked me, but you seem as though you're not so upset, you know?

PAUL: You know, I just figure, why bother? If people are gonna act like assholes, let them. What do I care?

MARY: Well, anyway, it's good to see you more relaxed.

PAUL: I'm glad you're happy.

[*Pause*]

MARY: Oh, mom has a message for you.

PAUL: Yeah, what?

[MARY *removes an envelope from her bag, and hands it to* PAUL, *who opens it.*]

PAUL: [*Reading*]
Dear Paul, I don't think that we have to pretend that I haven't been somewhat neglectful of my responsibilities, but I want you to know that it has nothing to do with you. I still love you, and believe me when I tell you that I still know you're my son. Even though I don't write often enough (I know I don't!) I still think of you all the time, and wish you were here. Your sister says you've asked for me, and I did feel a stab of guilt. It isn't as though I don't want to see you, it's just that this is a very bad time for me. It's hard to explain, so just believe me when I say I'll see you soon.
                                            Love, Mom.

[PAUL *looks over the letter once, and tosses it on the table.*]

MARY: Oh, Paul...

PAUL: It's all right, Mary. Don't say anything. I know what she's like by now, don't I? She's a bitch.

MARY: Paul—

PAUL: It doesn't matter.

MARY: It doesn't?

PAUL: Like I said a second ago, people are sick, and so let them be sick, learn to get along without them.

The Rennings Children

MARY: That depends on how many people you think are sick.

PAUL: A lot of weird characters out there, Mary. Gotta learn to be tolerant.

MARY: Every time I come here, you act so different... do you know what I mean?

PAUL: Are you asking if I have a split personality?

MARY: No, I know you don't. It's just that last time you were so angry, and today, you're a pussycat!

PAUL: I'm just better adapted.

MARY: To what? Better adapted to what? To this?

PAUL: Yeah.

MARY: I don't want you to become adapted, for God's sake!

PAUL: Well, what do you want from me, man?

MARY: You know what.

[*Pause*]

PAUL: I stopped having nightmares for a while, did I tell you?

MARY: No, you didn't. But that's great.

PAUL: But I had one last night.

MARY: A new one, or the same old...

PAUL: No, no, it was... I never had one that was like this... Let me tell you. You wanna hear it?

MARY: Not really, but...

PAUL: Well, it started out with me and Davy in this field of wheat, or something. I'm not sure what it was. Anyway, we're racing and playing Frisbee, right?... Then—wait, no, it started out with a whole bunch of us in the field, and then me and Davy were alone somehow... Then... Then... It was like the Frisbee we were throwing was razor-sharp on half of it... and we were playing a game where you have to catch it on the side that's not sharp? And somehow... I had control of the game, and he really wasn't into playing... but I made him... And, I knew it was wrong, man, but I didn't want to stop, you know?

MARY: Yeah?

PAUL: So then, we're both playing well, I kept catching good, and so did he. But then I started throwing it faster, lots faster, and he said, "Hey, not so fast, man," but I said, "It's cool, come on, come on," and just kept throwing it faster and faster, like a sick fuck—so finally of course, he makes a bad catch and his goddamn hand is practically cut in two, bleeding everywhere—

MARY: I don't want to hear any more.

PAUL: So what do I do, I throw the goddamn thing at him again and hit him in the face... [*Pause*] So then, I had this shotgun, somehow. It was really weird. The Frisbee changed into a shotgun, you know how things do in dreams... And he was supposed to catch the bullet—so I fired, but of course he couldn't catch the bullet 'cause his hand was cut up and his face, and there was blood in his eyes, and so bang! He's dead. Isn't that weird?

MARY: Paul, listen to me, honey, he is dead.

[*Pause*]

PAUL: What, Mary?

MARY: He's dead, honey. He's been dead for more than a year.

PAUL: Mary, shut the fuck up.

MARY: It's true.

PAUL: I don't believe that shit for a second, Mary. Not for a second. You're so thick, sometimes, Mary, I swear to God. Why don't you understand?

MARY: How can I understand? He's dead, he's—

PAUL: [*Grabbing her*] Shut up!

[*They freeze.* MARY *is very frightened.* PAUL *releases her and sinks back into his chair.* MARY *touches his hand.*]

MARY: Paul, I—

PAUL: I'm sorry, Mary.

MARY: Paul...

PAUL: You just shouldn't...

[*The* ATTENDANT *enters.*]

ATTENDANT: Is everything all right, miss?

MARY: Yes, thank you.

[*The* ATTENDANT *exits.*]

MARY: Paul, I'm sorry. I'm so sorry. Please, I don't know why I said anything. Please, honey, I'm sorry...

[PAUL *does not respond.*]

MARY: It's just that I don't understand why you got sick... I mean, I know you loved him, but sometimes... sometimes terrible things happen... you just have to face up to them. You can't drown yourself in your own guilt. Everybody has terrible things in their life. Look at me. Maybe I'm not in the hospital, but I feel like I belong in one, sometimes, I swear. But I know that my problems can be solved—eventually. You have to do the same thing. I know it's hard, but you used to be so good at it... Believe me, I know how

hard it is. You... Paul, are you listening to me?
PAUL: Yes.
MARY: Don't you understand what I'm saying? Nothing is that impossible to deal with. You are an intelligent, talented person. You have a lot up there, and you just can't let this destroy you. Please, Paul, you have to listen to me. It's important, honey.
PAUL: [*Lights a cigarette*] Forget it, Mary. It's nothing. I shouldn't have told you.
MARY: Paul, listen—
PAUL: Hey, look, man, don't feel bad. I don't care, I really don't. It's cool. [*Pause*] Everything's fine.
MARY: Okay.

[*Pause*]

PAUL: Anyway, besides that one dream, I haven't been, you know, bothered or anything.
MARY: Well, that's terrific.
PAUL: I do wish my mommy would come see me, though.
MARY: Don't waste your time worrying about her.
PAUL: I know, I know, she's screwed up, but she's still my mommy.
MARY: I really don't know how to get through to her. She keeps saying she'll see you, she'll write you, she'll do this, she'll do that... I just keep pounding and pounding at her until she finally does something. She doesn't even think you need her.
PAUL: Come on, man, I don't need her.
MARY: Then why?... What did you just say? Why do you always talk about her, and ask her to come see you?
PAUL: Because she's my mommy! That doesn't mean I need her, does it? Do you need her?
MARY: What?
PAUL: Do you feel that you need mom, that you require her existence in order to fulfill your own?
MARY: No, but I'm not—
PAUL: No. See? So how come you need her; how come you don't need her, and I do? Huh?
MARY: You know the answer to that.
PAUL: Because I'm nuts, and you're the Rock of Gibraltar.
MARY: You got it, kiddo.
PAUL: Some goddamn rock. [*Rises and crosses to the right exit.*]

Johnson! Hey Johnson!

[*Pause. The* ATTENDANT *enters.*]

ATTENDANT: Yes, Paul? Something I can do for you?

PAUL: How about getting me a pack of cigarettes, man? [*Gives him a dollar*] I know you're not supposed to, but you know how it is... Paul gets ugly without his smokes.

ATTENDANT: Okay, Paul, but just this one time.

[*Takes the dollar and exits.*]

PAUL: [*Walking around*] Nice guy.

MARY: Yes, he seems very... nice.

PAUL: Oh, yeah, he is.

[*Pause*]

MARY: Have you written any more poems?

PAUL: Yeah, one. I've been writing this one thing...

MARY: Can I hear it?

PAUL: No, man, I don't think so... It's hard...

MARY: Come on.

PAUL: No, Mary, I don't really want to... Sorry...

MARY: Okay, you don't have to.

PAUL: Sorry.

MARY: That's okay.

[*Pause*]

PAUL: [*Looking through his pockets*] Here, Mary, let me read it to you, 'cause I know you're really dying to hear it, right?

MARY: Right.

PAUL: [*Picks up his poem and walks around*] Okay, listen.

When you're on the outside
With your cars and your curls
Your bars and your girls
You own the fucking world
And plus you think you're real hip
And plus you think everything else
Is real hip too
But then you hear someone scream
Like an animal and take a breath
So's he can scream some more
And then you say,
"Hey, man, that's real fucked up. Wow."

Now you're inside 'cause the
Screaming blew your mind

The Rennings Children

They say don't live with us no more
Now I live with guys who piss
All over the goddamn floor
All alone in my army bed
A zillion volts run through my head
My insides turning into lead
The world is filled with streaks of red
I wish that I was finally dead
Until something said
"Hey, man, relax, and take what you can find
Just be yourself and forget your mind."

Gimme a bath, and a little room
A big glass window, a nice
Sunny day, a couple of eggs,
A nice place to sleep,
And then leave me alone
So I can rest.
[*Pause*]

MARY: Well, that's wonderful, Paul, that's just wonderful.
PAUL: It's the way I feel, man. Sorry if you can't relate to that.
MARY: It's not that I don't like the poem, I just don't really agree with what you're saying. I think—
PAUL: Yeah, Mary? What am I saying?
MARY: I'm saying that you are perfectly capable of getting out of this hospital if you tried.
[*Pause*]
PAUL: What's out there, Mary? [*Pause*] What is out there? Your life? Your dinky little life? The life I had? It sucks out there, Mary, you can tell by all the guys in here, okay? You can tell. So why are you on my back, every time you come to see me?
MARY: Because I can't stand it—
PAUL: No, hold on, I know it's just because you care about me, but you're not helping me. You understand? You're not helping me.
MARY: What would help?
PAUL: I don't know. But I don't need Mary Poppins.
MARY: You make me wonder, sometimes.
PAUL: Now, Mary, what kind of crock of shit is that? What made you want to say something as stupid as that?

MARY: If you could hear yourself, you might not think so.
PAUL: Just stop, Mary, okay? Just stop now.
MARY: Okay. [*Pause*] Okay, I'll stop. I'll leave you all alone. [*Pause*] How's it going with Dr. Pierceson?
PAUL: I don't know. Okay, I guess.
MARY: Do you like her?
PAUL: Yeah, she's a pretty cool old girl.
MARY: She's not old.
PAUL: That's an idiomatic expression, Mary.
MARY: Oh. [*Pause*] I've talked with her a couple of times. She seems like she's very intelligent.
PAUL: Yeah? I guess so.
MARY: And she is very nice.
PAUL: What do you talk about with her? You, or me?
MARY: You, of course.
PAUL: But of course.
MARY: I think she could really help you if you'd let her.
PAUL: As far as I'm concerned, Mary, she can help me all she wants.
MARY: Well, good.
PAUL: She's not like a lot of other shrinks, you know. Most shrinks are like, no matter how professional and comforting they are, you can tell that underneath they're really assholes, so why should you tell them anything? But Dr. Pierceson's real cool. She's not like that. She's nice.
MARY: That's great to hear.
PAUL: And you should meet some of the attendants at this joint, man, they'd crack you up. Johnson is a riot, Mary, I'm telling you. He's sort of on the Neanderthal level, but he has a good heart, you know?
MARY: Yeah.
PAUL: I don't know, I really used to freak out at this place... But you know? It's not really that bad here...
MARY: What did you say?
PAUL: I said I don't think it's so bad here.
MARY: Are you serious? [*Rises*] I can't believe that. I'm going. [MARY *starts to exit toward the right.* PAUL *jumps up and grabs her, spinning her around.*]
PAUL: Wait a minute! What the hell is wrong with you? What'd I say?
MARY: What's wrong with me? What's wrong with me? What's wrong with you? You like it here! Here's your little room

and you could just stay in here for the rest of your life, couldn't you?

PAUL: I didn't say that.

MARY: Then what are you saying?

[*Pause*]

PAUL: I wasn't saying anything! What...

MARY: Let go of my arm. [*Pause.* PAUL *lets go.*] I just want to say that I think you are such bullshit, sitting here every week, lying to me, telling me that you're trying so hard! You're trying! You're not doing anything!

PAUL: I am trying! I am trying!

MARY: That is such bullshit! How can you stand there and say that to me? You don't care what happens to you! And you don't care what happens to me, either—

PAUL: Mary, please—

MARY: Just leave me alone. As far as I'm concerned, you can sit here for the rest of your life and write poetry about sunshine and hot tubs!

PAUL: Mary—

MARY: Just go to hell.

[MARY *exits, right.*]

PAUL: MARY!

[*Pause.* PAUL *does not move. Silence. Slowly he falls to his knees and then to the floor, as the lights grow dim. The* ATTENDANT(s) *puts him on his feet and leads him off, right. The* ATTENDANT(s) *returns and removes the table, then moves the chairs to dead center, on inward diagonal angles to one another.* DR. PIERCESON *enters, and sits in the chair on the right. She is in her late thirties, dressed in a skirt, blouse, and white medical robe.* MARY *enters from the left and sits in the other chair. The lights come up to full.*]

DR. PIERCESON: We haven't really been able to get any sort of response out of him at all. He speaks, but usually in monosyllables, and very rarely. He seems to have almost completely withdrawn. For the moment.

MARY: Doesn't he talk to you?

DR. PIERCESON: Very rarely. Sometimes he'll talk to one of the other patients, but they're all starting to disregard him, too.

MARY: Wonderful.

DR. PIERCESON: I'm afraid that after your last visit, I haven't really made up my mind as to what exactly I ought to say, because I'm not really sure how I stand with you... But I certainly would like to advise against saying things that will upset him.

MARY: I know, I just...

DR. PIERCESON: Well, it's very hard seeing someone you love in an institution, and I know a lot of people who don't even deal with it as well as you do...

MARY: Which doesn't seem to be so wonderful lately.

DR. PIERCESON: No.

MARY: You ought to meet our family. Not one of them has even come to see him once. Not once.

DR. PIERCESON: Yes, I know. It bothers him a lot, too.

MARY: Bothers me.

DR. PIERCESON: Me too. [*Pause*] I get very angry sometimes, when I see parents who won't even try. I'm not saying your parents, because I don't know them, but some of the kids in here have parents that visit them once a year, and that's it. Once a year. It's amazing to me.

MARY: But I would have thought that you'd understand why that is—

DR. PIERCESON: Oh, I understand it, but sometimes that doesn't make it any less disturbing.

MARY: I know what you mean. There are a lot of things that I *don't* understand, though.

DR. PIERCESON: Such as...

MARY: Such as why he's given up. And he has given up. Why doesn't he want to get out of here anymore?

DR. PIERCESON: He's tired. [*Pause*] You read that poem. He's tired of trying, and he doesn't see any reward at the end of his efforts. He doesn't see what's so wonderful about the outside world.

MARY: I'm not so sure I do, either... but doesn't he understand that anything is better than being here?

DR. PIERCESON: If he could understand that, he probably wouldn't be in here.

MARY: But—

DR. PIERCESON: Mrs. Jones, you expect too much from him. He is a disturbed young man. You cannot expect the same kind of rational behavior that you get from most people.

MARY: I think he's a lot less disturbed than you seem to think he is.

DR. PIERCESON: I know. But it takes time, and it doesn't make it easier for him if everyone around him is pushing him. He has to be able to push himself.

MARY: But why doesn't he?

DR. PIERCESON: Because he isn't ready yet. And now, I don't know when he will be.

MARY: And now? You mean, now that I've set him back? [*Pause*]

DR. PIERCESON: Yes.
[*Pause*]

MARY: Well, you and I certainly have different ideas about how to deal with the problem.

DR. PIERCESON: Yes we do. And I would like to suggest that you let me handle it. It's my job. It's what I was trained to do, and that's why he's in this hospital and under my care.

MARY: I think I know my brother a little better than you do, Dr. Pierceson.

DR. PIERCESON: No doubt you do. But you suffer from the same delusion that a lot of people suffer from...

MARY: And what is that? [*Pause*] You can say anything you like; I won't be offended.

DR. PIERCESON: Well, Mrs. Jones, if your car broke down, and you took it to a professional repairman, you wouldn't feel yourself as capable as he, would you?

MARY: Well, considering the reliability of the garages these days...

DR. PIERCESON: Well, if your brother had some sort of physical disorder, such as an eye infection, and you took him to a specialist, you wouldn't give the specialist advice, and you wouldn't try to treat Paul yourself, because you know that the eye doctor has studied, and is a professional M.D....

MARY: Yes?...

DR. PIERCESON: But everybody has lived, and spent years with other people, so everyone is a psychiatrist, by virtue of experience. You've had twenty-five years of first-hand experience with human beings, and like everyone else, you feel that you are qualified to help them with their troubles, and you are, to an extent. But when someone is severely neurotic, or borderline, or a psychotic, neither you, nor any of the other people who feel qualified *are* actually capable of treating that person. Only someone who has trained, who has studied, who has learned about Freud, and Jung, and

Adler, and the countless other psychologists, only someone who has been working alongside of a hundred years of psychoanalytic theory is qualified to treat someone like your brother. The same way that only a surgeon who has been through training, and has had years of experience, is qualified to do open heart surgery.

[*Pause*]

MARY: Well, I don't really know what to say to that... I'm sorry, but I just can't believe that you don't think it makes any difference that I've known my brother for so long...

DR. PIERCESON: I think that qualifies you to be his sister, not his shrink.

MARY: But I'm not trying to be his shrink, I'm only trying to help.

DR. PIERCESON: I know that, and until last time, your visits have been very helpful.

MARY: Well, that's good to hear.

DR. PIERCESON: But I don't know whether it's a good idea for you to see him right now. I'm not saying it isn't, I'm just saying that I don't know.

MARY: I don't even know if he wants to see me. He must hate me now...

DR. PIERCESON: Do you want to see him?

MARY: Yes, of course I do.

DR. PIERCESON: Well, that's half of it.

[*Pause*]

MARY: How long is he going to be here?

DR. PIERCESON: Mrs. Jones, there's just no way I can answer that question now.

MARY: What do you mean, now? That's the same thing you said to me six months ago.

DR. PIERCESON: It's just not as simple as you seem to think. I don't know how to expl—

MARY: Well, God damn it, can't you do anything?

DR. PIERCESON: Yes, we can. [*Pause*] But it takes time.

MARY: [*Rising*] Of course it takes time. I don't know what else I would expect, really. No wonder he likes it here; everyone around him does nothing but agree with him. Well, doctor, how the hell do you expect him to get better if you just let him go on telling himself his friend is alive? Pretty soon he'll really start to believe it. Then he'll be in great shape—

DR. PIERCESON: He does believe it.

MARY: How can he? How can he possibly believe that? Where does he think Davy is?

DR. PIERCESON: I don't think he knows.

MARY: Well, maybe you'd better tell him.

DR. PIERCESON: He isn't ready yet. I could tell him, but he wouldn't believe me. It would just—

MARY: Well when will he be ready? How long are you going to let him rot in here? Is there something wrong with you? Don't you understand? He's my brother! I want to get him out!

DR. PIERCESON: I know you do. Please believe me. I want him to also.

[*Pause*]

MARY: [*Sitting again*] I know. Please forgive me. I'm a little tense.

DR. PIERCESON: That's perfectly understandable.

[*Pause*]

MARY: When can I see him?

DR. PIERCESON: I'm not sure. Hopefully soon. But we're just going to have to do this my way. You'll have to trust me.

[*Pause*]

MARY: All right. We'll do it your way.

DR. PIERCESON: Thank you.

MARY: [*Rising*] Well, I really have to go now. Thank you very much for everything.

DR. PIERCESON: [*Rising*] That's all right, Mrs. Jones. I'll be getting in touch with you.

[*They shake hands, and* MARY *exits left.* DR. PIERCESON *sits again. Pause. The* ATTENDANT *enters with* PAUL, *who is dressed in his hospital uniform. The* ATTENDANT *sits him in an empty chair.*]

DR. PIERCESON: Thank you, Mr. Johnson.

[ATTENDANT *exits. Silence*]

DR. PIERCESON: So, how do you feel?

[*Pause*]

PAUL: I'm getting pretty goddamn sick of that question.

DR. PIERCESON: Why?

PAUL: Look, Dr. Pierceson, don't play any shrink games with me today, I don't want to be shrinked.

DR. PIERCESON: Okay. [*Pause*] I just spoke with your sister.

PAUL: Yeah?

DR. PIERCESON: She's very concerned about you.

PAUL: I'm real concerned about her, too, man, she's nuts.
DR. PIERCESON: She wanted me to tell you that she's sorry.
PAUL: That's a lot of bullshit.
DR. PIERCESON: I'm not lying to you, Paul.
PAUL: I know you're not, she's lying, man, she's lying.
DR. PIERCESON: You think so?
PAUL: One more fuckin' shrink remark like that and I'm not gonna say another goddamn thing. I'm telling you she's lying. She's lying to herself, man, and to me, but she's lying to herself first and foremost. [*Long pause*] Man, what should I do? What if I gotta tell her something, and she's not gonna want to hear it? She's gonna freak me out... But I have to tell her, man, I just don't know...
DR. PIERCESON: Tell her what?
PAUL: Well, I sure as hell can't talk to you, you're trying to shrink me out. Call my sister, let me see her.
DR. PIERCESON: I really don't know if it's such a good idea at this time, Paul.
PAUL: Oh, no, Doc, please, I have to see her. Please.
DR. PIERCESON: I'll tell you what. The three of us can have a talk, how would that be?
PAUL: No, man, I gotta see her alone. Please, I won't freak out, I promise, please...
[*Pause*]
DR. PIERCESON: Well, all right, Paul. You can see her. I'll give her a call.
PAUL: Thank you.
[*The lights fade out.*]

Scene 4

TIME: *A few days later*
PLACE: *The visitors' room*
SETTING: *The same as before.* PAUL *enters, dressed in his street clothes. He lights a cigarette.* MARY *enters, and* PAUL *drops*

the cigarette, stubbing it out with his foot. They look at each other for a moment.

MARY: [*Approaching him*] Paul, I'm sorry, I'm so sorry.
PAUL: [*Putting up his hands*] I don't want to talk about it, Mary, I really don't.
MARY: All right. What do you want to talk about?
PAUL: I have to tell you something, Mary.
MARY: What? [PAUL *is silent. Pause*] Let's sit down.
PAUL: Go ahead.
   [MARY *sits, and watches* PAUL. PAUL *is silent. Long pause*]
MARY: Paul, what is it? Can't you even talk to me anymore?
PAUL: Am I supposed to be able to talk to you, man? Do you think it's easy talking to you? Is that what you think?
MARY: Paul, I said I was sorry, and I really mean it. I don't know what else to do. I—
PAUL: [*With sudden violence*] Well just SHUT UP! Let me think, for Christ's sake! Just shut up!
MARY: [*Tight*] All right, I'll shut up.
   [ATTENDANT *enters right.*]
ATTENDANT: Everything all right, miss?
PAUL: Hey, Johnson, why don't you get the fuck out of here and let me talk to my sister for once!
ATTENDANT: [*Angry*] Watch it, Paul.
MARY: [*Rising*] Please, Mr. Johnson.
ATTENDANT: [*Grudgingly*] All right, miss. But you call me if...
   [*He exits right.* MARY *sits down again.* PAUL *looks at her.*]
PAUL: I lied to you, Mary. I never stopped having those nightmares. I have them every night, baby. The nightmare is always the same goddamn one. Davy and me are driving on the West Side Highway. Sometimes we're stoned, sometimes we're not. [*Pause*] Sometimes we're wasted. It never makes a difference. We rev the car up, you know, go fast for kicks, since there's no one much on the highway, and no sharp turns for miles. And we go faster and faster, man. The dial just keeps going up and it doesn't stop. All the time we're laughing, and singing along with the radio. Then we see there's a lot more traffic than before and Davy starts getting kind of nervous. But I'm driving, and I don't care, and anyway, Davy's still laughing. But then he starts getting

real scared, because I just keep going faster and faster. And he starts begging me to slow down, but I don't. I just want to go, and I don't even really think about him at all. [*Pause*] Then... we hit something... I don't know what... But there's this sick crashing noise, and... I duck my head, and go through the windshield, but only my back gets cut up, and it feels like a billion little needles cutting into me. I go flying up, up, way up high, and I'm thinking that when I come down, it'll really hurt. But it doesn't. I just hit grass and go rolling. Then suddenly I'm walking up a hill, and I can see smoke up above. And I go and look, and there's the car, wrecked. And there's Davy. And... [*PAUL begins to cry.*] Half his face's been torn off, and he doesn't have no arm... But he's still alive. And... he's just shaking because he can't cry... because he's got no eyes left. Oh, God, and he stays alive for so long, just shaking and shaking, covered with blood... Blood everywhere, all over me, too... And finally he dies, and I wake up... Every fucking night, Mary! And I know it's not true! I didn't kill him, Mary. I really didn't. I couldn't have! I don't know where he is, but he's alive... I know it. I...

[*Long pause. PAUL weeps. MARY rises and goes to him, and he clutches her.*]

MARY: [*Soothing*] Paul, no. Don't cry. Please don't cry. Listen to me. Paul, listen to me. You didn't kill anybody. You didn't. But Paul. Paul. You can't go on like this... He's dead. You have to face it. You know it's true... Try to listen...

PAUL: NO! SHUT UP!

[*PAUL throws MARY away from him and upends the table. He smashes at the chairs wildly.*]

PAUL: HE'S NOT DEAD! HE'S NOT DEAD! HE'S NOT DEAD!

[*He goes toward her, grabbing her by the throat. The ATTENDANT runs into the room and flings PAUL away from MARY. The ATTENDANT jumps at him and pins him on the floor, twisting his arm behind his back. He jerks PAUL to his feet and drags him toward the right exit. MARY grabs ATTENDANT's arm*]

MARY: Stop! Leave him alone!... Please!

ATTENDANT: I'm sorry, miss.

MARY: STOP! STOP! For God's sake! Paul!

The Rennings Children

[PAUL *breaks free and runs to the extreme left of the stage. He stands there, apparently calm. The* ATTENDANT *goes toward him.*]

MARY: Please don't take him away. He stopped, can't you see? He stopped! [ATTENDANT *ignores her and walks toward* PAUL. MARY *grabs his arm and jerks him back.*] Can't you see? Please let me talk to him. Please.

ATTENDANT: [*Shaking off her hand*] I'm sorry, miss.

MARY: Let me talk to him! Do you want him to be crazy forever? For God's sake, what's wrong with you? Let me talk to him!

[*The* ATTENDANT *pauses, uncertain. He looks at* PAUL, *who is standing perfectly still, watching them silently, waiting.*]

ATTENDANT: All right. You go talk to him.

[MARY *crosses past* ATTENDANT *and approaches* PAUL *cautiously.* ATTENDANT *watches.*]

MARY: Paul, listen to me. [*Pause*] You're right. I'm sorry. You're right. I was wrong. He's...alive. I don't know where he is, that's all. But he's alive, I swear to God. [PAUL *is silent.*] Paul listen to me! I was wrong! I was wrong! You're right. Dr. Pierceson was right...I was wrong. [PAUL *is silent.*] Don't you hear me? Don't you understand? Why don't you say anything? What more do you want from me? You were right and you can stay here as long as you want, and I'll go back out there and rot! Is that what you want to hear me say? [*Pause*] Paul? [MARY *cautiously reaches out and touches his arm.*] Paul?

PAUL: [*Mocking her*] Mary? [*With sudden violence he slaps her across the face.*] You fucking bitch! Bitch! [*The* ATTENDANT *is across the room in a bound. He grabs* PAUL *and drags him toward the right exit.* PAUL *offers only the slightest resistance.*] [*To* MARY] Go back to your goddamn husband. Leave me the fuck alone! Christ, couldn't you help me? [*The* ATTENDANT *drags him offstage.* MARY *takes a few steps after them, then stops. She looks around the room. She picks up the fallen objects and furniture and sets everything up perfectly. She sits in one of the chairs.*]

CURTAIN

PRESENT TENSE

by John McNamara

CHARACTERS

NORM PRESCOTT
ANN ALLEN
JERRY MELNICKER
DOUG WILLARD
MOTHER'S VOICE
SHELLY
MARGIE EATON

The play takes place in the bedroom and in the mind of NORM PRESCOTT *on a Saturday morning. The action is continuous.*
We are in NORM PRESCOTT's *bedroom. It is the typical bedroom of a seventeen-year-old American male, circa late twentieth century. There is a single bed, which is unmade, a dresser and table and chair and a closet. A door to the right leads to the outside hall and the rest of the house; a door to the left leads to the bathroom.*
The wall behind NORM's *bed is covered with movie posters, college pennants and girlie pictures. Strewn about the room are various items of clothing, books, papers, dirty magazines. On the dresser is a photograph of a pretty girl about* NORM's *age.*
The lights come up and we see NORM PRESCOTT *lying on the bed, holding a phone to his chest. He tips his head up, looks us over for a moment and then addresses us.*

NORM: Excuse me, but how many people here are virgins? I know that's a really embarrassing question and there's no reason to raise your hands. Especially for the people here on their first date. It's just that a lot of things have been on my mind lately and basically one of them is sex... I've got nothing against sex. But unfortunately it's got nothing against me either. [*A nervous laugh. He clears his throat.*] Which is part of the problem, but not really. You see, I've got this girl friend, Ann Allen. We've been going together about three months. [*Shows us her picture from dresser*] This is her. She's a knockout, right? And she's also nice and wonderful and sweet and very smart. Let's face it, she's the light of my life and I never want to change the bulb. Everyone tells me how lucky I am. I think I heard one person tell Ann how lucky she is. My mother. Anyway, we've got this really wonderful teenage relationship...
[*Lights fade and come up centerstage only.* ANN ALLEN, *indeed a very pretty girl of seventeen, comes on. She eyes* NORM *lovingly and sighs.*]

NORM: Hi, Ann.

ANN: Oh, Norm. I've missed you so much. [*She kisses him.*] You look so handsome today. So virile, so...

NORM: Masculine.

ANN: Oh, yes, yes. Have I told you how lucky I am to have you?

NORM: Not since lunch.

ANN: I am. I'm so lucky to have someone so handsome, so virile, so... so...

NORM: Masculine.

ANN: Oooohhh, yes, yes, yes—!

NORM: [*Addressing us,* ANN *freezes.*] Oh, who am I kidding? It's not a wonderful teenage relationship. It's fraught with guilt, despair, hopelessness, jealousy, pity and fear. I feel like I'm living in a Dostoevsky novel.
[*Lights go to black. We hear two bodies rustling in the dark. Then* ANN *and* NORM's *voices are heard.*]

ANN: Don't.

NORM: Why not?

ANN: Because.

NORM: Because why?

ANN: Because... because. [*Silence*] Please, Norm.

NORM: But I'm not doing *that* anymore.

ANN: Well, I don't like what you're doing now, either.

NORM: Okay, why don't we draw up a series of boundaries, like the United Nations. Everywhere I can't go is communist territory.

ANN: I hate it when you get sarcastic.
[*A light is switched on.* NORM *and* ANN *are on the bed.* ANN *rolls off, tucking in her shirt.*]

NORM: Look, we don't *have* to do this. I mean, we could go for walks, go to more movies...[*A frustrated sigh*] ...play Scrabble.

ANN: Is this the only reason you want to go out with me?

NORM: No, of course not, Ann.

ANN: Everytime we do this, you seem to forget I'm a person, I have a mind.

NORM: Everytime we do this, you seem to forget I'm a person and that I have a *body*.
[ANN *throws up her hands in frustration.*]
I'm sorry. I didn't mean that.
[*He touches her arm gently. She turns to him and smiles. Then she kisses him gently on the lips. While they are kiss-*

ing, his hand reaches for the light and switches it off. Silence. Then—]

ANN: Norm!

NORM: Okay, that's it!

[*The lights come up.* ANN *is gone.* NORM *is gone.* NORM *is downstage, addressing us.*]

NORM: Every time! This happens every time! The Battle of the Blouse... And I know what you're thinking. That I'm just one of these Joes out for a good time. Love 'em and leave 'em. I realize I may seem very suave and devil-may-care to you, but I love Ann. I mean, I've been out with other girls before. Like...[*Thinks hard for a moment*] Like Mary Jo Jenkowski, who is so huge she is getting curvature of the spine. And... Sally Billings, who invented a whole new strain of social disease. The point of this being, I've been around, I'm no kid. But with Ann it's different. It's like I want to... to... own her. I think about her every minute of the day. When I'm walking, talking, sleeping, eating. Once I even sculpted her face in my mashed potatoes. But what makes it really rotten is, I have no idea if she feels the same way about me. Okay, she is my girl friend and she's never turned me down for a date—except the time she had her wisdom teeth removed. She said she didn't want to bleed on me. Other than that, though, dating is really good. But we never talk. Well, we talk, but it's never about anything...

[ANN *is holding a newspaper, scanning the movie section.*]

ANN: What about a comedy?

NORM: I want to see a love story.

ANN: I hate love stories. Let's see a war movie.

NORM: Do you love me, Ann?

ANN: [*Flips a page*] Did you get your allowance this week? Can we go to dinner, too?

[NORM *grabs the paper away and holds it behind his back.*]

NORM: If you don't love me, say so. I want to hear it. I can take it. When I kill myself I'll make it look like an accident so you won't be embarrassed.

ANN: You're a nut.

NORM: You do love me.

[*She hugs him tight, and in doing so, spots an item in the paper.*]

ANN: Let's see a monster movie.

[*Lights on* ANN *fade.* NORM *talks to us.*]

NORM: You see how distant she is? How she sidesteps even the subtlest questions? I could never figure out *why* she was doing this until two weeks ago, when...

[JERRY MELNICKER, *a friend of* NORM'*s, comes ambling on. He spots* NORM.]

JERRY: [*Chewing a piece of gum*] Hey, Norm, guess what I heard? You know Ann? You know, your girl friend? You know who she used to go out with? Doug Willard. For like six months. Isn't that bizarre? Who'd think that any girl who had Doug Willard would want to go out with you?

[JERRY *breaks up laughing. Then he pauses as if listening.*] What?... What are you getting so upset about?... Oh, yeah? Well, so's your mother.

[*Lights fade and* JERRY *disappears.*]

NORM: I know he's an idiot. I know he shouldn't bother me. But do you know who Doug Willard is?

[*The blaring horns of* "The Olympic Theme" *are heard as* DOUG WILLARD *moves onto the stage, dressed in only a bathing suit.* DOUG *is tall, tan and good-looking. He smiles a dazzling smile and his muscles ripple.*]

He's the captain of the football team, the captain of the swim team, the captain of the baseball team. The Commander-in-Chief of interscholastic sports.

[NORM *crosses over to this self-conjured fantasy of* DOUG.]

But the worst part is... I know him. In addition to everything else, Doug Willard is the editor of the school paper. And as an editor, let me tell you, he makes one hell of a swimmer.

[NORM *crosses over near his bed.*]

But I don't want to get into personalities, particularly since Doug is somewhat lacking in that area. Okay, yeah, you could say that he's relatively attractive in a physical sort of way but I... I've got... heh, heh, I...

[ANN *comes on. She eyes* DOUG *lustfully, crosses to him and throws her arms around him,* "The Olympic Theme" *continuing to play.* DOUG *lowers* ANN *to the ground, then lowers himself on top of her as a horrified* NORM *watches. Then* DOUG *begins doing push-ups, with* ANN *directly beneath him, counting.*]

ANN: One... two... three...

NORM: I've got nothing! What have I got? I'm skinny, I'm pale, I can't use after-shave because it gives me pimples.

[DOUG *and* ANN *have faded out and are gone.*]

It's stupid, right? Jerry didn't tell me he caught them in the back seat of a Thunderbird. He told me they *used* to go out together. It's over. [*He stands.*] Oh, yeah? Then why hasn't she called? Huh? Can you tell me that? Because tonight is the night of the prom. And this is something that Ann and I have been planning for weeks. And do you know what she told me the other day?

[ANN *appears, holding a telephone. At the opposite side of the stage,* NORM *holds one also.*]

ANN: ... oh, and I've kind of got some bad news.

NORM: Oh, yeah? What's that?

ANN: Well, I'm not sure I'm going to be able to make it to the prom Saturday night.

[*Pause.* NORM *looks ill.*]

Norm? Are you there?

NORM: Uh-huh.

ANN: I'm not sure or anything. It depends on if my Aunt Gladys gets better. You know the one who lives in Kalkaska? She's in the hospital and she's got gallstones and we might have to go up to visit her.

[*Pause again.* NORM *doesn't look any better.*]

Norm?

NORM: Mm-hm?

ANN: Are you mad?

NORM: No, no. Saturday's fine.

ANN: Okay, well, I'll see you in school tomorrow.

NORM: Right. Bye.

ANN: Bye.

[*They both hang up. Lights on* ANN *fade.*]

NORM: Do you know what time it is? Noon. It is no longer Saturday morning, it is Saturday afternoon. And guess who hasn't called?

[*He crosses up near the bed and looks at a tuxedo hanging there. It is only a little more garish than the typical prom tux—with lots of blue ruffle and trim.*]

I explained the whole thing to the guy at the tuxedo shop. You know how it's sometimes easier to spill your guts out to a total stranger? And he was very compassionate, gave me a special deal. I'm renting it by the hour. [*Looks at his watch*] Yep, there goes another two-and-a-quarter.

[*He hangs the tux up and sits on the bed.*]

Sure, I know what you're saying. You're saying they never

see each other anymore. Oh, yeah? Well I've got something to show you. It happened just the day before Ann called me to say that her "Aunt Gladys" was sick. It happened in school...

[*Lighting change. A bell rings. We hear voices, as if we are in a hallway. Several lockers appear.* ANN *walks on. She leafs through a textbook.* DOUG *comes from behind the lockers, his nose buried in a book as well. He runs into* ANN *and both their books fall to the floor. They bend over to pick them up, see each other.*]

ANN: [*Surprised*] Doug, hi.

DOUG: [*Equally surprised*] Hi, Ann, how are you?

ANN: Fine. I haven't seen you around school much lately.

DOUG: Oh, I've got all my classes in the morning.

ANN: That explains it. I've got most of mine in the afternoon.

DOUG: Yeah.

ANN: Well...

[*There is an awkward pause.*]

DOUG: Well...

ANN: I've got to get going.

DOUG: I'll see you later, then.

ANN: Bye.

[*They walk off in opposite directions. As* NORM *speaks, they freeze where they are.*]

NORM: Looked perfectly innocent, didn't it? I just happened to be in the hall when this happened. And I'm sure to the untrained eye that was just the chance meeting of two people who haven't seen each other in a long time. But to the expert.

[NORM *whips out a pointer.* DOUG *and* ANN *begin to move like a film being run backwards at high speed. They go quickly and silently through every move in reverse. Then, when* DOUG *is back at the lockers it begins to run forward again at normal speed.* DOUG *comes from behind the lockers and runs into* ANN. NORM, *pointer-in-hand, freezes the action.*]

Exhibit A. Doug running into Ann, a lame excuse so that two bodies lusting for one another can touch for a brief moment.

[*Action proceeds.* ANN *drops her books.* DOUG *reaches down, picks them up and hands them to her.*]

Let's take that again, in slow motion.

[*Action is rewound. Then, in slow motion,* DOUG *reaches*

down and picks up the books.]
Now, notice how as he bends over, his eyes toil over her legs. How her eyes stare at his back. And as he gives her the books, his hand is passionately drawn to hers. Now the conversation.

ANN: [*Playfully, a smile*] Doug...hiiii. [*She bats her eyes.*]
DOUG: Hi, Ann. [*Very macho*] How are you?
ANN: Fine. I haven't seen you around school much.
DOUG: [*Moves close*] Oh, I've got most of my classes in the morning.
ANN: Oooohhh. *That* explains it. I've got most of mine in the afternoon.
DOUG: [*Grins*] Yeah.
ANN: [*Expectantly*] Well...
DOUG: [*Eyeing her*] Well...
ANN: I've *got* to get going.
DOUG: I'll see you later then.
ANN: Bye.

[*They walk off in opposite directions.* NORM *steps forward to say something, then all at once* ANN *and* DOUG *turn, look at one another and rush into each other's arms. They fall to the floor and tear each other's clothes off.*]

NORM: Stop it! Stop it!! Stop it!!! Haven't you two got any sense of decency?

[*The lights come down on* DOUG *and* ANN. *They fade out.*]

NORM: Okay, so I'm a little paranoid.
MOTHER'S VOICE: Norm!
NORM: Yeah, mom?
MOTHER'S VOICE: Your friend Jerry is here to see you.
NORM: All right, send him up.

[*For reasons which we will see in a moment,* NORM *quickly begins picking up the* Playboys *and* Penthouses *spread around the room. He stuffs them into a drawer of his dresser, under his bed, under the covers and under the pillow.*]

JERRY: [*Off stage*] Norm, hey, Norm...

[JERRY *enters. During the following scene he systematically goes through the room and finds the* Playboys *and* Penthouses *in the drawer of the dresser, under the bed, under the covers and under the pillow.*]

JERRY: Hey, Norm, y'know tonight? What are you doing tonight?
NORM: [*A glance at the tux*] I dunno. Why?
JERRY: Great, great. There are these two girls I met last night.

They go to the junior college and we were talking and they want to go out tonight. But you know how girls are, they want to go together so I've got to find somebody else and I thought, "Hey, your old buddy Norm'll help you out," soooo...

NORM: Aw, I dunno, Jerry.

JERRY: Hey, you think they're ugly, right? Well I've got a picture of them right here.

[*He takes a snapshot out of his back pocket and hands it to* NORM.]

JERRY: I told them I was gonna have to go around looking for another guy to go out, so I made them take that picture in the Foto-Booth at the mall.

NORM: Which one would I get?

JERRY: Either one. They don't care. [*He is looking at one of the magazines, suddenly gets an idea.*] Maybe, y'know, we could switch off half-way through the night.

NORM: Wow. Boy, Jerry. That blond one. She's really...

JERRY: You like her, huh?

NORM: Yeah.

JERRY: Her name's Shelly. I told her all about you.

NORM: You did?

JERRY: Sure. They would have come over with me but I didn't want you to be embarrassed.

NORM: Embarrassed? No way. I think she's—Hey, what am I saying? [*Hands the picture back*] I can't go out with other girls. What about Ann?

JERRY: Oh, Ann shmann, you shouldn't tie yourself down the way you do.

NORM: No, Jerry, I'm sorry. I can't do it.

JERRY: But Norm—

NORM: It just wouldn't... feel right. [*He lies down on the bed and puts the phone on his chest.*] Ann's going to—er, she's supposed to call soon.

JERRY: What do you mean.

NORM: She's going to call me and tell me whether we're going to the prom tonight.

JERRY: Wait a minute. Let me get this straight. The prom is less than seven hours away and you still don't know if you're going?

[NORM *doesn't answer. He clutches the phone tighter.*]
You let her treat you like that?

NORM: Well...

JERRY: You let her push you around like that? Norm... how long have we known each other?

NORM: [*A lament*] A long time, Jerry.

JERRY: That's right. A long time. I'm your buddy, Norm. I care about what happens to you. And believe me when I say I know how these things go. I do it to girls all the time. It's called the Old Put-Off.

NORM: The Old Put-Off?

JERRY: Sure. She called you... two days ago?

NORM: Three.

JERRY: Same difference. And she said she didn't know what was happening, some family crisis was going, but she'd let you know today.

NORM: Yeah.

[JERRY *chuckles wisely.*]

JERRY: Oh, Norm...

NORM: Th-the Old Put-Off?

JERRY: The Old Put-Off.

[NORM *takes the phone off his chest and sets it on the dresser. He sighs.*]

Look, Norm, you think I like seeing you like this? You think I haven't noticed the way you've been acting? Mumbling, moaning, twitching... You're like an ad for Preparation H. Look, I'm not saying Ann's not a great girl. I think she's great. Everybody says she's the best.

NORM: What does *that* mean?

JERRY: It's just an expression. But Norm, Ann is not the earth and sky. You're not stranded with her on a desert island, you know?

[*In the course of this speech,* JERRY *has made his way around to where the tuxedo is hanging. He eyes it for a moment, looks at* NORM, *raises an amazed eyebrow, then continues.*]

I'm gonna go home and try and get my dad's convertible. Give me a call if you change your mind. And remember. We're talking about junior-college girls. A once-in-a-lifetime chance.

[JERRY, *with several of* NORM's *magazines under his arm, walks out. Before* NORM *can say anything, he is gone.*]

NORM: The Old Put-Off. How could I be so stupid? Of course. The Old Put-Off...

[*He rolls off the bed and rubs his forehead with the palms of his hands. Then he looks up.*]

God, you should have seen that girl in the picture. The blond one, Shelly.

[SHELLY *appears, her golden locks fluffed up around her heavily made-up face. She is dressed in a tight, red skirt and a white blouse.*]

I wonder what she would have been like?

[NORM *walks over to* SHELLY. *He grins.*]

I know what she would have been like. She would have been really dumb... and really easy.

[*He walks close to* SHELLY, *stops and gives her what he thinks is his sexiest look.*]

Hi, baby. Come here often?

[SHELLY, *noticing him for the first time, turns and looks at him.*]

SHELLY: Beat it, creep.

NORM: I can't even have fun in my imagination.

[SHELLY *fades out and disappears.*]

Anything's better than real life, though. Can you believe that? The Old Put-Off. I should have seen it weeks ago, when I started pressuring her... all because I couldn't get her bra off myself.

[*He picks up a bottle of cologne off the dresser and splashes some on.*]

I mean, we all know how it goes, don't we? Let's face it, Ann feels abused by me, like I don't really love her anymore but that's just an excuse so that she can do what she really wants. You see, the present boy friend...

[*Indicates himself*]... abuses the present girl friend.

[ANN *appears, frozen in a spotlight.*]

In which case, the present girl friend goes rushing back to the past boy friend.

[DOUG *appears in a spotlight of his own. Then both he and* ANN *unfreeze and run into each other's arms.*]

DOUG: Ann, Ann. What's wrong?

ANN: It's... it's... oooohhhh...

DOUG: Ann, you've got to tell me.

ANN: It's Norm.

DOUG: Norm? Your present boy friend?

[NORM *points to himself again to clarify things.*]

ANN: Yes. Him.

DOUG: What is it? Has he... abused you?

ANN: Oh, Doug, let's not talk about it. I'm just glad I'm here with you.

DOUG: I'm glad you're here too, Ann. I've missed you a great deal.

ANN: And I've missed you.

DOUG: There are no regrets then? About us?

ANN: [*The good sport*] Oh, a few. But you know I'll always love you, even if I am going out with some little schmuck who tries to take my bra off on the couch.

[*Both* DOUG *and* ANN *turn and look at* NORM. NORM *sighs and looks away.*]

DOUG: What do you say, huh? One more... for old times' sake?

[*This catches* NORM *off-guard. He spins around, wide-eyed.*]

ANN: [*A shrug*] Sure.

[*They fall to the floor and tear each other's clothes off.*]

NORM: Stop it!! Stop already!!! Jesus, you two ought to have your hormones removed! [*The lights come down on* DOUG *and* ANN *and they melt away.*] What's really going on here? Why hasn't she called yet? Why am I sitting here slowly going out of my mind? [*Thinks a moment*] Maybe the secret is just to be aloof, play the field, not tie yourself down to one person. Like Doug. Maybe if I was more like him. God, you should see the way he is with women. There's this one girl who works on the paper. Margie Eaton...

[DOUG *appears wearing a button-down shirt and glasses.* MARGIE EATON, *eighteen and beautiful in a cheerleaderish sort of way, walks on.*]

DOUG: Uh, Margie...

MARGIE: Yes?

DOUG: About this article you wrote for the school paper.

MARGIE: Did you like it, Doug?

DOUG: Oh, yes. Very much. You've got a terrific sense of the language.

NORM: I wonder who read it to him.

DOUG: But I think it'll need a rewrite.

MARGIE: Oh?

DOUG: I think we should go over it... together.

MARGIE: *Oh.*

[*She moves close to him.*]

DOUG: [*Removing the glasses*] My place? Eight o'clock tonight?

MARGIE: Oh, Doug, sure!

[*Then all at once, MARGIE reaches over and tears DOUG's shirt open, revealing a Superman "S" underneath. NORM turns and looks at us, just as surprised as we are. DOUG and MARGIE fade out.*]

I've really been spending too much time alone.

[*He shoves his hands in his pockets and moves aimlessly around the room.*]

I don't want you guys to get the wrong idea about Ann and me. Things haven't always been this horrible. I mean, they actually used to be pretty good, pretty fun. [*He smiles at a memory.*] I remember this one time...

[ANN *appears. She is holding something behind her back.*]

ANN: Hey, Norm, close your eyes, I've got a big surprise for you.

NORM: What is it?

ANN: Close the eyes and you'll find out.

[NORM *closes his eyes.* ANN *takes a step toward him.*]

NORM: No, forget it. I don't trust you.

[*He opens his eyes.*]

ANN: Don't trust me? Norm, what is an emotional commitment, what is a relationship? It's based on trust. So if you're committed to me, you have to trust me.

[NORM *gives in and closes his eyes.* ANN *takes out a water pistol and squirts water in his face.*]

ANN: Happy April Fools' Day!

NORM: It's not April Fools' Day!

ANN: Every day with you is April Fools' Day.

NORM: [*Shielding his face from the onslaught of water*] Hey, what is this? What'd I do?

[ANN *stops shooting and steps away.*]

ANN: You thought I forgot, didn't you?

NORM: Forgot about what?

ANN: The frog.

NORM: [*Innocently*] What frog?

[*At the same time, he makes a move for the gun.* ANN *darts away and squirts him a good one in the face.*]

ANN: That big, slimy, ugly green frog that I found in my locker a week ago. And it had that note around its neck that said, "Ann, something terrible has happened, kiss me quick. Love, Norm."

NORM: You think that *I* did that?

[*She squirts him.*]

ANN: Yep.

NORM: Boy, talk about your emotional commitments and your trust. You think that I'd do something like that? Endanger the life of a frog, jeopardize the fact that you might have frog-a-phobia. *Jerry* would do something like that.

[*Listening to this,* ANN *is stupid enough to lower the gun to her side.*]

NORM: You're the woman in my life, the person that I cherish and respect the most. I don't know why you think that I did it but...

[*At that moment,* NORM *lunges for the gun and gets it.*]

ANN: Oh, you creep!

NORM: Ah-ha!

[*He holds her at bay. She puts her hands up.*]

NORM: That's it. Just stay like that.

ANN: Don't you dare, Norm.

[*He raises the barrel*...]

ANN: No, I'm serious, don't you dare.

[*He laughs sardonically*...]

ANN: The fun and games are over, Norm... Norm, this is a new blouse.

[NORM *fires.* ANN *squeals and starts to run, but he cuts her off by shooting the floor in front of her.*]

ANN: No, not my good penny loafers!

[NORM *puts the gun down. They are both laughing hard.*]

ANN: You really did put that frog in my locker, didn't you?

NORM: [*Nods*] And you never kissed it.

[*They put their arms around one another.*]

ANN: I knew it couldn't be you. The frog was too good-looking.

[*Before* NORM *can respond,* ANN *kisses him. And just as he is starting to enjoy it, she pulls the gun out of his hand and squirts viciously.*]

NORM: Go on, shoot. I've got a high rate of saturation.

[*She shoots.* NORM *goes after her.*]

Now you're going to get it!!

[*He chases her and she runs out of the room.*]

MOTHER'S VOICE: Norm!

NORM: Yes, mom?

MOTHER'S VOICE: There's someone here to see you.

NORM: It's probably Jerry again. Two wasn't enough so he went out and found triplets...

[DOUG WILLARD *appears in the doorway and strides into the*

room. NORM *jumps as if seeing a ghost and we realize this is no fantasy.*]

DOUG: Hey, little fella, how ya doin'?

NORM: Ah, Dou-Dou-Dou...uh...

DOUG: Mind if I come in?

NORM: Ah, n-n-n...uh...

DOUG: Nice room. Very nice.

NORM: Ah, w-w-w...uh...

DOUG: [*Sees tux—unconvincingly*] Nice tux.

[NORM *sits on the bed, very weak. Then he notices the picture of* ANN *and lays it face down.*]

DOUG: You feel okay?

[NORM *manages a nod.* DOUG *opens a notebook he is carrying.*]

DOUG: Listen, the reason I stopped by was, I want to talk to you about this article you wrote for next week's issue.

NORM: Article?

DOUG: The football article. You remember.

NORM: Oh, yeah. That.

DOUG: Only one thing bothered me about it and I'm a little embarrassed to mention it but... you don't mention me once in the article. I mean after all, I am the quarterback and I think that entitles me to a, uh, passing reference.

[*To* DOUG WILLARD, *this is cleverness at its very limit. He laughs heartily.*]

NORM: I guess it depends on your view of football. Do you really see the quarterback as the key to the game?

DOUG: Absolutely. You see, this is a good article but it's got just one flaw.

NORM: What's that?

DOUG: It's boring. I think sports articles should be exciting, encompass the thrill of the game. Now take that pass I made in the second quarter. The way I faded back, ignoring the three linemen coming at me. Then I just tossed that ball...

NORM: ...to one of the linemen coming at you. He intercepted and made a touchdown.

DOUG: Well, I think you get the idea anyhow. I'd like to see a re-draft by tomorrow. It'll go to press on Monday.

[*He hands* NORM *the article.* NORM *glances down at it.*]

DOUG: By the way, do you have a bathroom I could use? It was kind of a long drive over here.

NORM: Oh, yeah, sure. [*Goes to bathroom door and opens it*] It's right in here.

DOUG: Thanks.

[*He goes inside and closes the door behind him.*]

NORM: Jesus, this is something I never expected. But do you see what I mean? He's got all the brainpower of a corn flake. And he wants me to rewrite the article...Rewrite the article?... That's funny. He never stopped by the house to ask me to rewrite before. What the hell is he up to? It's got to have something to do with Ann. This is just too much coincidence. First that meeting in the hall. Then her Aunt Gladys gets sick. Hah! Who does she think she's kidding? Nobody has an Aunt Gladys.

[DOUG *and* ANN—*locked in an embrace—appear in a spotlight.*]

ANN: When you tell him, Doug, be gentle. For a skinny little wimp, he's pretty nice.

DOUG: I'll just tell him the truth. That I dumped you for another girl but now I want you back. And since he means absolutely nothing to you, you never want to see him again. And if he ever does come near you, I'll push his face through the back of his head.

ANN: Oh, you're such a romantic.

DOUG: I know.

ANN: [*Breathing heavily*] Oh, Doug, Doug, Doug, Doug...

DOUG: [*Also breathing heavily*] Ann, Ann, Ann, Ann...

[*They paw at each other, grope, grab, kiss, fall to the floor and—*]

NORM: Stop it, stop it, stop it, stop it!!!!!

[DOUG *and* ANN *both get up, brush themselves off and walk out. At the last moment,* ANN *turns to* NORM, *puts her hands on her hips and sticks her tongue out at him. Then she fades out and disappears.*]

NORM: Christ, I'm driving myself crazy!

MOTHER'S VOICE: Norm! Someone else is here to see you!

NORM: Hah! Someone else is here to see me, someone else is here to see me! Suddenly half the English-speaking world is knocking down my door! Mr. Popular all of a sudden...!

[ANN *appears in the doorway.*]

ANN: Hi, Norm.

[*When he sees her,* NORM *screams and jumps. Again, no fantasy.*]

NORM: What are you doing here?

ANN: Well, I would have called but—

[*From offstage, a toilet flushes.*]

ANN: Oh, do you have company?
NORM: Company? Company, oh, God, that's right. Oh, no. Oh, no, here it comes, the big axe, the final scene...

[DOUG *steps out of the bathroom. Ever the class-act, he is zipping his fly.*]

DOUG: You know something little fella—[*Sees* ANN, *a quick zip*] Ann...
ANN: Doug...
NORM: Why couldn't I live in a room with a back door?
ANN: What are you doing here?
DOUG: Oh, me and the little fella were just working on a football article. I didn't know you and Norm were friends.

[ANN *smiles*.]

DOUG: So... how's everything?
ANN: Good. How about you?
DOUG: Couldn't be better. Listen, I was just leaving. Could I give you a lift?
ANN: No, I just got here.
DOUG: Oh. Well, I'll wait. Say, why don't we have lunch?
ANN: Doug, I don't think you understand—
DOUG: I know this great hamburger place—
ANN: I came to see Norm.

[*A pause as* DOUG *considers this*. ANN *crosses over and stands near* NORM.]

DOUG: What do you mean? You mean you came to... see Norm?

[*A nod from* ANN]

DOUG: [*Short laugh*] What, are you guys... going together or something?
ANN: Yes. We are.

[DOUG's *laughter is hysterical. He cannot contain himself as he looks at* NORM *and* ANN.]

ANN: What is so funny?
DOUG: [*Taking a breath*] Oh, nothing... nothing.
ANN: No, I want to know what it is you find so humorous.
DOUG: [*Managing a straight face*] No, no. It's nothing. Really. Listen, I've got to get going...[*Takes out a pencil and scribbles on the corner of a notepad*] But, uh, you can call me sometime, Ann.

[*He tears off the corner of the paper and hands it to her.*]

ANN: [*Taking it*] Oh, can I?
DOUG: Yeah, absolutely.
ANN: Well I don't think I will, Doug. [*Starts to tear the paper to bits*] And I don't want you to call me either. In fact, I

don't ever want you to speak to me again, because if you do I'll push your face through the back of your head.

[*On this, a double-take from* NORM]

DOUG: Hey, Ann—

ANN: Go on, leave. I didn't come to see you.

[DOUG *gets his books and angrily turns to exit.*]

NORM: Yeah, that's right. And one more thing, Doug.

[DOUG *walks out of the room, oblivious to* NORM. NORM *calls after him through the doorway.*]

NORM: I don't ever want you to call me little fella again, because I happen to have a norm and it's Name!

[*It is a moment before* NORM *realizes his mistake. When he does, he slips his hands into his pockets and smiles sheepishly.*]

ANN: Can you believe the nerve of that guy? What a jerk.

NORM: Yeah. Tell me, despite the fact that he's tall, muscular and handsome, what did you ever see in him?

ANN: I'm sorry I'm late.

NORM: [*Goes to tux, stands in front of it so* ANN *can't see it*] Oh, that's okay. I was just kind of sitting around anyhow, not doing much.

ANN: I just stopped by to say that if you want, I can go to the dance tonight.

NORM: Your Aunt Gladys is all better?

ANN: The gallstones turned out to be gas.

NORM: [*Taking the tux off the wall*] Then...then I'll pick you up around seven.

ANN: Okay.

[*She leans over and kisses him. He starts to kiss her back but she breaks away with a laugh.*] I'd better get going. I've only got six-and-a-half hours to get ready.

NORM: Well, if you work straight through you should be able to make it.

ANN: I'll see you tonight.

[NORM *sits on the bed with his tux as* ANN *goes out of the room. He leans back, staring at the ceiling.* ANN *comes back into the room. She pauses in the doorway, looking at him.*]

ANN: Hey, Norm?

NORM: Yeah?

ANN: I have a confession to make.

NORM: Oh?

ANN: You asked me what I saw in Doug? Something I never

told you was...one day while Doug and I were still going out, I was in the hall at school. And I saw this guy trying to open his locker. He wasn't exactly what I'd call handsome, but he was definitely cute. And he stood there, spinning and spinning the dial of that lock, trying and trying to get that locker open. Then he started hitting it. Then kicking it. And when that didn't work, he started talking to it. "C'mon," he said, "will you please open up?...Look, if you let me hang my jacket up, I'll share my lunch with you." I laughed so hard there were tears rolling down my eyes. And I thought right there, forget Doug Willard and meet this guy.

NORM: Wow.

[ANN *hugs him tight, crushing the tux against him.*]

Wow.

[ANN *kisses him on the cheek, gets up, waves a good-bye and goes.*]

Wow. What a great girl. What an *intelligent* girl. To fall in love with me at first sight. I always knew Ann was something special, something terrific. To just see me in a hall and fall immediately and completely in love. My gosh...[*He thinks it over a moment.*] ...my gosh. To fall in love with me after just seeing me? How many guys does she see in a day? A hundred? Two hundred? She must fall in love two hundred times a day... with every guy I know...

[Suddenly JERRY *ambles onto the stage in a spotlight.* ANN *appears downstage of him.*]

ANN: [*To* JERRY] Oh, God, the way you walk. It drives me mad.

[JERRY's *face has a "Who me?" look on it.*]

NORM: Oh, no, it's happening again.

ANN: I love you.

[ANN *crosses to* JERRY *like a panther stalking its prey. With one hand she pushes him back and sprawls him on the floor.*]

NORM: Oh, no, I can see it coming.

ANN: I love you. I love you.

[*She starts to close in on* JERRY, *who is starting to hyperventilate.*]

ANN: Use me, abuse me, toss me away like an old kleenex.

[ANN *comes down. They tear each other's clothes off.*]

NORM: HEEEEEEEEEEEELLLLLLLLPPPPPPPPP!!!!!!

[*Blackout*]

COLEMAN, S.D.

by Anne Pierson Wiese

CHARACTERS

LAUREL, a tall, pretty girl of about seventeen. She has an air of sophistication, and yet there is a rather wide-eyed look of innocence about her.

HOPE, a shorter, rather plain girl of about seventeen. In contrast to Laurel, she is very simple in demeanor.

TERRY, a tall, handsome boy of about eighteen. He is straightforward in appearance, very unsophisticated, and yet there is a quality of intelligence and hidden depth about him.

Scene 1

It is late morning. LAUREL *is sitting on the floor of a front porch reading a county paper. She is wearing a flowered sundress, no shoes, and a ribbon in her hair. As she reads,* HOPE *begins to sneak down from among the audience.* LAUREL *glances up, sees* HOPE, *but pretends not to have noticed. As* HOPE *continues to sneak around the side of the stage,* LAUREL *stands up, arches her back and bends over to touch her toes. While* LAUREL *is stretching down,* HOPE *reaches the end of the porch.* LAUREL *turns her head and looks at* HOPE *calmly.*

LAUREL: Hi, Hope.
  [HOPE *looks surprised and then both girls begin to laugh.* LAUREL *comes down porch steps and they hug each other, laughing.*] Next time you decide to sneak up on me, try taking off your shoes first! How are you, Hope?
  [HOPE *sits down on porch steps, looks up at* LAUREL.]
HOPE: I'm real good.... Laurel, ain't you never gonna stop growin'?
LAUREL: Hopey Olsen! I haven't grown one single centimeter since last summer! I think you're shrinking.
HOPE: You have too grown. I bet you got at least a couple more inches since last year.
LAUREL: I haven't—I promise. I just measured myself—really.
HOPE: Well, you look real good, anyway. Maybe you can be a model. I hear they gotta be tall.
LAUREL: [*Laughing*] Will you stop insulting me?
HOPE: [*Looks worried*] Gol, I'm sorry—I didn't mean to.
LAUREL: [*Sits down beside* HOPE] I was just joking, Hope. So, how is everything?
HOPE: All about the same as usual, but, Laurel?
LAUREL: What?

HOPE: Well, there is one thing different—but, tell me about you.
LAUREL: You know about me, Hopey.
HOPE: Sure, but there's always somethin'... Say, how's your grandma doin'? I've been meanin' to come by and see her, but you know, what with one thing and another... I bet she's real glad to see you.
LAUREL: Yeah... you know Grandma—she loves having us grandkids underfoot all summer. I'm certainly glad to be here... Oh, I know something I've forgotten to tell you. I meant to when I wrote last time, but, well, I was accepted to Harvard.

[LAUREL *can't keep a big smile off her face.*]

HOPE: Oh, is that that college you wanted to go to so bad?
LAUREL: Yeah.
HOPE: That's super. I figured you'd get in, 'cause they probably don't get a lot of real smart girls like you. They probably don't get all that many girls, anyway.
LAUREL: Sure they do. The ratio at Harvard is about sixty-forty.
HOPE: Oh. I never knew that many girls went.
LAUREL: Of course. Look at you—
HOPE: Me?
LAUREL: Well, yeah. You're going to Dakota State this fall.
HOPE: Laurel, that's part of the one thing different. I ain't goin'.
LAUREL: But...
HOPE: [*Rushing*] I don't want to no more.
LAUREL: Hopey, last summer you said—I mean we talked about, well, when I said I wanted Harvard more than anything in the world, and you said you wanted—Hope, what happened?
HOPE: I decided not to. That's all.
LAUREL: But you didn't say in your letters...
HOPE: I *just* decided.
LAUREL: I don't understand—are you kidding? [*Suspiciously*] Hope, you *are* kidding.
HOPE: I ain't. I'm not foolin'.
LAUREL: *Hope.*
HOPE: Laurel, I mean it—really—I ain't foolin'.
LAUREL: Hope, I... why?
HOPE: I told you. I just decided not to.
LAUREL: There must be more than that. Hope, you wanted to

go. I was there when you *dreamed* about it. You *wanted* to go away.

HOPE: Laurel, I ain't interested no more. I wanna stay here, in Coleman.

LAUREL: [*Puzzled*] I don't believe you. Hope, you're crazy. It wouldn't cost you anything, and... Listen, you want to *be* someone. You, you want to *do* things. Hope, what are your plans?

HOPE: Laurel, I ain't smart enough to do them things, anyway, so it's just as well I don't go. Just forget it. I ain't goin'. Listen, we'll have a great time this summer. There's a good movie showin' at the drive-in tonight.

LAUREL: [*After a long silence*] All right, Hope. But I want to know why you're not going. You can at least tell me why.

HOPE: I told you.

LAUREL: No, you didn't. Don't you think I know you better than that? I haven't spent every summer since I was born in Coleman for nothing. I know you. And damn it, Hope, why?

HOPE: I'll tell you, Laurel, but not now. I wanna talk with you first. I, I wanna do things with you. I want it to be... the same. It will be, Laurel, won't it?

LAUREL: Oh, Hope. It'll always be the same. Of course it will. Of *course* it will. In fact, why don't we call up Terry and Ben, now, and ask them about the movie tonight, just like last year?

HOPE: No. I mean, not tonight.

LAUREL: [*She peers into* HOPE's *face.*] Tell me what's bothering you. Please. [*Speaks in exaggerated tone*] Tell me *all* about it, and I'll diagnose it and find the antidote, immediately. Hope?

HOPE: Find the what?

LAUREL: The antidote—the remedy—the cure.

HOPE: I know the cure but I ain't gonna do it.

LAUREL: Hope? Do... what?

HOPE: I'm pregnant, Laurel. I'm real happy about it, actually. Me and—Terry, we're engaged. We're gonna buy one of them new houses on Center Street—real cute, and we're gonna do a room over special for the baby. I hope it's a girl, kinda, but either way it'll be nice. We're just gonna love that little girl, Laurel, me and Terry. I guess maybe you think it's kinda strange—it bein' Terry and all, but it—it just happened, and, well, you'll be here for the weddin'. [LAUREL *is looking straight ahead. She doesn't say anything.*] You can be my maid-of-honor, Laurel. I'm havin' blue and white colors—you look real good in blue—Laurel... Oh, Laurel, please don't be like that. I'm sorry about Terry and all—I mean, I know last summer you guys, well... But, we're real happy, now, and don't that count, don't it, Laurel? If I'd thought that you were real serious about him, I'd never have let it happen this way, but I, I kinda knew you weren't, and... Laurel? Laurel, he said for me to give you a kiss for him the moment I saw you. He said, give her a big kiss. Laurel?

[HOPE *looks at* LAUREL *for a long moment and then gets up to leave. As she stands,* LAUREL *catches her hand but remains seated and still doesn't quite look at her. Hands are loosely clasped. Lights fade.*]

Scene 2

Same front porch, later that afternoon. Whistling is heard offstage and TERRY *walks slowly into view from somewhere behind the house. He jumps over the picket fence at the side of the porch and walks up the porch steps. He goes to the door and knocks, smoothing back hair. No one answers. He knocks again, louder, still there is no answer. He steps back off the porch and peers up at windows. As he is looking, the screen door opens and* LAUREL *comes out, still wearing sun-dress and ribbon.* TERRY *walks up to her and stares down at her. They stand looking at one another for a long moment and then* LAUREL *puts her hand out.* TERRY *takes it and they shake hands quickly.*

LAUREL: Hi, Terry.
TERRY: Hello, Laurel. How's everything?
LAUREL: Oh, all right, I guess. I mean, great, you know?
TERRY: Yeah.

LAUREL: How about you?
TERRY: Well, I guess you talked to Hope.... You girls. I bet she's been over here fifty times already, today, huh?
LAUREL: No, I mean, yes. I talked to her—once. She, well, she explained everything.
TERRY: Yeah, I figured she would.
LAUREL: I—I'm happy for you guys.

[LAUREL *brushes past* TERRY *and walks down porch steps.*]

TERRY: Laurel, you don't have to—Yeah, thanks. Everyone's all excited. About the wedding, I mean. Huh, I sure can't believe it. I mean, me bein' married and all.

[LAUREL *sits on grass bank in front of the house as she speaks.*]

LAUREL: Well, I—it seems strange to me, too. But you and Hope—you'll make great parents—and really, you know, it's just that I keep forgetting how old we're getting. It seems strange, but, I mean, lots of things seem strange, now, like drinking coffee, and being able to drive. Getting married's kind of the same—you know? It's like—

[TERRY *interrupts and as he is speaking he moves to sit next to Laurel.*]

TERRY: Yeah, you're right. It is the same—getting married. Married. Hope told me you were accepted at Harvard.
LAUREL: Yeah, I was.
TERRY: You sure don't look too thrilled about it.
LAUREL: Oh, I am. It's just, well, you know, it seems pretty unreal right now.
TERRY: It'll be real soon.
LAUREL: I know.
TERRY: When are you leaving?
LAUREL: I guess I'll go back to New York in August.
TERRY: Then to Harvard?
LAUREL: Yeah. Terry?
TERRY: What?
LAUREL: It's nice to be here again, I mean, you know, here in Coleman.
TERRY: Wish I could say the same.
LAUREL: Terry—
TERRY: What I meant was—I wish I could go to your place, New York, and then I'd come back and say about how it's so nice to be back in Coleman—you know?
LAUREL: I guess. Terry?

TERRY: Huh?

LAUREL: Are you—staying here next year?

TERRY: I thought you said Hope explained....

LAUREL: She did. I mean, you're not—going to the university?

TERRY: No.

LAUREL: Oh.

TERRY: We talked so much last summer, Laurel. I guess you must think I'm pretty dumb. Probably I am, I don't know, but, Laurel, Hope's gonna be my wife, and... Laurel, my kid's gotta know who his dad is. My kid, he's gotta *have* a dad, even if he is only a roadworker.

LAUREL: Terr, maybe you guys can go to school. [TERRY *stands up*.] Sure, of course you can! Terry, why not? Lots of people with kids take part-time, and—

TERRY: Stop it, Laurel.

LAUREL: Why, Terry? You can't give up—just like that. You can't do that—

TERRY: [*Interrupting*] Laurel, I said stop it. Just don't go trying to make me dream again.

LAUREL: Terry, you have a right to do this. You, you have to. Terry, you're *giving up*. You're *quitting*. You just can't—

TERRY: *Damn it*, Laurel. What do you want me to do? Hope and I—we *have* to do this. Do you think if I had a choice, I—oh, hell. I didn't—mean that. Laurel, you'll be here for the wedding.

LAUREL: What does that matter? Terry, this is your life. This is real.

[*They stare at each other for a long moment and then* TERRY *sits down on the porch steps.*]

TERRY: Oh, what's real, anyway? I don't even know anymore. I don't even think I care. It's just that...

LAUREL: What, Terry?

TERRY: I don't know, Laurel. I really don't.

[LAUREL *sits next to him on steps.*]

LAUREL: Terry?

TERRY: I guess it's just that, well, Laurel... *you're* so real—to me, I mean. All of a sudden, it's all so real—but not the *right* real. I mean, I can almost forget that it's not last summer, that there is no university, that there is no—I don't want—Laurel, I don't want it to be real like this—don't you see?

LAUREL: I'm not sure I see.
TERRY: Laurel, you've gotta see. I mean, last summer, last summer you always saw.
LAUREL: Terry, this isn't last summer.
TERRY: I know it ain't last summer. I didn't mean that—I—
[LAUREL *rises and moves away a little.*]
LAUREL: Oh, I know. Course I know, Terr.
[TERRY *rises, too, and comes toward* LAUREL.]
TERRY: Laurel—
LAUREL: Terry, why don't you and Hopey go away—to school together with the baby.
TERRY: Laurel, I don't even have a job, yet.
LAUREL: I thought you said you could get one with the road crew—
TERRY: [*Interrupting*] Yeah, I'll get one with the road crew—sure.
LAUREL: Then why can't you—
TERRY: I can't fix fences and go to school at the same time.
LAUREL: But, Terry, you can't just—
TERRY: It *ain't* gonna work. Laurel!
LAUREL: What?
[TERRY *moves very close to* LAUREL.]
TERRY: I want you to know that I—
LAUREL: Terry, it's all right. You don't have to say anything—not one, single thing.
TERRY: Okay. I won't say it. You know it.
LAUREL: I—
TERRY: You what?
LAUREL: Terry—Hope's coming over—soon.
TERRY: You what, Laurel?
LAUREL: I—oh, all right, Terry. I *don't* know it. I wanna hear it. I want you to— [TERRY *takes her face in his hands and kisses her lightly.*] I'm sorry, Terry.
TERRY: Please, Laurel, don't be—not yet.
[LAUREL *pulls away and then reaches for his hand.* TERRY *lifts his other hand to stroke her hair. Then* LAUREL *starts toward the door.*]
LAUREL: I, I'll go in and see if you and Hope can stay for supper. Okay Terry?
[TERRY *nods his head slowly.* LAUREL *goes into house and* TERRY *stares at the door. He sits down on steps and stares*

at the ground. After a minute, HOPE *walks onstage.* TERRY *doesn't look up. She reaches* TERRY.]

HOPE: Terry?

TERRY: [*He stands up quickly.*] Scared me—

HOPE: That's real funny. I tried to sneak up on Laurel this morning, but she heard me. You better get your ears checked.

TERRY: Yeah.

HOPE: Ain't you seen Laurel yet?

TERRY: Yup. She just went in the house for a minute.

HOPE: She looks real good, don't she?

TERRY: Yeah.

HOPE: Every year it seems like she gets taller, and smarter, and . . .

TERRY: And?

HOPE: Oh, I don't know.

TERRY: Yeah, well, she's still Laurel.

HOPE: Sure. Terry?

TERRY: What?

HOPE: I looked at one of them houses today. It was real nice— right on the corner of Center and Josephine. [TERRY *doesn't answer.*] It's—it's only a few blocks from the Seven-Eleven, so maybe I could work—

TERRY: Hope, we already talked about this. I don't want you working.

HOPE: Oh, Terry, I don't mind. It's a long time before the baby comes, and after we can get mom to sit with it—

TERRY: [*Interrupting*] How many times do I have to say it?

HOPE: But I know we need the money, so why can't—

TERRY: *Damn it,* Hope—If we're going to get married, and have a family, then we're going to do it right. Do you understand? If there's going to be a baby, there are going to be two parents, and those parents are going to be *you* and *me*. My child is not going to spend his life with his grandmother, or a sitter, or anyone but his parents. He's *not* . . . Damn it, if I'm giving up college it's got to be for something. Don't you see? You should. You're giving up something, too. Hope, if we can't at least make the right life for our child then you might as well get rid of it, *right now*.

HOPE: Terry . . . [HOPE *sits down on the porch steps*] You ain't mad because I told Laurel about everythin', are you? [TERRY *is looking at her almost accusingly.*] Oh, Terry, don't be mad. Please don't. I, I thought you'd like it better if I told her. I didn't want to. I was scared she'd hate me. Oh, Terry, you ain't mad at me, are you?

TERRY: No.

HOPE: Terry—Terry?

TERRY: I said I ain't mad at you, didn't I?

HOPE: I'm sorry, Terry. You know I'm real sorry.

TERRY: It's okay.

HOPE: It ain't okay, is it? You hate me, don't you?

TERRY: No—not you.

HOPE: It is me, ain't it? Me and the baby?

TERRY: NO.

HOPE: Terry, *please* don't hate me.

[*His expression changes. He sits down next to* HOPE, *and puts an arm around her.*]

TERRY: Hope, I don't hate you. You've gotta believe me. This is just very hard in some ways. [HOPE *puts her head down.*] Hope, Hope... don't. We'll be okay—all right? We grew up together, and we'll make it okay, all right? [HOPE *lifts her head.*]

HOPE: You want to go to the university real bad, don't you?

TERRY: Nah, not all that bad, Hope.

HOPE: I can tell. You and Laurel both. That's all you guys ever talked about.

TERRY: Hope—

HOPE: Terry, I'll make it okay for you. I'll try real hard.

TERRY: I know—you'll try, I'll try...

HOPE: Don't you wish the baby was here?

TERRY: Yeah.

HOPE: If it was here, everythin'd be okay. It's just right now all there is is waitin'.

TERRY: Uh-huh.

HOPE: You know, for the baby and all...

[*The screen door opens and* LAUREL *comes out onto the porch. She leans against the porch railing.*]

LAUREL: It's okay about supper.

HOPE: Supper?

TERRY: Oh, I forgot to tell you.

LAUREL: Can you stay for supper, Hope?

HOPE: Terry, we were supposed to eat over to your house,

tonight. Ain't your mom expectin' us?
TERRY: Well, I told her we'd eat over here—I figured Laurel'd ask us to.
HOPE: Oh.
LAUREL: Terry! Are you, by any chance, taking me for granted?
TERRY: Would I do that?
LAUREL: Given the opportunity? Probably.
TERRY: Now, Laurel, is that anything to say to a guest?
LAUREL: Guest? I don't see any guest. [LAUREL *walks behind* TERRY *and* HOPE *and sits down next to* HOPE.] Us females have to stick together, right, Hope?
TERRY: Well, that's that. If you guys are gonna gang up on me, I'm through.
[TERRY *begins to pull up blades of grass at his feet.*]
LAUREL: What movie's at the drive-in, tonight?
HOPE: *Dressed to Kill*—it's supposed to be real scary.
LAUREL: Well, if it's anywhere near as scary as that one we saw last summer—remember the one, the one with the dead little boy coming out of the water—all green?
TERRY: Oh, yeah.
[TERRY *and* LAUREL *exchange glances.*]
HOPE: Remember, you guys were so scared you slid all the way under the dashboard and Ben and me... It was real scary.
LAUREL: Yeah. Hey, Terr, some of us like a front lawn.
TERRY: Oh, sorry.
HOPE: Are you sure it's okay about supper? Me and Terry could eat at the cafe or somethin'.
LAUREL: Of course it's okay. Grandma's expecting you.
TERRY: Laurel?
LAUREL: Hmnnn?
TERRY: Do you know what classes you're taking next year?
LAUREL: You mean, at Harvard?
TERRY: Yeah.
LAUREL: Not for sure. I guess I'll definitely be taking an English. They're supposed to be hard for freshmen, but I want to. And some French literature course, probably.
HOPE: You mean, it's like books in French?
LAUREL: Yeah. It's like an English, but in French.
HOPE: You'll do real well, Laurel. I know you will. You better write me and Terry, too. Tell us all about everythin'. I bet you'll have a real nice roommate.
LAUREL: I hope so.

TERRY: You...
LAUREL: What?
TERRY: Forget it.

[TERRY *jumps up and walks off around the corner of the house, stepping over the fence.*]

HOPE: He seems real restless, don't he?
LAUREL: Everyone gets restless, sometimes.
HOPE: Yeah, I guess.
LAUREL: Hope, did you ever think about—about not having it?
HOPE: No, I ain't never thought about that.
LAUREL: Hope, maybe...
HOPE: Laurel, it don't make a difference. I know you're worryin' and all, but college just don't matter to me like it does to you, and I—
LAUREL: [*Interrupting*] But how can you be *sure*, Hope? How can you know? Oh, Hope, I'm not saying it would be easy—I know it wouldn't, but please, give yourself a chance, at least a *chance*. Oh, Hope, give Terry a chance.
HOPE: [*Standing*] I didn't know he mattered all that much to you, Laurel.
LAUREL: [*Stands also*] I—Hope, no. I mean, that's wrong. He doesn't. I mean, he does, but not like that... Hope, I just care so much about both of you, I—oh, Hope, don't think that....
HOPE: We're gonna be real happy, Laurel.
LAUREL: Oh, I know you are. I know you will. Oh, Hope, of course. And the baby—it'll be happy, too. I just can't wait. I'll fly straight out the minute I hear, and...
HOPE: Oh, will you, Laurel? Fly out, I mean.
LAUREL: On my own two wings!

[TERRY *reappears out of the screen door.*]

TERRY: Supper's on. Your grandma told me to drag you two in the house somehow. Coming?

[LAUREL *and* HOPE *walk to the door,* LAUREL *disappearing inside first.*]

HOPE: Terry, did you know that Laurel's got wings?
TERRY: Of course. So've you and I. Difference is, she uses hers.

[*They enter house. Lights fade.*]

Scene 3

Same front porch, about two weeks later. It is late afternoon. Lights come up and voices are heard offstage, laughing, etc. After a minute, LAUREL *and* HOPE *appear from offstage, with their arms full of packages.* LAUREL *is wearing a flowered dirndl skirt, blouse and sandals.* HOPE *is wearing jeans and nondescript top. They reach the grass directly in front of the porch steps and* LAUREL *lets all her packages fall onto the ground with an exaggerated sigh. She stops, looks at* HOPE *nervously.* HOPE *is putting her packages carefully on the porch steps.*

LAUREL: Don't tell me there was anything breakable in there...
HOPE: Gol, I forget—I don't think so.
  [HOPE *sits on porch steps,* LAUREL *sits on grass.*]
LAUREL: I guess I'd better check and make sure.
  [LAUREL *starts opening bags with* HOPE. *They pull out white tablecloths, napkins, doilies, and some fake flowers. Then* LAUREL *holds up a set of tall, white candles, one of which is broken.*] Oh, darn, I'm sorry, Hope. I'll go downtown and get you some new ones tomorrow.
HOPE: Never mind, Laurel.
LAUREL: I'll even get you two sets.
HOPE: You don't have to. It's just a candle. Look, these'll be real pretty on the tables, huh?
  [*She holds up a tablecloth.*]
LAUREL: Yeah. Are you sure we got enough?
HOPE: I think so. We're usin' them long tables—Reverend Larson said it made seatin' and all easier. I guess if we use three cloths on each table we'll have enough, but maybe—Laurel, what are you doin'?
  [LAUREL *is putting a wreath of flowers on her head, trying to make it stay.*]

136

LAUREL: I'm making my headdress for the wedding—you know—maid-of-honor bonnet?

HOPE: Laurel, you ain't never gonna get those to stay like that, and besides, I wanted all blue and white colors—

[LAUREL *takes off flowers.*]

LAUREL: Hope, I wasn't serious.

HOPE: Well, gol, Laurel, how'm I supposed to know?

LAUREL: *Hope*.

HOPE: I mean it. I wish you'd either be serious or—Laurel, ain't you ever...

LAUREL: What?

HOPE: Do you always know what to say? I mean, sometimes, don't you say somethin' real dumb, 'cause you couldn't think of nothin' else, and then wish you hadn't?

LAUREL: I don't know—sure, I guess so.

HOPE: But you always sound like, well, like you had it all planned out or somethin'.

LAUREL: Oh, good. I'm predictable.

HOPE: I didn't mean it like that—I'm sorry.

LAUREL: It's all right. You can say what you think without apologizing all the time.

HOPE: I know I ain't as smart as you, but I can't help it, Laurel. I can't help the way I am.

LAUREL: That's dumb, Hope. I wish you wouldn't put yourself down all the time.

HOPE: I ain't puttin' myself down.

LAUREL: You are, too. Hope, why, *why* won't you give yourself a chance? I just don't understand you. You could at least try, just *try* to let yourself have a chance. *One* chance. That's all it takes, Hope. You know, I don't know what happened to you. I don't know you anymore. Hope, how could you not care like this? How?

HOPE: Laurel, ain't you heard anythin' I've said to you? College don't matter to me like it does to you. It ain't never mattered like that. Sure—I thought about it, once, but that's all. I just thought. Thoughts ain't real.

LAUREL: No, they're not real. You've got to make them real, Hope. Nothing's real if you don't make it that way. Do you think I just dreamed about Harvard, and "poof," I was in? Not by a long shot, Hope. I worked damn hard to make that dream real for myself, and you could too. You used to want to—what happened?

HOPE: I don't want to leave Coleman.
LAUREL: Well, that's all very nice, Hope, but did you ever stop to think about Terry? Did you ever give him one goddamn thought? How could you? How *could* you? Hope, you're destroying him—all his dreams. He wanted college so badly—more than you'll ever know. He worked so hard to make enough money. He dreamed so hard to make it all real, and you're just smashing that dream to pieces. Did you ever think about Terry?
HOPE: Terry—
LAUREL: [*Stands up.*] Yeah, Terry. Remember him? The guy you're gonna marry? Jesus, Hope. Did you ever think about anyone but yourself? Terry had dreams, too—he had plans, too. You may not care much about yourself, but you have no right to end his dreams. You just can't do that. Hope, why can't you at least let him make his own decision? He never will, you know, as long as there's that baby, as long as—Oh, Hope, why are you doing this?
HOPE: I thought you and Terry weren't never serious last summer.
LAUREL: Never serious? No, no, Hope, we were never serious.
[LAUREL *walks up the porch steps past* HOPE *and goes into the house.* HOPE *sits among the packages and the lights fade.*]

Scene 4

Same front porch. Two more weeks have passed. It is dusk. TERRY *and* LAUREL *sit at the top of the steps facing each other, with their backs against the two front poles on either side of the steps.* LAUREL *is wearing the same sun-dress again, and no shoes. Their feet rest on the top step, their toes just touching.*

TERRY: Well, I guess this is really my last night, I mean, the wedding tomorrow and all.

LAUREL: I know what you mean.
TERRY: Yeah. You always do.
LAUREL: Oh, Terry, not always.
TERRY: *Yes,* always.

[TERRY *covers* LAUREL's *bare toes with his feet.*]

LAUREL: You seem very sure of yourself, tonight.
TERRY: No, I ain't sure of myself, but I'm sure of you.
LAUREL: It should be the other way around, Terry.
TERRY: I guess so, but it's not. Laurel?
LAUREL: Yeah?
TERRY: I'm kind of glad it's this way. At least, I'm glad that there's someone to be sure of.

[LAUREL *swings her body around so that she is sitting straight on the steps, profile to* TERRY.]

LAUREL: Oh, Terry.
TERRY: What?
LAUREL: Terry, it's all wrong.

[TERRY *moves down a step, and closer to* LAUREL. *He leans forward.*]

TERRY: What do you mean?
LAUREL: I mean, you *can't* feel that way, you—
TERRY: But I do, Laurel.
LAUREL: Terry, it's just not right. I'm gonna be gone soon, and then...
TERRY: And then I don't know what I'll do. I just don't know.
LAUREL: Terry, that's not fair... Terry, it's not fair to me, or you—or Hope.
TERRY: And you still believe in "fair"? After all this, it's still there for you?
LAUREL: Well, there's always fair...
TERRY: No, there ain't. There never was, I just didn't know it.
LAUREL: Terry—
TERRY: I mean it, Laurel. It's like all this time I've been seeing something one way, and now—now it's all different...
LAUREL: [*Grabs his hand*] It's not different, at least I don't think so. Oh, Terry, it's just us that make it different. We *make* it that way. Don't you see?
TERRY: No. I don't see. I don't see anything anymore.
LAUREL: But you can't stop trying. Oh, Terry, you've got to keep trying. If you stop, everything will stop. If you don't—
TERRY: Oh, Laurel...

[*Suddenly* TERRY *puts his head into* LAUREL's *lap and his arms around her.* LAUREL *stares down at him a minute and then starts to smooth his hair.*]

LAUREL: Terry, listen to me. Everything will be all right. We can make it all right—I'll help you. Terry, we'll find a way for you to go to college. We'll find a way. I promise you. Oh, Terry, I promise you.

[TERRY *sits up. They stare at each other and then they hug one another for a long time. They separate and* TERRY *takes* LAUREL's *hands.*]

TERRY: Laurel, I love you.

LAUREL: I know. What are we going to do?

TERRY: I don't know.

LAUREL: We could always—

TERRY: What?

LAUREL: Flee across the border? That wasn't very funny—sorry.

TERRY: It's okay. It might work, except that I don't want to live in Nebraska. Sorry—that wasn't funny either.

LAUREL: I guess this really isn't a very funny thing.

TERRY: No. Laurel?

LAUREL: What?

TERRY: Harvard's a long ways away.

LAUREL: [*Stands*] I know. Maybe I could—

TERRY: No.

LAUREL: Terry, Harvard doesn't really matter...

TERRY: Yes, it does. You know it does.

LAUREL: But we'd be together, and...

TERRY: Laurel, I can tell Hope something.

LAUREL: [*Sits down again*] What do you mean?

TERRY: I'll tell Hope to forget it. I'll tell her that I'm going to school in the East. I could find a job—we could have an apartment.

LAUREL: Something small.... I could work, too.... and the baby?

TERRY: It can go to HELL. No, no, I didn't—

LAUREL: I know you didn't mean it, Terry. It's okay. I know. Really, I—

TERRY: But you don't. You *don't* know, Laurel. I can't make you understand. Oh, Laurel, I want you to. I want you to.

LAUREL: Terry—

TERRY: See, everything's all gone, Laurel. I thought... I wanted,

I wanted—out.
LAUREL: And you can't say that to Hope?
TERRY: I don't know.
[*Lights fade.*]

Scene 5

Same front porch, later that night. It is about 10:00 p.m. HOPE *appears from offstage, walks up porch steps and knocks on door.* LAUREL *opens it.*

HOPE: Laurel, I was wonderin' if you'd seen Terry. I ain't and—[TERRY *appears behind* LAUREL *in the doorway and steps out onto the porch.*] Oh, I was over to the church—you know, settin' up the tables and all—everythin' looks real pretty. I just lost track of time. Your blue dress is all hemmed, Laurel. It's hangin' up over to the church. Mrs. Stacy sure worked hard finishin' those outfits.
LAUREL: Well, I'm glad you got here before Terry ate us out of house and home. He just dropped by, so I fed him, and we were talking...
TERRY: Yeah, we were talking, and...
LAUREL: I'll be right back.
[*She goes into house.* TERRY *walks to the edge of the porch.*]
TERRY: We were talking, Hope, and—
HOPE: It looks so pretty, Terry—over to the church. I ain't never seen it so pretty. Everythin's all white and blue and gold. The flowers ain't comin' till tomorrow. It'll look even nicer then. Terry, I—
TERRY: Hope, I just don't...
HOPE: I just want to say one thing. See, I know I ain't real tall, or pretty, or any of them things, but, Terry, all I ever wanted was to make it better for you. I wanted to make it all right. And Terry, I'll be the best mother—I promise.
[TERRY *turns away from* HOPE *and stands at the edge of the porch staring off into the darkness.* LAUREL *comes quietly*

out and stands unnoticed by the screen door. She looks from TERRY *to* HOPE *and then stands watching* TERRY. HOPE, *too, is watching him. After a long silence* TERRY *goes quickly down the steps of the porch. He stops and turns his head slightly toward the porch.*]

TERRY: Hope, if it's a girl, let's name it Laurel.

[TERRY *walks swiftly offstage.* HOPE *walks down steps as if to follow him and pauses just below porch.*]

HOPE: Laurel, you should be at the church around ten o'clock tomorrow.

LAUREL: [*Speaks very viciously*] Are you going to have a television set after you're married, Hope? I hope so—you'll have nothing else to do. Are you going to have a radio? A dishwasher? A vacuum? Oh, but I forgot the baby—I guess you will be busy after all. Are you going to have a car, Hope? Of course. It'll sit in your driveway and rust because you'll have nowhere to go. Do you think it's gonna be *fun*, Hope? Are you gonna have a good time? Is it gonna be worth it? Are you gonna buy a new house every five years, or keep the same one for fifty? Are you gonna have a waterbed? I hear they're in. Are you gonna mow the lawn, or is Terry? Are you gonna have a garden? That way, you'll produce something worthwhile. Are you ever gonna read another book in your life? Are you gonna let Terry? Are you gonna put your baby through school? What the hell are you gonna do, Hope?

HOPE: You know, Laurel, I was always real impressed when you started talkin' about your dreams—about your plans—about what's real and what ain't real. I always thought you was real smart because of all that. I thought you was a real carin' person. But you ain't carin'. You only care about one person, and that's you. I guess it was real fun for you to come out here and play like you was one of us—pretend that we was the same. I guess you liked havin' real lives to play with, 'cause that's all you've been doin' this whole time, ain't it? Playin'. It's fun, ain't it, to be part of a sad story for a while, long as you can step on a plane whenever you get tired of hurtin'. It's all a big joke, ain't it? Somethin' to write about when you get back to your own life. Well, I wish you'd take that plane tomorrow, because I want my baby, and I want my husband, and you'd take 'em both if you could.

LAUREL: Hope—I—

HOPE: I don't need you no more. I didn't never need you. You can go home to your city, and your college, and you can stay there.

LAUREL: Unfortunately, Terry doesn't seem to feel the same way.

HOPE: I don't care. You just go away and we'll be happy. You think we won't, don't you? You think I can't make him happy, and you're glad, ain't you? Well, you're wrong, Laurel. [HOPE *continues more quietly.*] See, we grew up together, me and Terry. We come from the same thing, Laurel. We belong to the same place, and that's a lot. I know you can't understand that—I wish you could, kind of, but you can't. You're just different, Laurel.

LAUREL: I'm different?

HOPE: See, you're real, but a different real from me and Terry, now, because you ain't never had no dreams smashed.

LAUREL: You said you didn't care.

HOPE: I didn't never want nothin' but college, nothin' but out, never. But it's different, now. It's gotta be, because there ain't no other way. Don't you see, all your talkin' about chances and all, that was for before—when it made a difference. Now there's gotta be a whole new set of chances for me, and for Terry. That's why you're different. You've still got those first dreams. Me and Terry, we have to find new ones.

LAUREL: But, we make our own dreams, Hope—don't we?

HOPE: Don't you see? All that, Laurel, all that about makin' dreams—that's only a dream, too. It's a real dream for you, but not for me no more—not for me.

LAUREL: Hope?

HOPE: What, Laurel?

LAUREL: I never meant to play—I know it's over, now, but I never meant to play.

HOPE: It's all right, Laurel. I didn't never mind. Just, don't forget about it's bein' over.

LAUREL: I won't. Hopey?

HOPE: Yeah?

LAUREL: I wish I could give you some of my dreams.
[*Lights fade.*]

EPIPHANY

by *Jennifer A. Litt*

CHARACTERS

LIONEL J. PERRY, sixteen to seventeen years old
RICHARD TAVERNER, sixteen to seventeen
MR. WOOLWEAVER, thirties
ASBURY, eighteen to nineteen
TWEED, eighteen to nineteen
MEDBOURNE, seventeen to nineteen
HERSHEY, nineteen
PROCTOR, eighteen to nineteen
McGOVERN, fifteen to sixteen
WARNER, thirteen
EVANS, thirteen
STOWE, sixteen to seventeen
CHURCHILL, fifteen to sixteen
CLIVE JARRETT, sixteen to seventeen
DR. MAPES, Headmaster, early fifties
MRS. LANE, mid-thirties
GEORGINA LANE, sixteen
HORACE LANE, sixteen
MR. WILLARD, sixties
FITZSIMMONS, sixteen to seventeen
ISOBEL (IBBY) JARRETT, sixteen
PHIPPS, a butler, sixties
HARRIS, a gardener, very elderly
OTHER BOYS; OTHER MASTERS

ACT I

Scene 1

Thomas More College for Boys, Surrey, England. The year is 1912. As the house lights dim very slowly to blackout, S. S. Wesley's "Blessed Be the God and Father" is played, to measure 60. As the music plays, a soft, grey light comes up on the house. By this light, there appears a darting white will-o'-the-wisp, descending from the back of the theatre to the stage. As it approaches, we see that it is a boy, trying to be silent and keep within the shadows. He is barefoot and dressed in a long white nightgown. Nervous, frightened, and cold, he reaches a staircase that leads up to the stage, by a winding route. He rests with hand pressing heart at the foot of the stairs; he trips up the first few loudly.

PERRY: Shit!!

[*Motionless for some moments in fear and pain, he looks about warily. Then he creeps up the stairs, all the way up to the up left platform. Breathing deeply, he knocks quietly on* TAVERNER's *door. With* PERRY's *knock, lights come up gradually on* TAVERNER's *study-bedroom. In this room are a chest of drawers and a desk, strewn with papers, books, a cap, inkpots, and a lamp. Various games equipment is lying on the floor, and there is a pile in the corner. Some clothes have been tossed over a chair, some more over the bedstead. The impression is one of comfortable untidiness.* TAVERNER *is in bed, asleep.* PERRY *speaks urgently in a low tone.*] Taverner! Taverner, open the door! [*Silence from within.* PERRY *looks nervously about. He drums on the door.*] Oh, please open the door! [*Silence. He knocks louder and looks about fearfully.*] Are you awake? Taverner, please be awake! [*Sleepily,* TAVERNER *mumbles inside his room. The lights are fully up by now.*]

Oh, wake up, old man! It's Perry! Come, let me in!

TAVERNER: [*More awake*] Perry?

PERRY: Yes—I'm at the door!

TAVERNER: Hold on a sec'. [*He gets up, patters to the door, unbolts it.* PERRY *immediately pushes in, shuts and bolts the door, and leans back against it, quivering.* TAVERNER *takes him by both hands.* PERRY *looks up after a moment, relaxes and smiles. They kiss each other's lips and then draw back, still holding hands.*] Your hands are cold.

PERRY: Mmm-hmm. Yours are lovely and warm. [*Suddenly shudders*] Jemimah, I don't enjoy that!

TAVERNER: What is it?

PERRY: [*Moves nervously about*] No matter how silent I try to be, I always fall or sneeze or something. I keep expecting that I shall run into a master or prefect and get expelled. It's a perfect nightmare!

TAVERNER: It is, it's awful.

PERRY: [*Realizing quickly how he must sound*] But it's well worth the trouble.

TAVERNER: [*Smiling, sitting on the bed by* PERRY] Thanks. I wish I could come to you, Perry.

PERRY: Oh, bother you! If you were caught out in the passage after lights, you'd never be made a prefect.

TAVERNER: Still, it's not fair, really.

PERRY: Oh, go to the devil! Who used to come and see me every night all through Third and Fourth Form, Richard Taverner?

TAVERNER: Well, what else could I do? You wouldn't even admit to liking me until I turned up every night for a week and pressured you into a confession.

PERRY: I was too shy. I *was* a bit of an idiot. But I didn't like you at the *very* first. You were too pushy.

TAVERNER: That's because I knew I liked you the moment I saw you, even before I knew you. I *was* rather pushy.

PERRY: How could you love somebody you didn't even know?

TAVERNER: Shot if I know, it's just this feeling, *you* know, that you get about certain people.

PERRY: I don't.

TAVERNER: Well, I do, and I did about you—the very first time I saw you.

PERRY: When was that?

TAVERNER: At Prayers, on the first morning of term, when we

Epiphany

were just starting Third Form. We were all singing the hymn, except you weren't. You were just sitting there, looking homesick.

PERRY: I was, rather, my first term at school.

TAVERNER: You looked it—besides being awfully good-looking.

PERRY: [*Smiles at* TAVERNER; *a thought strikes*] Speaking of first terms, did you know there's a new boy coming this week?

TAVERNER: No—is there? Who is he?

PERRY: I don't know... [*Intimately*] I don't want to talk about it now. [*Shudders*]

TAVERNER: What's the matter? Cold?

PERRY: Nervous. [*Shakes himself*] You know why I'm so nervous, don't you? Because of the time I was caught.

TAVERNER: But that was ages ago!

PERRY: Still, it could happen any time. And I'd have to think of a new excuse.

TAVERNER: What did you say the last time?

PERRY: Told 'em I was sleepwalking.

TAVERNER: And they believed you?!

PERRY: It was only Honor Society. They do it all the time themselves.

TAVERNER: Don't they, though. You're lucky you didn't have to explain to the Head.

PERRY: I know. The boot.

TAVERNER: But it's not likely you'd be caught, is it? You're awfully quiet.

PERRY: I'm well-practiced. "With love's light wings did I o'erperch these walls/For stony limits cannot hold love out."

TAVERNER: Oh, I'd forgotten! I've something for you!

PERRY: [*Joking*] Oh, you shouldn't have.

TAVERNER: [*Rummaging on his desktop*] Where'd it disappear to?

PERRY: A single rose?

TAVERNER: Got it!

[*Brings book to* PERRY]

PERRY: What is it?

TAVERNER: It's a crib *Romeo and Juliet*—you know, with translations in it.

PERRY: [*Moving to the window for light*] How very handy. Thanks awfully. Don't you need one?

TAVERNER: I've got two.
PERRY: Well, thanks. [*Flips through the pages as he speaks*] Awfully. "O speak again bright angel."
TAVERNER: I've got two.
PERRY: [*Looks up uncomprehending, then laughs*] Oh, pathetic! "Shall I hear more or shall I speak at this?"
TAVERNER: Like it?
PERRY: Never read it.
TAVERNER: Mr. Willard's such a *bore*. It mightn't be a bad play with another master.
PERRY: [*Looks back at book, laughing absently*] "Dost thou love me? I know thou wilt say ay, / And I will take thy word. Yet if thou swear'st / Thou mayst prove false. At lovers' perjuries, / They say Jove laughs."
TAVERNER: Oh, give over. Of course I love you, but it's cold. Come to bed. [PERRY *puts book by bed and hops in.*]
PERRY: Shove over, then. Can I borrow your slippers for the way back?
TAVERNER: Yes, of course. [*Pause*] Warmer?
PERRY: Yes, thanks, but you've got all of the pillow, you hog! [TAVERNER *sits up, a little bit annoyed.*]
PERRY: I didn't mean it, love. [*Pause. Seriously*] I do love you—awfully, Taverner.
TAVERNER: I love you too—awfully.
[*In a short ensuing silence they turn their attention to matters beneath the blankets. Blackout*]

Scene 2

Two days later, 4:15 in the afternoon. The school chapel. The light coming in through the stained-glass windows is meager. The sound of a heavy rainfall accompanies the following dialogue. MR. WOOLWEAVER, *at the altar with a clipboard, is calling the roll of the entire school, who are seated in pews and on the floor, talking to each other but standing and answering when their names are called. The school prefects,*

Epiphany

ASBURY, TWEED, MEDBOURNE *and* HERSHEY *wander through the aisles with their canes trying to keep order*. PROCTOR, *also a prefect, is flirting with* McGOVERN. STOWE *sits with* CHURCHILL. TAVERNER, PERRY *and* JARRETT *are very downstage, alternately pantomiming and conversing aloud. The lights come up suddenly, the noise with them.*

WOOLWEAVER: Stowe.
STOWE: Here, sir.
WOOLWEAVER: Strong.
BOY: Here, sir.
WOOLWEAVER: St. Thomas.
BOY: Here, sir.
WOOLWEAVER: Tailor.
BOY: Here, sir.
WOOLWEAVER: Taverner.
TAVERNER: Here, sir.
WOOLWEAVER: Tefts.
BOY: Right-oh, sir!
WOOLWEAVER: Thayer major.
BOY: Yes, I'm here, sir.
WOOLWEAVER: Thayer minor.
BOY: Here! Sir!
WOOLWEAVER: Thayer tertius.
EVANS: He's sick, poor chap.
WOOLWEAVER: Really? [*Marks clipboard*] Tilford?
BOY: Here, my liege.
WOOLWEAVER: Townsend?
BOY: Here, sir.
WOOLWEAVER: Trenton.
BOY: Yes, your highness.
WOOLWEAVER: Tucker.
BOY: Yes, your worship.
WOOLWEAVER: Oh, come off it, boys! Tuke!
BOY: Yes, sir.
WOOLWEAVER: Turner.
BOY: Present, sir.
WOOLWEAVER: Tweed.
TWEED: [*Prefect*] Oh! Here, sir!
WOOLWEAVER: Tyler-Patrick.
BOY: Yes, I'm here, sir.
WOOLWEAVER: Utley major [*Pause*] Utley major? [*Another*

pause. WOOLWEAVER *marks clipboard.*] Utley minor?
BOY: Here, sir.
WOOLWEAVER: Where is your brother, Utley minor?
BOY: Dunno, sir.
WOOLWEAVER: Just a shot. Victor major?
BOY: Here, sir.
WOOLWEAVER: Victor minor?
BOY: Yes, sir.
WOOLWEAVER: Wade?
BOY: Oh-so-present, sir.
WOOLWEAVER: Quiet! Wagstaff.
BOY: Here, sir.
WOOLWEAVER: Walker.
BOY: Here, sir.
WOOLWEAVER: Wallace.
BOY: Yes, sir.
WOOLWEAVER: Wallingford.
BOY: Here I am, sir.
WOOLWEAVER: Warner.
WARNER: Oh, sir, call me but love and I'll be new baptized!
[ASBURY, *who is fortuitously close to* WARNER, *lashes out at him with his cane, first with one hand and then the other, in an admirable manual maneuver.*]
WOOLWEAVER: I take it you're present.
WARNER: [*Smarting*] Yes, sir.
[*The callover either freezes or continues in pantomime, as the focus shifts to* JARRETT, TAVERNER, *and* PERRY.]
JARRETT: Look at that! Asbury can cane with both hands! He's ambidextrous!
TAVERNER: I'd give my right arm to be ambidextrous.
PERRY: [*Impressed*] Is he really?
JARRETT: No, Perry, I was joking.
PERRY: [*Reflectively*] I should think it would be awfully confusing to be ambidextrous.
TAVERNER: Why confusing?
JARRETT: Well, for instance, whatever would happen to *droit du seigneur*?
PERRY: Yes, he could only use it if he'd had an arm shot off!
[*Pretends to be an amputee*]
TAVERNER: Yes, everything *is* made for the right-handed, like shears. And inkwells are on the right side of the desk. Rather

Epiphany

inconvenient for the poor left-handed chaps.

JARRETT: I never thought of that. You know, I'll bet it would be a jolly sight easier on them if everyone was right-handed. Their ink smears like a bugger, too, when they write.

PERRY: They ought to follow the dictates of society and be right-handed. [*Raises fist*] Right is Might.

TAVERNER: You're right. I think it's the left-handed people who make all the trouble in the world—sinister, you know?

PERRY: Jarrett, I thought you were right-handed.

JARRETT: We *know* Taverner is right-handed.

TAVERNER: Of course.

PERRY: Never would he break a rule.

JARRETT: Perish the thought.

[*General noise again; focus shifts.*]

WOOLWEAVER: White. [*Pause*] White?

BOY: Oh! Here, sir.

WOOLWEAVER: [*Irritated but in control*] If you'd keep the noise down, everyone would be able to hear his name, and we'd be done sooner. Obviously, if it weren't raining we'd be on the cricket field. However, it is, and we must contend with the acoustics in here, which do not happen to be ideal for noisy callovers, though fine and good for music. Where was I? White is here?

BOY: Yes, sir.

[*Focus shifts again.*]

TAVERNER: [*Slightly defensive*] Well, it is important—to follow school rules, I mean. [*To Perry*] I really wish you would more. I worry about you.

PERRY: Well, I don't go about seeing if I can break any records for disobedience or anything like that. You make me sound like a walking felon.

TAVERNER: No, it's just that I hate to see you get into trouble. [*To* JARRETT, *laughing*] You I don't care about. I suspect you enjoy catching it.

JARRETT: No I don't—I'm just a smart aleck.

PERRY: You're just puerile and obnoxious. [*To* TAVERNER] So are you, in your own way.

JARRETT: [*Without the tenderness of* PERRY'*s rebuke*] You are, you know, Taverner. Have you been in any trouble at all this term?

TAVERNER: [*Defensively*] Yes! [*Thinks*] Mr. Drake caught me

bagging a muffin from the dining hall last week.
JARRETT: Yes, I'm sure you were nearly given the sack for that one.
TAVERNER: Oh, shut up, Jarrett.
ASBURY: [*Hissing*] Keep quiet, you three!
PERRY: Yes, SIR! [JARRETT *snarls and claws at* ASBURY's *departing back.*]
JARRETT: [*A new thought*] Hey, did you know there's a new boy coming to college?
PERRY: Hay is for horses.
TAVERNER: Of course we did.
PERRY: Bloody tick. New ticks are always the worst.
TAVERNER: When is he supposed to be coming?
JARRETT: Today or tomorrow. I wonder how old he is.
PERRY: He's probably a runt.
TAVERNER: Why is he coming now? In the middle of the term and all.
JARRETT: Maybe he was sacked from someplace.
PERRY: Yes, Thomas More seems to attract everyone else's rejections.
TAVERNER: How can you say that about your own school?!
JARRETT: With luck he'll be a fag and we won't have to bother about him.
PERRY: Righto.
[*Focus shifts.*]
WOOLWEAVER: Winston minor.
BOY: Here, sir. [*Over this line, someone has a coughing fit.*]
WOOLWEAVER: Boys! Is Winston minor present?! [*He is answered by several coughs; more and more boys join in the fun. The noise builds.*] I suppose I'll have to send his name up to the Head, then.
BOY: [*Shouting*] I'm here, sir!
WOOLWEAVER: Oh, you are? Then you'll do me two hundred lines for insufferable insolence! [*The coughing continues.*]
BOY: I will not, you old bastard—wasn't me!
WOOLWEAVER: What was that, Winston minor? [*He is answered by even louder coughing. Even* TAVERNER *puts in his two cents.*] I'll give every one of you an imposition! Now pipe down and behave yourselves! [*They do not, of course. The prefects are trying very hard to shut up the boys.*] Winston tertius.
BOY: Here, sir!

Epiphany

WOOLWEAVER: Wynn.
BOY: Here, sir!
WOOLWEAVER: Boys! Enough is enough! Now shut up or I shall go straight to the Head! [*The coughing has nearly run its course anyway. It tapers off.*] Yancy.
BOY: Here, sir!
WOOLWEAVER: Yates.
BOY: Here.
WOOLWEAVER: Here what?
BOY: Here, SIR.
WOOLWEAVER: Younger.
BOY: Here, sir.
WOOLWEAVER: Zachary.
BOY: Finally.
WOOLWEAVER: [*Puts clipboard down, picks up items from lectern*] Mr. McGovern, here is your shirt. Next time, don't forget it by the stables.
[MCGOVERN, *good-looking, claims shirt amid wolf-whistles, etc.*]
HERSHEY: Give it a stroke, McGovern!
WOOLWEAVER: Evans—your history book?
EVANS: Oh, thanks. [*Claims*]
WOOLWEAVER: Taverner—[WOOLWEAVER *holds out slip of paper.*] The Headmaster wishes to see you in his study immediately, if not sooner.
BOYS: [*Immediately*] Taverner, we're shocked and ashamed! Ooooh, naughty, naughty! Too bad your suit of armor's in the laundry, Taverner! etc.
[TAVERNER *claims the chit in shock and returns to* PERRY.]
PERRY: What have you done?
TAVERNER: I swear, Perry, I haven't done a thing!
[PERRY *laughs sarcastically.*]
WOOLWEAVER: For those of you who may not know, there is a house cricket match tomorrow—the Head's house versus Mr. Willard's house [*Cheers from boys*] at which attendance is not compulsory.
STOWE: What if it is still raining, sir? Will they call it off?
WOOLWEAVER: We never call off cricket for rain, Stowe. We call off the rain for cricket.
PERRY: Trust Crater-Face to ask such a silly question.
WOOLWEAVER: The next callover will be at Prayers tonight; and I wish to see the choir at seven o'clock in the chapel—

here—please. [*Boys begin talking, making as if to leave.*] Do be quiet—you're not dismissed yet. [*Groan.* WOOLWEAVER *waits for absolute silence.*] Now you are dismissed. Go to class.
[*The school gets up and exits with a roar and several coughs.*]

Scene 3

Immediately following. As the school empties the stage, PERRY *and* TAVERNER *are discovered at the foot of the stairs leading to the* HEAD's *study (up right platform). As the scene is played, they mount the stairs, reaching the top at the end of the scene. We break in on the middle of the boys' conversation.*

TAVERNER: No, Perry, there isn't! Except...
PERRY: Oh, stop it! I've told you any number of times, no one saw me!
TAVERNER: Well, everyone knows, just the same—all the chaps. Have we got an enemy?
PERRY: No!! It's not that, everyone likes you, Taverner. It's something else.
TAVERNER: It can't be anything else! You know how good I've been all term. Now it's a dead cert I won't get a prefectship.
PERRY: Oh, one thing won't ruin your chances. He probably wants to warn you of the evils of stealing muffins, or something half-witted like that.
TAVERNER: Don't be so damned flippant! This is very serious to me!
PERRY: Well, don't be so damned conscientious, it's probably nothing at all. This can't do you any harm, not after setting such an example all term.
TAVERNER: But it can—you don't understand. You're not concerned about being a prefect or not, but in the Fifth they only take the chaps with totally spotless records, and now mine's, umm... spotted! It's not fair.
PERRY: [*Quite calm now*] Well, if you're sure—and *I* can't think that you've done anything—I suppose you can't get into any trouble, then. [PERRY *looks around. They are com-*

pletely alone. Suddenly kisses TAVERNER's *cheek.*] Good luck. I hope this hasn't ruined your chances.
[PERRY *runs down the staircase and into the darkened classroom down left.*]
TAVERNER: [*Although* PERRY *has already disappeared*] Thanks. [*Turns dejectedly to the door and knocks*]

Scene 4

With TAVERNER's *knock, lights come up on the* HEAD's *study. This, like all the Thomas More sets, is austere, although not bleak, like* TAVERNER's *bedroom. The main feature is a large desk, which is severely neat. There are two other chairs beside the one* DR. MAPES *is using. In these are* MRS. LANE *and* GEORGINA. LANE *is standing up behind his mother's chair. Tea is served. As soon as* TAVERNER *enters, that is the end for* GEORGINA. *She is smitten. It's love at first sight.* TAVERNER *doesn't notice this mere girl until they are introduced.*

HEAD: Come in. [TAVERNER *does so, shuts door.*] Ah, Taverner. Come here.
TAVERNER: [*Looking about in confusion*] You wanted to see me, sir?
HEAD: Yes. [*Smiles kindly*] Why the long face? You're not on the carpet, boy.
TAVERNER: I'm not in trouble?
HEAD: [*Probing*] Should you be?
TAVERNER: [*Confused*] Well, no, I— [*The light dawns.*] Oh, is this the new boy, sir?
HEAD: Yes, it is. Madam, this is the boy I told you about. Taverner is also in the Fifth Form— [*To* LANE] You'll be together in form, and he shall be your host, so to speak, until you've settled in. [LANE *smiles at the vastly relieved* TAVERNER *in a friendly way.* TAVERNER *nods in acknowledgment.*] Now, Taverner, this is Mrs. Lane [MRS. LANE *stands, they shake hands.* TAVERNER *is about to say "How do you do?" but the* HEAD *ploughs on.*] and her son Horace.

LANE: [*Shaking* TAVERNER's *hand, bright and friendly*] Hello.
TAVERNER: How do you do?
HEAD: And this young lady is Miss Georgina Lane, Horace's sister.
[TAVERNER *now really sees her for the first time and for the rest of the Act is as moon-eyed as can be portrayed. The two are hypnotically attracted to one another. All thoughts of* PERRY *have vanished from anyone's mind.*]
TAVERNER: How . . . how . . . [*The lights dim on the study, but* TAVERNER *and* GEORGINA *are illuminated. They freeze during the following insert.*]

Scene 5

MR. WILLARD's *classroom. The events in Scene 5 are occurring simultaneously with those in Scene 4, only in another part of the school.* WILLARD, *in scholastic black gown, is seated on the edge of his desk with book in hand. The Fifth Form is seated at long tables on benches (forms), facing him.* PERRY *and* JARRETT *sit in the front row, with two empty seats behind them. All boys make a semblance of paying attention. A very few are genuinely interested, others merely daydream. Some are whispering; a few notes are passed.*

WILLARD: We have now reached, gentlemen, the masked ball at which Romeo and Juliet meet. Through it all, we are inundated with that archaic idea which scholars term "Elizabethan Love." You might all take notes. [*Pause while boys ready themselves*] Now then, Elizabethan love is that special species of love to be found only in Elizabethan plays. Romeo sees Juliet across a crowded room and falls passionately in love with her. It happens so fast that one almost misses it. Romeo asks a servant:

"What lady's that which doth enrich the hand
Of yonder knight?"

at which point he sights her. The next instant he is burning:

"Oh, she doth teach the torches to burn bright!
It seems she hangs upon the cheek of night
As a rich jewel in an Ethiop's ear—
Beauty too rich for use, for earth too dear!"

If you notice, Shakespeare has mixed his metaphors just a touch right there. "She hangs upon the *cheek* of night as... in an Ethiop's *ear*." Found it?

McGOVERN: Ethiop's... ear.

WILLARD: Anyway, Romeo has been smitten very violently in the space of about thirty seconds. *That* is Elizabethan love. That alone is an example of why Shakespeare wrote it in 1594. He could not seriously have written it in 1912. You understand why not. Perry?

PERRY: [*Stands, uncertain. Hasn't, of course, been listening*] Well, he's dead, sir. [*Giggles from boys*]

WILLARD: [*Humorless*] Anyone else? I just told you the answer. How about Fitzsimmons?

FITZSIMMONS: Well, the styles are different now, sir.

WILLARD: In what way?

FITZSIMMONS: The theatre is more melodramatic, they don't write real tragedies now, do they?

WILLARD: Ah, for a moment I thought you had it right. McGovern?

McGOVERN: [*Stands*] Because there aren't the same popular beliefs now as then, sir.

WILLARD: Yes! Correct! We of the Edwardian age know that there is no such thing as Elizabethan love, or enduring love at first sight. That sort of bosh was in vogue in 1594. Now we are compelled to acknowledge the nonexistence of such a thing. Of course, in the context of the play it makes sense, and it does happen—in the play. *Because* it is a play. You remember: "That willing suspension of disbelief, for the moment, which constitutes poetic faith." In any intelligent, true-life situation, however, a lasting love is based on common likes, dislikes, goals, and ideas. To love a person, one must know him, or *her,* very well, and be able to deal with all the pitfalls in her character. Only then can love bloom. It isn't as sudden and fierce a thing as pictured here; and I personally hold Act I, Scene 5 to be an illustration of shocking lust. That, though, is not the scholarly opinion. Real love is only fostered in the minds of mature and intelligent

adults. [*All the boys are slightly embarrassed by this tirade. They murmur. Most disagree.* PERRY *fidgets angrily.*] For example, none of you have ever loved [*This last is extremely irksome.*] , and you've especially not loved someone you've only seen for half a minute. [*Emphasizing*] When you grow older, you'll learn to distinguish between immature infatuation and real intelligent love. [*The boys are silent as* WILLARD *pauses to let this wisdom sink in.*] Now look at the same scene, lines ninety-four to one hundred seven.
[*Lights dim on Scene 5 and all freeze.*]

Scene 6

Lights come up again on the HEAD's *study, where all are in the positions in which we left them. They unfreeze and the* HEAD *addresses* TAVERNER, *whose eyes seldom stray from* GEORGINA's.

HEAD: Lane is entering school today. It's the middle of the term, of course, but this is a special case. He's never been to Public School before, and we only hope Thomas More College will be a good experience, don't we Lane?

LANE: Yes, sir.

HEAD: Lane was at Lawrence Park until—

TAVERNER: [*Interrupts, because the name shocks him out of his session of worship*] Lawrence Park? Isn't that a progressive school, sir?
[*To get the proper feeling into this line, substitute the words "leper colony" for "progressive school."*]

HEAD: [*Soothingly*] It *was*, until last March, when it went bankrupt. He's been trying to catch up with our curriculum in the meanwhile at home. We thought it a sound idea to start him at Thomas More as soon as possible. [*Turns to* LANE *briskly*] Now, then, Taverner, we've put Lane in the study at the end of your row, in Number Ten. I'll get the key, and his trunk will be there by the end of Fifth Lesson. I

Epiphany

want you to take him straight to class—that [way he can] meet the other boys and generally get the feel of things. [*Gets key from desk*] Here's the key. [TAVERNER *doesn't respond.*] Come and get the key. [*This was more sharply said and* TAVERNER *is startled into a reaction. Dreamily he moves to* HEAD *and takes the key.*] What lesson do you have now? Where should you be?

TAVERNER: English Lit., sir, with Mr. Willard.

HEAD: Hand me that chit, then.

[TAVERNER *hands* HEAD *slip of paper given him by* WOOLWEAVER.]

MRS. LANE: [*Clears throat*] What literature are you studying, Master Taverner?

TAVERNER: [*After pause*] Oh! Shakespeare, ma'am. *Romeo and Juliet*.

HEAD: Have you ever read Shakespeare, Lane?

LANE: Oh, yes, my sister and I were just reading *Romeo and Juliet*.

HEAD: [*What he hoped was an encouraging smile was really a look of patent disbelief. He holds out chit.*] Here, Taverner, here is a note for your master.

[*The lights dim on the* HEAD'*s study. The five characters freeze.*]

Scene 7

MR. WILLARD'*s classroom again.* STOWE *and* CHURCHILL *are standing in their places, reading aloud.*

CHURCHILL: [*As Benvolio, although he is not even pretending to act*]
"Come, he hath hid himself among these trees
To be consorted with the humorous night.
Blind is his love and best befits the dark."

STOWE: [*As Mercutio, not acting either*] If love be—

WILLARD: Pardon me, Stowe, I meant to stop earlier. There are some literary devices we missed. Go back to line thirty-one, gentlemen. Somebody tell me what sort of literary device "He hath hid himself" may be. [*Pause. No hands are raised.*] I'm waiting, boys. [*A tentative hand goes up.*] Ah, Mr. Churchill.

CHURCHILL: [*Stands*] An... alliteration, sir?

WILLARD: Good. [CHURCHILL *sits.*] The next is "the humorous night." [*No hands*] Stowe will tell us.

STOWE: [*To his neighbor, as he stands*] Will I? [*Uncertainly, to* WILLARD] It's not an apostrophe, is it, sir?

WILLARD: No.

[STOWE *sits.*]

STOWE: Oh.

WILLARD: Anyone? Fitzsimmons?

FITZSIMMONS: [*Stands. At first confident, then realizes he is wrong*] It's a pa...

WILLARD: Yes! What is it?

FITZSIMMONS: ...Paradox? [*Pause.* WILLARD *begins brooding.*] A most ingenious paradox?... Sir?

WILLARD: It's an example of personification, children. The night itself has no humorous qualities until you imbue it with human characteristics. All right.

STOWE: If love be blind—

WILLARD: [*Thundering*] Did I give you leave, Stowe?

JARRETT: [*To* PERRY] Just keep on interrupting poor old Crater-Face, that's right.

PERRY: How rude.

WILLARD: There is one more literary device we've not identified. "Blind is his love." Who'll tell me what it is? [*Long pause. No hands are raised.* WILLARD *gathers his wrath.*] You ought to know these literary devices! *Any*body? [*Pause*] Say something brilliant, somebody.

JARRETT: Cogito ergo sum.

WILLARD: What does Perry say?

PERRY: [*To* JARRETT, *frantically*] Where are we?

[*Lights dim.*]

Scene 8

Lights up on HEAD's *study; the five unfreeze.*

HEAD: I suppose, then, this is...good-bye. Madam?
[MRS. LANE *rises and crosses to* LANE, *taking his hands in hers, formally. She is very aware of their lack of privacy.*]
MRS. LANE: Horace... [HEAD *takes* TAVERNER's *arm and draws him back.*] I want you to write home every week. Will you?
LANE: [*Very upset*] Yes, mum.
MRS. LANE: Good. Now, remember all I've told you, and I'm sure you'll have a splendid time. [LANE *responds to impulse. Disregarding the situation, he grabs and hugs* MRS. LANE, *hiding his face. Stiffening, she gently peels him off.* HEAD *and* TAVERNER *look away in embarrassment.*] Good-bye, darling.
LANE: [*Quietly*] Good-bye, mummy.
GEORGINA: [*Gets up and crosses to* LANE, *with a beautiful unity of movement*] Bye, Horsey.
[LANE *nods.*]
HEAD: [*Breaking the silence*] Well, Lane, you'd best be off.
[MRS. LANE *looks up quickly and kisses* LANE's *forehead.*]
MRS. LANE: Good-bye, darling.
HEAD: Mr. Willard expects you both very soon. [*Turns, sees* LANE's *coat*] Oh! you can't forget your gabardine, Lane. [*Gives it to* LANE] Take it with you—that would be the best thing. Go now. Go! Oh, and Taverner, thank you.
TAVERNER: Yes, sir. [LANE *looks back at his mother. She is intent on preserving her dignity and gives him a patronizing nod.* TAVERNER *tries to tear his eyes away from* GEORGINA.] Thank you, sir. [*He manages.*] Come on, old man! [*The boys exit.*]
HEAD: [*As the door closes*] I'll be keeping a close eye on him, madam. I foresee some slight trouble with him settling in here.
[*Blackout on* HEAD's *study.*]

Scene 9

MR. WILLARD's *classroom. All boys in their seats.* WILLARD *is lecturing.*

WILLARD: Shakespeare's plays fall into two main categories: tragedy and comedy. The tragedies are the better-known and more popular. Shakespeare was a very traditional playwright, for the most part. He crafted his plays along traditional lines and although his stories were never original, he constructed them along the lines of drama set down by Aristotle. In Elizabethan times, however—which were when? Who will tell me the years of Elizabeth's reign? [*No hands*] Nobody? I'll have to make Mr. Drake aware of the disgraceful lack of attention in his history lessons. Ah—Stowe?

STOWE: 1558 to 1603, sir.

WILLARD: Correct. Now, what was I saying? Shakespeare's tragic heroes. His tragic heroes are not regular, everyday, common men. They are exceptional men, as well tragic heroes ought to be. They've all got their one tragic flaw; for example, Caesar's ambition, or Hamlet's procrastination. This tragic flaw proves their undoing, and they all die.

JARRETT: [*To* PERRY] Amen.

WILLARD: The comedies are all light, featuring a boy meets girl, boy cannot have girl, boy gets girl pattern. They all end in marriage. Well, Shakespeare does not adhere religiously to this pattern on all occasions. Before he'd quite perfected his craft, the patterns were apt to be less readily discernible, *Measure for Measure,* for example. This group of plays is termed the Problem Plays. Scholars don't know quite what to make of them.

JARRETT: [*Disgusted, to* PERRY] Why don't they just watch them, and not try to pull them apart so much? It's bad enough we've got to analyze every bloody sentence.

Epiphany

PERRY: [*To no one in particular*] God, I'm bored. [*Stretches*]

WILLARD: Some scholars put *Romeo and Juliet* in the Problem Plays category, as well. It begins like a comedy, and if one unfamiliar with it saw it performed, he would assume it was a comedy until—well, until Mercutio's death.

PERRY: [*To* JARRETT] A *comedy?!*

JARRETT: [*To* PERRY] I'm splitting my sides.

[JARRET *is very unhappy with this whole lecture—he is bored, and he thinks that all the information is pointless. He has taken the inkpot out of the inkwell and is amusing himself by dipping the nib of his pen into the ink and splashing the ink at the desk or at* PERRY. PERRY *soon joins in, splashing ink at* JARRETT. *Involved with their game, they get a trifle carried away.* WILLARD *notices.*]

WILLARD: In comedy, you see, the obstacle to the marriage or the reunion of the young lovers is often a parental one, as in this case. It is overcome in comedy and the lesson is marriage. But in *Romeo and Juliet*, it is not overcome. The climax is reached very dramatically—[*Here* JARRETT *somehow contrives to spill ink all over the desk, splashing both* PERRY *and* WILLARD. PERRY *wipes himself with a handkerchief.* WILLARD, *enraged, explodes.*] Mr. Jarrett! Learn to show some respect! I've watched you disrupt my lesson long enough. [*The entire class is enjoying this diversion.*] You'll remember, Jarrett, that you aren't a prefect and you're not too big to receive a caning from me!

JARRETT: I'm sorry, sir.

WILLARD: "I'm sorry!" You'll come to my study at seven o'clock tonight, *then* you'll be sorry!

JARRETT: Yes, sir.

[*The classroom door opens,* LANE *and* TAVERNER *enter.* WILLARD *stops.*]

TAVERNER: [*Holding out chit*] I was seeing the Head, sir. This is the new boy, his name is Lane.

[*All the boys watch* LANE *intently, whispering to each other.*]

WILLARD: [*Stands, fixes gown, takes chit, holds out right hand for* LANE *to shake*] How do you do? [*Doesn't expect or get an answer. Gives chit a cursory glance, then peers at it.*] What does this say?

TAVERNER: It's from the Head.

WILLARD: Ah. [*Tosses it into the waste-paper basket*]— Lane. [*Gets book for* LANE] Here's a book, Lane, and you may sit anywhere you like for now. We're studying *Romeo and Juliet*, and we're on page [*Consults copy on desk*]...eighteen. Boys! [*All whispers cease, but all eyes follow* LANE *as he sits next to* TAVERNER *on the form behind* PERRY. *As* TAVERNER *passes,* PERRY *touches him and grins.* TAVERNER *looks at* PERRY *absently, but does not respond.*] Where was I? [TAVERNER *dips pen dutifully. To* LANE *and* TAVERNER] I'd gone off on a tangent. Let's read on, gentlemen. Act II, Scene 2. Who would like to be Romeo? Taverner? And the lovely Juliet? McGovern, would you be so kind?

McGOVERN: [*Stands*] Yes, sir.

[FITZSIMMONS, *at the back of the classroom, whistles at* McGOVERN. *The class laughs.*]

WILLARD: Who did that? I want to know this instant! [*The class grows quiet. All faces are as stiff as pokers.*] Was it Churchill?

CHURCHILL: Oh, no, sir.

WILLARD: Was it Fitzsimmons?

FITZSIMMONS: [*Not looking at* WILLARD] No, sir.

WILLARD: Look at me and say that.

PERRY: [*To* JARRETT, *exasperated*] Christ!

LANE: [*To* TAVERNER, *pointing to* PERRY] Who's that?

TAVERNER: That's my best chum, Perry.

LANE: He looks very nice.

TAVERNER: [*Misconstrues* LANE's *comment and is very taken aback*] Yes, he's nice-looking.

FITZSIMMONS: [*After a short pause, looks straight at* WILLARD] No, sir.

WILLARD: [*Unconvinced*] You'll do me a hundred lines, just the same, Fitzsimmons.

FITZSIMMONS: Yes, sir. [*Laughing, to his neighbor*] Fair's fair.

WILLARD: Romeo?

TAVERNER: Uh,

"He jests at scars that never felt a wound.
But soft, what light through yonder window breaks?
It is the East, and Juliet is the sun.
Arise, fair sun, and kill the envious moon,—"

WILLARD: Desist, my boy. We've got a classical allusion on our hands, besides a wealth of other literary devices. [TAVERNER *and* McGOVERN *sit.*] Who is the moon to whom Romeo refers? [*Stumped silence*] Come now, what

Epiphany

goddess is the moon? This is Second-Form material!

STOWE: [*Stands*] Venus, sir.

WILLARD: Not Venus. Somebody else?

FITZSIMMONS: [*Stands*] Isn't it—no. [*Sits*]

WILLARD: [*Pause*] No, Fitzsimmons, it isn't. I cannot believe you don't know this! Jarrett, tell us.

JARRETT: [*Stands*] It's Diana, sir.

WILLARD: Why didn't you speak earlier? Taverner, continue, please.

TAVERNER: "Who is already sick and pale with grief,—"

WILLARD: Who is? [*Pause*] The moon is.

TAVERNER: "That thou her maid art far more fair than she.
Be not her maid since she is envious,
Her vestal livery is but—"

[*The church bell rings.* TAVERNER *immediately shuts up and sits down. Boys collect things, and stay seated, though barely restrained.*]

WILLARD: Oh, go on. Class dismissed.

[*With a roar of relief, the boys get up. While* WILLARD *gathers his belongings and leaves, they cluster around* LANE. *The crowd hides him. It is apparent that though challenging, the group is friendly enough. Finally,* TAVERNER *rises above the crowd, standing on a form.*]

TAVERNER: Shut up, shut up! [*Slowly, they do so.*] Now, one at a time.

McGOVERN: [*Mockingly*] Yes, granny.

TAVERNER: [*Lunging at* McGOVERN *good-naturedly*] Shut up McGovern, you beast.

[LANE *is now in the clear, sitting on a form, his coat over his knees. The pace is very fast, eager, undisciplined.*]

FITZSIMMONS: What's your name?

LANE: [*Friendly, smiling at them*] Hello! I'm Horace Lane.

STOWE: Well, *you*'re friendly, aren't you?

LANE: Yes! What's your name?

[*Pause.* TAVERNER *is cringing for* LANE.]

FITZSIMMONS: Uh—tick—you don't speak to us that way.

CHURCHILL: Keep your head down and be respectful—new tick.

LANE: [*Confused*] Sorry.

FITZSIMMONS: So, *what*'s your name?

LANE: Horace Lane.

McGOVERN: Oh, *Horace* Lane.

CHURCHILL: His name's Horse?

[*Chorus of "Neigh," "Giddyup," etc.*]
TAVERNER: [*Uncomfortable*] His name's Lane.
JARRETT: Oh, sorry, granny.
[TAVERNER *grimaces at* JARRETT.]
STOWE: Where were you before you came here?
LANE: Lawrence Park.
PERRY: Where? No such place, ducky.
CHURCHILL: No, Perry, his name's Horsey, not Ducky.
[TAVERNER *catches* PERRY's *eye.* PERRY, *guilt-stricken, retires to the sidelines to watch the taunting develop, a non-participant.*]
FITZSIMMONS: Well, where did you go to school?
LANE: [*More exasperated*] Lawrence Park!
STOWE: Keep your voice down, tick!
FITZSIMMONS: [*Simultaneously with* STOWE] Never heard of it.
CHURCHILL: You've heard of it Fitzsimmons—that's the progressive school that's just closed, and good riddance.
JARRETT: Progressive school? [*Begins laughing*] You went to a progressive school? How did you ever pass our entrance exam? [*To group*] They don't give lessons at progressive schools.
LANE: They do!
JARRETT: No they don't, it's rubbish like farming and—and ditch-digging.
LANE: Well, what's wrong with learning farming? It's useful!
CHURCHILL: Is that your ambition? To become a farmer?
[*Pause*]
McGOVERN: You stupid progressive ass!
[*Short pause, then the next lines come in a torrent.*]
FITZSIMMONS: Why in hell did they let you in?
McGOVERN: How do I spell my name?
STOWE: What comes after six?
JARRETT: He must have bribed the governors.
FITZSIMMONS: 'Fraid we don't teach weeding the vegetable garden here, Horsey.
STOWE: Giddyup, Horsey! Faster!
McGOVERN: But sir, why should I do my Latin? I'm going to dig ditches when I grow up!
CHURCHILL: Sorry, Horse, no farmers allowed.
[*The taunting crescendoes. Up till this point it has been semi-coherent, now it just becomes a shouting mass. In the tumult, we hear—*]

TAVERNER: Stop it, now!
[TAVERNER *and* PERRY *stand away, uncertain what to do.* LANE *sits with bowed head. Maybe, or maybe not, accidentally,* STOWE *joggles* LANE. *The rest follow suit, mostly pushing* STOWE *into* LANE.]

CHURCHILL: Go for him, Crater-Face!

McGOVERN: Take his coat! [*They attempt this, but* LANE's *grip is too strong. He turns his back and struggles into his coat. He is very close to tears, but does not give in. The boys perceive his armor* [his coat] *and the taunting dies.* TAVERNER *goes over to* LANE, *not looking at the other boys. He takes* LANE's *arm.*]

TAVERNER: I'll take you to your room. Come on...Lane.
[TAVERNER *and* LANE *exit by the classroom door. All the boys follow them with their eyes, panting. With the slam of the door comes the blackout.*]

CURTAIN

ACT II

Scene 1

MR. WILLARD's *classroom. It is neat, orderly, and empty of people. The time is two months later, a July afternoon during the school's holidays.* PERRY *enters the classroom, holding a letter. He sits on a form and rips the letter open. It is read by* TAVERNER *offstage over the PA system.*

TAVERNER'S VOICE: Dear Perry,

I've been thinking of you so much since I got home for the holidays. I think it's a rotten job that you've to stay at school for the hols. I don't see why your parents couldn't have gone to the Continent during the term or taken you with them, or something. What sort of a stunt do they think they're pulling? What was that literary device? You'd better write me. I've not heard from you in simply ages. It's a very selfish thing, you know, never to answer my letters.

We've not done much—rather a bore at home, actually. Tomorrow, however, I shall be going to Somerset to spend a fortnight with Jarrett. It sounds awfully jolly, if we can avoid his sister and her chum. There is little I find more offputting than a couple of giggly females.

I'm so excited about next term! I was so afraid that I wouldn't be made a prefect, so I'm awfully relieved. It's Jarrett and I, we're the only Fifth Formers who've got the promotion. With such a big change, I imagine my work is going to go rather to the devil, but I don't really care. I'm just so glad that I was chosen! Don't worry, I'll be nice to you, although I can think of a few chaps I'll really enjoy giving the cane. No, that's not true, really. One can't take advantage of one's position. It's not fair.

I hope you're not too frightfully bored. Who else is staying over the hols? Is it mostly Sixth Formers who've to swot for the Army Exam? I should expect so. Write me back soon. I do miss you.

Yours, etc.
Taverner

[*At this point,* LANE *enters nervously, with some schoolwork. He doesn't want the rejection he knows is in store for him.*]

LANE: Perry...

PERRY: [*Turning*] Huh? [*Disgusted*] Oh, bugger off!

LANE: [*Immediately*] I'm sorry. [*Begins leaving.*]

PERRY: Oh, Lane, I'm sorry. What do you want?

LANE: Just a bit of help.

PERRY: Latin again?

LANE: Right.

PERRY: You know how stupid I am. I can't help you.

LANE: Everyone else is out. Really.

PERRY: So I'm your last resort? Oh, sit down! [*He grabs the paper.*] "Change each singular to plural," is it? Read it.

LANE: "Agricola puellam portat." [*Pause*] I don't know.

PERRY: Well, what's it mean?

LANE: Ummm...the sailor—the farmer—no, I don't know. What's the use of it anyway? Who cares?

PERRY: You care, because if you don't do it you'll get your ears pinned back. The farmer, that's right. Now puellam...G—g—

LANE: [*Overlapping*] Ummm...give, to give!

PERRY: It's a noun, you silly ass!

LANE: Oh! Girl!

PERRY: Oh, well-played! Now, portat...

[*The lights dim to blackout.*]

Scene 2

Mid-July, one day later. It is late morning on a beautiful sunny summer's day. The lights come up on a visually lovely set, in sharp contrast to the bleak sets of Thomas More. This is the "rose garden" at the Jarretts' country estate. Flower beds form three sides of a square, the side nearest the wings boasting a trellis climbing with roses. The trellis is one of those arched affairs, with a path underneath leading to the house. The grey stone wall of the house is just visible, but the French doors are open, the path stopping at the threshold. The two flower beds perpendicular to the curtain-line hold a profusion of flowers of various species. The middle one is raked, and is planted in a pattern which shows up in blooming roses. A backdrop may show a gazebo, or something similar.

There is music coming from within the house—Tchaikovsky's "Sleeping Beauty" waltz, played on an early twentieth-century model gramophone. In the garden, two girls waltz very seriously to the music. They are JARRETT's *younger sister* IBBY, *and her bosom-buddy from dancing school,* GEORGINA LANE. GEORGINA *is dressed in a simple but very flattering white dress.* IBBY *is in sensible sky-blue. As they dance, they seem to be pulling at each other.*

IBBY: Stop leading, Georgina! I'm being the man this time!
GEORGINA: Oh, was I leading again? I am sorry.
IBBY: You're always leading. [*They dance.*] That's better. You know, everyone you dance with won't be such an oaf as those boys at the cotillion.
GEORGINA: Oh, all boys are oafs. [*Pause. They dance.*] On the dance floor, anyhow.
IBBY: What do you mean by that?! [IBBY *laughs. The music stops abruptly.* IBBY, *outraged, speaks as* GEORGINA *twirls her along, unconcerned.*] Who did that?! [GEORGINA *sings the melody.*] Who turned the gramophone off?
[JARRETT *enters through the French doors, in a hat.* GEORGINA, *seeing him, immediately pirouettes into his arms, leading aggressively.*]
GEORGINA: That wasn't at all nice.
JARRETT: [*Amused, but uncomfortable*] I had to make myself heard, you know. [*Pause. They dance.*] You know something? You ought to let *me* lead.
IBBY: What do I keep telling you, Georgina?
GEORGINA: Lead, then. Turn the music back on, Ibby.
JARRETT: No! I didn't come out here to dance! [*Laughing, he pushes her off.*] I came out to say that I'm going to the station to pick up my chum. Do you want to tag along?

Epiphany

IBBY: Are you going on Sultan?

JARRETT: No—how could we get back with his bags, then? James is taking me, silly.

IBBY: Well, I certainly don't want to come—ugly.

GEORGINA: Can your chum dance?

JARRETT: Like an angel.

GEORGINA: [*Pointedly; she does not like to be teased.*] Does he have a big nose?

JARRETT: [*Touches nose self-consciously*] Why do you always talk about my big nose?

GEORGINA: Because I'm angry that you turned our music off. Does he?

JARRETT: No. In fact, he's quite a nice-looking chap.

IBBY: Is he the little fellow who's always borrowing your clothes?

JARRETT: [*Thinks*] No—that's Perry. This is the big fellow who wins all our cricket matches for us. He's the one who's going to be a prefect with me next term.

IBBY: Oh, him. What's-his-name—Thompson, or something?

JARRETT: Something like that. So you're not coming? Miss Billings thought it would be nice if we all met him.

IBBY: Well, the grippe has obviously impaired Miss Billings' judgment. I think your chum would find it frightful if we all went to meet him.

GEORGINA: Besides, it would probably be boring.

JARRETT: Are you calling my friend boring?

GEORGINA: I don't know yet. [*Straightening JARRETT's tie*] What does he look like?

JARRETT: A boy.

GEORGINA: No, specifically.

JARRETT: He's got—umm—two eyes on the right side of his face and a nose in the palm of his left hand.

GEORGINA: Oh, now you're teasing me! Go away!

IBBY: Yes, do.

JARRETT: I plan to. Only don't ride off before I come back. I might be some time.

IBBY: Of course we'll wait for you—we'll make a proper outing of it.

GEORGINA: But only if you apologize for teasing me.

JARRETT: [*Preserving his dignity*] I am truly sorry for teasing you, Miss Lane. Shall I kneel?

[*He takes off his hat and bows slightly*]

GEORGINA: [*Enjoying it*] No, that won't be necessary. You are dismissed.

[*Obediently,* JARRETT *turns and exits, jamming his hat on his head.*]

IBBY: [*After* JARRETT's *exit*] You do flirt a lot, don't you?

GEORGINA: [*Absolute contrition*] Oh, does it bother you?

IBBY: Well . . . no, it doesn't *bother* me, only—

GEORGINA: [*Brightly*] Well, you can flirt with Mr.—Thompson when he comes, and you won't feel so left out.

IBBY: I'm afraid that's hardly my forte, Georgina.

GEORGINA: No? Then I shall teach you. He shall be your first conquest.

IBBY: [*Giggles*] Barkis is willing. [*Reflects*] But only if he isn't as much a Philistine as my brother. All he talks about is school. Clive is positively obsessed with school.

GEORGINA: Oh, Ibby, your brother's lovely. Shall we waltz some more?

IBBY: No. I get enough of that in London, practicing with a broom in front of Miss Billings. Especially now that she's ill—I want to do something naughty!

GEORGINA: Like?

IBBY: I can't think of anything. [*Thinks*] Yes I can.

[*She yanks her hair from its braided bun. There is a small basket under the trellis from which* IBBY *grabs a comb and deposits her hairpins.*]

GEORGINA: Oh, do let me fix it! [IBBY *hands her the comb and sits on the ground.* GEORGINA *kneels behind her.*] We used to spend hours doing this at Lawrence Park.

IBBY: Shhh! Don't say that name! Mama doesn't know, you know.

GEORGINA: [*A bit nonplussed*] Oh. Sorry. But we did, anyway. We'd do each other's hair, and eat the food that we'd smuggled into the dormy. And we'd talk about the girls we hated and the boys we liked.

IBBY: [*Cannot imagine life at a co-educational institution*] Did you see the boys much?

GEORGINA: Heavens, yes—all the time! We had lessons with them, we worked with them, we ate with them; all we didn't do was sleep with them.

IBBY: How very odd.

GEORGINA: No, it was great fun! Every girl always had a beau—

well, most girls. Not the ugly ones, or the fat ones. But we almost always had a beau. It was terribly exciting. The whole school used to pass notes at assembly.

IBBY: What sort of notes?

GEORGINA: Why, love notes, of course! "Meet me behind the girls' lav after cooking class," or sometimes they were from a secret admirer. Or the best kind of note: "My dearest...uh, Georgina, I do love you and I think you're ripping. Wear a red ribbon if you like me back. Love...Cameron Blake." He was my last beau before the school closed.

IBBY: What did you *do* with your beaux?

GEORGINA: Cameron used to take me on walks and pick me wildflowers. We'd go into the broom closet.

IBBY: Georgina!

GEORGINA: [*Giggling*] Well—we did. Everyone did. But I got fairly sick of Cameron after a few weeks. He was always chasing me into the boot-cupboard by the boys' box-room.

IBBY: That sounds fairly...intimate.

GEORGINA: [*Sourly*] It was so *intimate* that my entire left side was bruised from rubbing against the plaster. But he was awfully sweet. Do you know what he did? He wrote me poetry. Actually, I think he got one of the masters to do it. But it was so darling. He wrote an ode to my eyebrow. He thought I had lovely eyebrows.

[IBBY *turns her head around to look at* GEORGINA'*s eyebrows.* GEORGINA, *who was holding* IBBY'*s hair in a position to be pinned, sees what the style looks like from the front, makes a face and quickly takes it out.*] Uh—how shall I do your hair?

IBBY: [*Dryly*] Use your overactive imagination. I don't see what he could find to say about your *eye*brows.

GEORGINA: Oh, it was beautiful! It went like this—I know it by heart.

[*She sits back on her heels, using the comb to gesture. Feelingly*]

A brow of Heaven-chiseled arc—
My captive soul can but remark:
"Fair Helen's beauty rivalled is!"
How each desires that eyebrow; his
To touch, to love, to idolize
That bit of fuzz above her eyes.
Ensculpted, wingèd like the dove

Describes the eyebrow of my love.
Each perfect hair in Heaven gilded.
Upon demise, sweet Hera willed it
To adorn my worshipped's face—
The pure epitome of grace.
The beauty of that brow divine,
To gaze upon't: my life's design.
[*Pause*] Oh, isn't that *splendid?!*
[*Combs* IBBY's *hair rapturously.*]

IBBY: [*Impressed but objective*] It's silly.

GEORGINA: [*Stops in mid-stroke*] Oh, you've not an ounce of romance in you! Apologize or I shan't do your hair!

IBBY: I'm sorry. But I want it down anyway. [GEORGINA *makes a face at her back.*] And I *do* have romance in me. Just not silly romance. [GEORGINA *is pouting.* IBBY *stands, runs fingers through hair. She looks at* GEORGINA, *exasperated.*] I certainly wouldn't *mind* someone writing that for me. [*She tries again.*] If Cameron was so romantic, why did you break off with him?

GEORGINA: [*Instantly all right*] Oh... [*Takes down own hair as she talks, catches a braid at the back, leaving the rest loose.*] it got boring. He was a bore... Most boys are, you know. He just wasn't... perfect.

IBBY: Oh, come now, who's perfect.

GEORGINA: Someone.

IBBY: Who?

GEORGINA: Just someone. I don't know yet. The boy who's perfect is the one that you know the moment you see him. It's an electric attraction.

IBBY: Yes, but that doesn't *really* happen.

GEORGINA: Just because it never happened to you! It happens if you believe it will. I know exactly what will happen.

IBBY: [*Challenging*] What will happen, then?

GEORGINA: Well, it will start out that we'll see each other, and we won't speak a word. And then he'll take my hands in his, and he'll look deep down into my soul, and say, "I love you." And... and he'll bring me flowers, which I'll wear in my hair. And he'll kiss my eyes and my hair and my hands and... and he'll treat me like a goddess. And then... and then he'll adore me.

IBBY: [*Breaking the mood*] And then you'll decide that he's a bore.

Epiphany

GEORGINA: Oh, but he won't be! He'll be beautiful, and he'll be exciting, and he'll be charming, and he'll dance like an angel! There, how can you possibly say you don't want that to happen to you?

IBBY: [*Has to smile*] I can't.

[PHIPPS *enters through the French doors.*]

PHIPPS: Luncheon is ready, Miss Isobel.

GEORGINA: Oh, Ibby, wouldn't it be lovely to eat out here?

IBBY: Miss Billings never lets us eat outside. She says that there are too many insects.

GEORGINA: I haven't seen a single fly since I got here. Anyhow, she's ill. *She'll* never know.

IBBY: [*Looks up at window, at* GEORGINA, *at* PHIPPS, *at feet*] Bring our luncheon out here, Phipps.

PHIPPS: I'll see what your mother says, Miss.

IBBY: Very well. [*To* GEORGINA] But we can't make a mess.

GEORGINA: Make a mess? Why should we make a mess?

IBBY: Well, I'm just saying...

GEORGINA: [*Teasingly*] You mean I can't *pick* one?

[*Moves menacingly close to the trellis*]

IBBY: Only if you ask Harris. We're in the gardener's domain. Gather ye rosebuds while ye may, and all that.

GEORGINA: What? [IBBY *laughs.*] Clive *has* been a long time.

IBBY: The trains are sometimes unreliable. I do hope he gets back soon, though, otherwise we won't have much time to ride. And there are such capital rides around here!

[PHIPPS *reenters.*]

PHIPPS: Miss Isobel, you may eat in the rose garden. [*He goes back off and reemerges with a small table on wheels, with a lunch on it, followed by four small seats of some kind.* GEORGINA *sets the seats up industriously;* IBBY *stands and watches.*]

IBBY: [*Imperiously*] Thank you, Phipps. That will be all. [*In a normal voice*] Oh, I'm famished.

GEORGINA: [*Inspecting the dishes, with* IBBY] Oooh, cold chicken and cucumber sandwiches! Oh, and vegetables—horrid. I could eat that whole platter of chicken, I'm so hungry.

IBBY: But you'd vomit. [*They giggle madly.*] But why are there four seats?

GEORGINA: For the boys, of course.

IBBY: Oh, does that mean that we have to wait for them?

[*They look at each other, each deliberating.*]

GEORGINA: No. After all, they wouldn't wait for us.

IBBY: I do hope Miss Billings has got her windows shut. She'd have my liver if she heard us! [*Mischievously*] Let's eat! [*They serve themselves.* GEORGINA *takes a cucumber sandwich.*]

GEORGINA: I hate cucumber sandwiches—they're ridiculously small. I could put that whole pile in my mouth at once.

IBBY: No you couldn't.

GEORGINA: Yes, I could. D'you want to see?
[*Begins stuffing her mouth.* IBBY *begins to panic, although she is laughing.*]

IBBY: Stop! Stop! I believe you! Where *did* you learn your table manners, wench?

GEORGINA: [*With a full mouth*] I've got good table manners when I'm in company. [*Swallows*] Well, at least there are some left for you. Oooh, that was a lump. [*She holds her chest.*] We used to do that sort of thing all the time at Law— at school. Only the food wasn't as good. In fact, the food was positively vile.

IBBY: Clive always complains about the food at Thomas More. Says they get burnt porridge and rancid butter.

GEORGINA: I expect they do, because Horace says the same thing. He says they get soup with no meat in it, only fat and gristle.

IBBY: Oh, how horrid! Clive said he once found a long red hair in a piece of shepherd's pie.

GEORGINA: Oh, how dis*gust*ing! Would you pass me the chicken, please? We had rats in our lav at school.

IBBY: Oh, *did* you?! I never quite believed Clive's stories, but I suppose I do now—they check with your brother's.

GEORGINA: Yes, but I'm not sure if I believe all *my* brother says. Some of the things he writes are rather incredible.

IBBY: What?

GEORGINA: Well—for instance. Supposedly, one evening he was in his study and a group of boys barged in and grabbed him, and carried him to the fourth floor of their dormy, and held him upside-down out of a window by his ankles . . . But doesn't that sound rather savage? And do you know what *else* he said?

IBBY: What else?

GEORGINA: Shhhh. [*Looks around. Speaks in a hushed tone.*] All

Epiphany

right. Now, I don't know whether to believe this or not, but he says the boys have love affairs with each other, just as if it was boys and girls! And that they kiss, and walk about hand-in-hand, and all sorts of things!

IBBY: [*Shocked, intrigued, awed with the wickedness of their conversation*] That's horrid! It's *so*...wicked, and...decadent! [*Resolutely*] I don't believe it!

GEORGINA: Neither do I.

IBBY: How could a boy love another boy?

GEORGINA: Oh, Horace says that one of the boys sort of plays the girl—you know, a younger boy who still sings treble.

IBBY: Maybe Clive's chum is really his lover. Maybe that's why he was so eager to have him up.

GEORGINA: I wonder which one is the girl. Oooh, I'll bet they're holding hands right now! [*Wild giggling*] Oh, Clive must absolutely hate my flirting with him!

[*Voices are heard offstage, coming closer.*]

IBBY: That must be them now!

GEORGINA: Romeo and Juliet.

IBBY: I dare you to ask them if they're in love.

GEORGINA: I dare you!

IBBY: What if they said "Yes"!

GEORGINA: I'd probably vomit.

IBBY: And *I'd* never make my conquest.

GEORGINA: And that would be an even bigger tragedy.

[GEORGINA *stops abruptly as* JARRETT *and* TAVERNER *enter through the French doors.*]

JARRETT: Hallo—mama said you waited lunch for us, but you've not.

IBBY: Mama was wrong. This is... [*Wants an introduction*]

JARRETT: This is my august friend, Mr. Richard Taverner. [JARRETT *grabs* TAVERNER'*s arm and pulls him to the table.*] Come ahead, don't be shy. [*Gracelessly, only because he has to*] This is my sister Ibby and her friend, ummm, Georgina Lane.

[TAVERNER *sits across from* GEORGINA, *intoxicated, enraptured, hypnotized. They cannot stop looking at each other. The* JARRETTS, *in their quick and self-absorbed way are serving and setting up, unaware of the attraction.*]

IBBY: Georgina, pass the chicken, please. How much chicken do you want, Mr. Thom—uh, Taverner?

[GEORGINA *looks at* IBBY *perplexed until she comprehends the request. Then she relocates herself and passes the chicken, staring at* TAVERNER *again.*]

JARRETT: Give him a lot, he's not eaten since four this morning.

IBBY: How was your trip?

TAVERNER: [*Trying to pull himself together*] All right. [*Smiles nervously*] Thanks.

[IBBY *hands him his plate.*]

JARRETT: [*When* TAVERNER *doesn't eat*] Why don't you eat? You said you were starving.

TAVERNER: [*Looks at* JARRETT, *then laughs at himself*] I am. [*Eats wolfishly; so does* JARRETT]

IBBY: Do hurry, though. If we want to ride to the river we'll have to start very soon.

JARRETT: Oh, Taverner, you'll love to ride here! We've got the most capital places to ride to.

TAVERNER: Riding? Now?

JARRETT: No, when we've finished.

TAVERNER: But I've not even unpacked.

JARRETT: [*Unmoved*] Horrors.

IBBY: You can't unpack first, or there won't be time. It's a long way. Would you like a cucumber sandwich?

JARRETT: I would. [*Takes platter, throws some on* TAVERNER'*s plate, some on own plate*] Would you like one, Miss Lane?

GEORGINA: [*Who hasn't eaten a bite since* TAVERNER'*s entrance*] No thanks, I've already had one.

[IBBY *giggles.*]

IBBY: You can borrow some of my riding clothes, Georgina. Did you bring yours, umm...

JARRETT: Taverner.

TAVERNER: Yes, but I really don't think I can go. I got up at four o'clock this morning to catch the train, and I'm just not up to it.

JARRETT: Beast! I warned you we were going riding at the station.

TAVERNER: You can still go. Please don't let me stop you.

JARRETT: But I wanted you to come. [*He says that very sincerely.* IBBY *makes to exchange a meaningful glance with* GEORGINA, *but sees that she is still distracted.*]

IBBY: Wake up, Georgina.

GEORGINA: [*Astonished, her mind totally elsewhere*] Oh, have I been asleep?

Epiphany

IBBY: [*Laughing*] No—maybe with your eyes open. Aren't you finishing?
GEORGINA: Finishing what? [IBBY *looks at her curiously.*] Oh, my food! No. I mean yes!
JARRETT: Were you drinking or something while I was gone?
GEORGINA: Why do you say that?
JARRETT: Because of the way you're acting.
IBBY: How dare you talk to my friend that way?!
JARRETT: Don't shout at me, Ibby! I'll shout back louder, and I'll scrag ya, too!
IBBY: You're so ugly!
GEORGINA: [*Laughing at them*] You sound like my brother and me!
JARRETT: Oh, you have a brother?
GEORGINA: [*Surprised*] Yes! He's at your school.
TAVERNER: Didn't you know that, Jarrett?
JARRETT: [*Looks from* TAVERNER *to* GEORGINA, *digesting the last exchange. Throws his napkin on the table*] Well, I'm all ready to go. How about you, Ib?
IBBY: I'm ready. Come along, Georgina, we'll fix you up with—
GEORGINA: No, I don't think I want to go.
JARRETT: Oh heck, not you too!
GEORGINA: I—[*Smiles uncertainly, looks apologetic, gestures ignorance*] . . . Not today.
JARRETT: [*After a moment*] We'll have to do something else, then.
GEORGINA: No, you must go. Really!
 [JARRETT *and* IBBY *look at each other, considering, and at their guests, who are staring at each other.* IBBY *looks knowingly back at* JARRETT.]
IBBY: All right then. We'll be back sevenish. You can ring when you want all this cleared away.
JARRETT: But Ibby, we can't just leave them here! What are they going to do? Spread manure? [*Indicating flower beds*]
IBBY: Come *on*, stupid!
 [*She drags him off, protesting.*]
 [TAVERNER *and* GEORGINA *put their hands on the table and hold each other.*]
GEORGINA: Hello.
TAVERNER: Hello. [*Pause*] It's a shame you didn't go riding.
GEORGINA: No, it isn't, really.
TAVERNER: No? I thought it sounded rather jolly.

GEORGINA: [*Beginning to lure him*] Yes, but there would be too many people there.
TAVERNER: [*Still on top of things*] Well, I'm glad you stayed behind... to keep me company.
GEORGINA: [*Immediately*] Are you really?!
TAVERNER: [*Startled but truthful*] Well—yes.
GEORGINA: Good, because I'd far rather be here with you than off with them.
TAVERNER: [*Almost with trepidation; he senses the answer might be momentous.*] ...Why?
GEORGINA: [*Seizing the opportunity*] Well, because...Richard—do you believe in fate?
TAVERNER: I—uh—I suppose.
GEORGINA: [*Dramatically*] Fate brought me here to be with you!
TAVERNER: [*Wavering*] Well, but...I mean...
GEORGINA: [*So positive*] But you must believe in fate! You do, don't you?!
TAVERNER: [*Unable to resist her*] Yes.
GEORGINA: I thought I should never see you again...No, that's not true. I knew I should see you someday.
TAVERNER: Did you?
GEORGINA: Yes. I knew we had to meet again.
TAVERNER: Yes, I suppose we did.
GEORGINA: Because I feel...Richard?
TAVERNER: Yes?
GEORGINA: Richard, tell me how you feel about me!
TAVERNER: I don't quite know. [*Thinks*] I think you're... beautiful.
GEORGINA: Do you *love* me?
TAVERNER: I—I—
GEORGINA: I love you, Richard. [*Spurring him on*] I know all sorts of boys, and I've never felt this way about any of them, except you!
TAVERNER: [*Finally*] This is just like a dream.
GEORGINA: [*Jumps up*] No! No, it's not a dream! It's the realest feeling I've ever had! Truly, truly, in your heart, don't you know it's real?! Listen!
[*She runs off and puts on the* "Sleeping Beauty" *waltz and dashes out again. She grabs him and begins to dance with him, swift and graceful. After a while, he takes her hands and leans her up against the rose-colored trellis. He looks at her solemnly.*]

Epiphany

TAVERNER: Yes. I do love you.

GEORGINA: I know you do.

[*She reaches above her on the trellis and picks a flower. She presents it to him. He breaks off a thorn and fastens the flower to her dress. He then turns around and picks roses like a madman. He brings her an armful. She purposefully presents him her braid, and he fastens roses there. He fastens roses wherever he can (within reason) and she clings to him. He fastens one last one in her hair, and kisses her hair. She slowly turns around to offer him her face. She is obviously in charge, manipulating him, although he does not realize this. She closes her eyes, he kisses her eyelids. He kisses her lips and neck. Then she puts her hands on his shoulders and gently forces him to kneel. He holds her hands again and kisses them, passionately. In her simple white dress and crown of roses, she does now resemble a goddess. He kneels at her feet. Incidentally, the rose bed is a wreck.*]

TAVERNER: [*In wonder*] You are... a goddess.

[*She holds her hands slightly cupped before his face. Obediently he takes them and buries his face in them, kissing them.*]

GEORGINA: [*Pressing for perfection*] Do you adore me, Richard? [*In a whisper*] Do you adore me?

TAVERNER: [*Far gone*] ... Yes.

[*They hold this pose until the blackout.*]

Scene 3

One week later, about 2:00 p.m. The lights come up on the rose garden. The mess and disorganization left by TAVERNER *and* GEORGINA *has been cleared away.* HARRIS *kneels by the edge of the rose bed with a basket of rose plants by his side. With a spade he plants new roses, very slowly but very industriously. The table is still in the middle of the garden.* IBBY *is seated there, in gloves and a hat, tapping her foot. Her hair*

*is in ringlets, a far cry from the plain bun of Miss Billings'
regime.* IBBY *looks as if she is waiting for something. To pass
the time, she plays with the folds of her skirt, arranging it over
her shoes. She hums the "Sleeping Beauty" waltz rather tunelessly.
Her attention wanders to her hands, moving them gracefully,
pulling her gloves tighter. With a graceful sweep she
picks up her drawstring-purse. She fancies each of the different
ways she proceeds to hold it. Self-consciously she pushes a
ringlet back over her shoulder.*

TAVERNER *enters through the French doors. He looks tragic
and brave and walks with a purpose.* IBBY *giggles in order to
get his attention.* TAVERNER *sees* IBBY *and stops. He looks ever
so slightly annoyed.*

TAVERNER: Oh, hello Ibby.
IBBY: [*There is a pause while she smiles invitingly.*] Hello, Richard. [*Hardly noticing her,* TAVERNER *goes back to the French doors and peers into the house. He paces.*] Why don't you sit down?
TAVERNER: [*Looks at* IBBY, *then back through the French doors, then back at* IBBY.] I suppose I ought. [*He sits across from* IBBY.] I thought you'd be with Georgina.
IBBY: I've done my bit. All she's doing now is thanking mama.
TAVERNER: [*He feels he must make conversation; that is what one does with girls, isn't it?*] I suppose you're quite sorry your chum is leaving.
IBBY: Well . . . somewhat.
TAVERNER: [*Cannot imagine anyone not being heartbroken at today's event*] You're not sorry?
IBBY: Well, of course it is a shame. But she is a bit wearing, you know. [*Pause*] Besides, now I might have a better chance to . . . get to know you.
TAVERNER: [*Absolutely not realizing her game; confused and innocent*] Oh. Right.
IBBY: [*Nearly seductive*] And you me.
TAVERNER: [*Thinks*] Well . . . that would follow, wouldn't it?
IBBY: [*Tosses her head*] Who knows what would follow?!
TAVERNER: [*Looks at his watch*] Mm . . . hmm. What time is Georgina's train?
[*Lights dim on rose garden.*]

Scene 4

Lights come up brightly on the up right platform. It is completely bare except for a footlocker and GEORGINA. *She is kneeling down in front of it, fiddling with the lock.* JARRETT *enters.*

JARRETT: Oh, hello Georgina.
GEORGINA: [*Looks up*] Hello, Clive.
JARRETT: [*His tone, throughout this scene, is almost schoolmasterly—patronizing and detached.*] So we're finally packing you off.
GEORGINA: [*Jiggling the lock*] You might not be, actually. I think there's something wrong with this lock. It's loose.
JARRETT: Dear me, what inferior craftsmanship.
GEORGINA: Maybe you can tell if it's broken. [GEORGINA *moves aside.* JARRETT *pauses, knowing he is expected to check the lock. Then he kneels and jiggles it.*] See what I mean?
JARRETT: [*Unimpressed*] What, this tenth-of-an-inch it's moving? I think your worldly possessions are safe, Georgina.
GEORGINA: [*Sits back, gazing at* JARRETT] Good. I'm so relieved.
JARRETT: [*Chuckles unbelievingly as he sits on the footlocker*] God!
GEORGINA: I'm quite sorry to be leaving, you know.
JARRETT: [*Dryly*] I can imagine.
GEORGINA: Are you?
JARRETT: I'm not leaving
GEORGINA: [*Shakes her head in mock exasperation*] Are you sorry that *I'm* leaving?
JARRETT: [*A bit disgusted*] Taverner certainly is.
GEORGINA: [*Pleased with herself*] Yes, I know. But I'm sorry for another reason as well.
JARRETT: Do tell.
GEORGINA: [*Primping*] I'm sorry I didn't get to know you bet-

ter, Clive. [*Pause*] What I *do* know I like so much.
JARRETT: [*Humorously*] And just last week you said I had a big nose.
GEORGINA: [*Immediately*] Don't be silly, you don't have a big no... [*Looks at him*] Well... You *have* got a big nose... but I think it's rather charming.
JARRETT: Charming? You think my nose is *charming?*
GEORGINA: It gives your face such interesting character. It makes you look... urbane.
JARRETT: Now why don't you try to dig your way *out*, Georgina?
GEORGINA: [*Sits next to* JARRETT *on the footlocker*] I like your nose. [*Laughing softly, he bows slightly to her.*]
JARRETT: Thank you. I like *your* nose.
GEORGINA: I like you.

[GEORGINA *looks* JARRETT *right in the eye. He breaks the gaze, gets up, crosses down, looking startled. He stands still and looks back at her.*]

JARRETT: Your train leaves at 3:06. Hadn't you better get that taken downstairs?
GEORGINA: Yes, I had.
JARRETT: Shall I ring for you?
GEORGINA: [*Smiles at him mischievously*] Certainly not. I'm quite capable.

[GEORGINA *gets up and walks straight to* JARRETT, *looking at him in the eye again. An imaginary bell-pull hangs just beside* JARRETT's *head. She reaches out and pulls it. Still looking at him, she laughs, if I may say so, deliciously. Blackout.*]

Scene 5

Lights up on IBBY *and* TAVERNER *seated at the table in the rose garden.* IBBY, *looking brazen, tosses her head.*

IBBY: Do you like my new hairstyle, Richard?

Epiphany

TAVERNER: [*Studies her hair; politely*] It's very nice.

IBBY: [*Encouraged*] Thank you. [*She fondles a ringlet.*] It's lovely and soft, too. [IBBY *shakes her head; the curls spill forward.*] It's awfully soft.

TAVERNER: [*For lack of anything better to say*] Hair is.

IBBY: [*Nods at* TAVERNER, *uncertain what to say next. Pause*] Mine's softer. Feel it.

TAVERNER: Oh, I believe you, Ibby.

IBBY: Oh, just touch it!... I should like you to, really.

[IBBY *leans forward. With basically no alternative,* TAVERNER *reaches out and touches a few curls.*]

TAVERNER: [*Without conviction*] Lovely. [IBBY *grabs and holds the hand in her hair.* TAVERNER *snatches it away.*] Now look—Ibby—please—

IBBY: [*Giggling*] Don't you like that? I did.

[*In the pause,* IBBY *reaches out for* TAVERNER'*s hair.* JARRETT, *in a hat, enters through the French doors, silently. He looks mightily surprised at the scene in front of him.* TAVERNER, *who is facing him, looks at* JARRETT *helplessly.*]

TAVERNER: Excuse me, but—uh—Miss Jarrett—

JARRETT: So, Taverner, how's the vermin?

IBBY: Oh! [*Swiftly,* IBBY *draws her hand back and turns around to see* JARRETT. *Mortified*] What are you doing here?

JARRETT: Just watching you imitate Georgina.

[*Since that is exactly what* IBBY *was doing, she is enraged and flies at* JARRETT. *She pushes him so that he stumbles.*]

IBBY: You're a *pig*, Clive!

JARRETT: [*Laughing*] You're a copycat.

IBBY: I'm not!

[*She stalks out through the French doors.*]

TAVERNER: Thank you *very much*, Jarrett.

JARRETT: *Thank* you? I thought you liked to be flirted with.

TAVERNER: You thought I liked that?

JARRETT: Yes. The new Taverner. [*A bit sourly*] Lady-killer. Gallant. [JARRETT *looks at* TAVERNER *sideways.*] Eh?

TAVERNER: [*Defensively*] You're bonkers, Jarrett.

JARRETT: Huh. [JARRETT *takes off his hat and spins it on his finger. He drop-kicks it, trying to make it land on his head. After a pause*] Where's your hat, man?

TAVERNER: Well, I'm not coming.

JARRETT: You're not coming? Why ever not?

TAVERNER: Because I—really don't want to.

JARRETT: Well [*He kicks his hat.*] —neither do I, particularly, but we've got to. It's only polite.
TAVERNER: Georgina will understand.
JARRETT: I wouldn't bet on it.
TAVERNER: Well, I do know her a little better than you do, Jarrett.
JARRETT: [*Laughs softly*] I suggest you run in and get your lid.
TAVERNER: [*Thinking how dense* JARRETT *is*] If you must know, Jarrett, I'm not going because I feel the good-bye I say to her here will be much more meaningful than any I could say to her at the station.
[*He stands, uncomfortable; he looks at his watch.*]
JARRETT: Meaningful? What do you think this is? Antony and Cleopatra? Romeo and Juliet? [*Coolly,* TAVERNER *sits on the table and regards* JARRETT, *unblinking and unmoved.*] I think *you*'ve gone bonkers.
TAVERNER: I really don't see where bonkers comes in when—
JARRETT: Oh, don't you? Tearing the flower garden apart—worshipping that girl as if she were some sort of goddess—she acts just the same with me as she does with you, and you don't see me slobbering all over her.
TAVERNER: She does *not* act—
JARRETT: And besides all that, haven't you forgotten somebody? Where does—
TAVERNER: Jarrett, you obviously cannot understand any of what's happened to me this week.
JARRETT: [*Sarcastically*] Eureka.
TAVERNER: [*Very seriously; not patronizing*] Jarrett—I've grown up. Maybe somewhat more than you have. You'll just have to bear with me, because I don't think you can understand.
JARRETT: [*Does not want to fight; willing to believe* TAVERNER *knows something he doesn't; calmly, after a pause while he looks inside his hat*] All right, Taverner. I'm sorry I said what I did.
TAVERNER: It's all right. [*Pause. They look away from each other.*] Uh—Jarrett?
JARRETT: Yes?
TAVERNER: Would you do me a favor?
JARRETT: Yes. What do you want?
TAVERNER: . . . Would you fetch Georgina out here for me?
JARRETT: [*Looks up at the sky*] I— [*Reconsiders*] All right.

[*As JARRETT leaves, he touches TAVERNER's arm gently and looks at him, as if to apologize.*]

TAVERNER: [*Warmly*] Thanks.

[JARRETT *exits*. TAVERNER, *still sitting on the table, runs his fingers through his hair, trying to neaten it. He fixes his tie, pulls his blazer into place, and lifts his leg up onto the table. Taking out his handkerchief, he spits on his shoe and then wipes it until it shines. He repeats the procedure with the other shoe. Getting down, he clears his throat a few times, and attempts a debonair attitude, leaning against the table. He looks at his fingernails archly; he sees that they are dirty and starts to clean them with those on his other hand.* GEORGINA *enters.* TAVERNER *quickly thrusts his arms behind his back.*]

GEORGINA: [*Seeing* TAVERNER's *hatless state*] Why, Richard, you aren't even ready.

TAVERNER: I know I'm not. I'm not coming.

GEORGINA: You're not coming to see me off? How uncaring of you. Don't you care?

TAVERNER: Don't I *care*.

GEORGINA: And I had such a lovely good-bye planned for the station. Oh, how tiresome of you, Richard.

TAVERNER: [*Takes* GEORGINA's *hands and deals sensibly with the situation*] No, it's really not. Can you imagine trying to say good-bye with a horde of porters stepping on our heels?

GEORGINA: [*Rather sweetly pouting*] Yes.

[*Pause*]

TAVERNER: I shall write you.

GEORGINA: Naturally. I shall write you too—libraries.

TAVERNER: I can probably get myself invited to stay with my aunt and uncle in London next hols. Then we could see each other all the time.

GEORGINA: Next hols? Richard, I'll come up and visit you at school.

TAVERNER: [*After a pause*] You'll do what?

GEORGINA: Visit you at school. I'll pretend I've come to see Horace.

TAVERNER: No, Georgina, you can't possibly.

GEORGINA: Why not? [*Slightly challenging*] Clive will see me, anyway.

TAVERNER: Not if I can jolly well help it.

GEORGINA: Then where shall we meet?

TAVERNER: I don't know. By the chapel, perhaps? That's quite secluded, round the north side.

GEORGINA: Oh, how terribly romantic! We hadn't a chapel at Lawrence Park.

TAVERNER: Hadn't you?

GEORGINA: No, darling. [*Church bells begin faintly. There is only one stroke, signifying the half-hour.*] Oh, listen! I shall have to go in a moment. [*Pause*] You won't come?

TAVERNER: No.

[*They look at each other.*]

GEORGINA: Well?

TAVERNER: [*After pause*] I want to say something meaningful, and deathless. But there's nothing to say. [*Pause*] There are so many things running through my head, but I know they're the same as are running through yours, so there's not much point in saying them, is there?

GEORGINA: There's ever so much to say! How about... "I love you"?

TAVERNER: Well, that was one of the things running—I *am* botching this up. [*Pause*] I love you.

GEORGINA: [*Beaming, whispers*] I love you.

[JARRETT *enters, waving a letter. He is about to speak, but sees that his two guests are in the midst of a tender moment. He looks away. Neither* TAVERNER *nor* GEORGINA *have seen him, as they are looking at each other. With delicacy and restraint, in blatant contrast to the previous scene,* TAVERNER *kisses* GEORGINA *tenderly but shortly. Looking back,* JARRETT *sees them moving apart and decides it is all right to speak.*]

JARRETT: The post came, and there's a letter for you, Taverner. [*To* GEORGINA] You know, if we don't push off, you'll miss your train.

GEORGINA: [*Nods*] Right. Off we push, then. [GEORGINA *looks back at* TAVERNER *archly; she winks at him. She turns and starts to exit, tweaking* JARRETT'*s chin fondly as she passes him.*] Come along, handsome.

[GEORGINA *exits.*]

JARRETT: [*Unmoved by* GEORGINA'*s flirtation, gives letter to* TAVERNER] Adieu... Casanova.

[TAVERNER *stands still, staring at the French doors, while* HARRIS *goes back to work, chuckling noiselessly.* TAVERNER

lifts the hand holding the letter and waves after GEORGINA. *He remembers the letter and regards it uninterestedly. Then he reads the return address and looks extremely perturbed.*]
TAVERNER: [*Meaningfully*] Oh, God.
[*He plants his feet and steels himself to read the letter. As* TAVERNER *rips open the envelope,* PERRY'*s voice is heard over the PA system.*]
PERRY'S VOICE: Dear Taverner,

I hope you are fine. How are your hols? I can't begin to explain the excitement of stopping at school over the hols. I'm sorry I've been so bad about writing you. It's not because I've not been thinking of you, because I have, an awful lot. It's because there was a terrific fire which burnt the entire school to a crisp and also my letter-paper. Anyway, congratulations! You're a prefect! I'm *so* proud, although I knew you would be. I can't imagine why Jarrett would be promoted, too. He's awfully clever, but he's so cheeky, I don't think he deserves it. Not that I'm one to talk, I mean, I wouldn't promote me, either. It's beastly boring here. There are a few Sixth Formers swotting up for the Army Exam, as you said; also a slew of small boys who've absolutely no respect for their elders. And me. And that scab on life's complexion, Lane. He's being tutored in everything, so that he'll be caught up by next term, they hope. It's quite sad, really. He's always asking me for help at his lessons, and following me around, and I can't find it in my heart to be truly nasty to him. The horrid bit is that I think he's crushed on me. I'm not being conceited, it's just that I'm the only one who's halfway decent with him. I can't help comparing the two of you. Luckily, you got me first. Oh, how is Jarrett's house? As jolly as you expected? I hope you've managed to keep away from the giggly females. I can't wait to see you again, as I miss you *terribly*.

As ever,
Perry

P.S. You left your gray sweater here, it slipped behind your bureau. Can I borrow it?

TAVERNER: [*Dazed*] Damn. [*Then, distraught, he crumples the letter and envelope and throws them on the ground, accidentally at* HARRIS. *As he throws them, he exclaims*] Damn!! [HARRIS *turns to* TAVERNER *accusingly, sitting back on his heels.* TAVERNER *walks over apologeti-*

cally and picks up the paper.] Excuse me.
[*Measures 67-106 of the Wesley are played and the lights come down to blackout.*]

CURTAIN

ACT III

Scene 1

As the houselights dim, and the curtain opens, the Wesley piece is continued from measure 107-117. Onstage, MR. WILLARD's *classroom is illuminated. It is late September, two weeks into the Michaelmas term, Monday evening, just before 7:00. In contrast to its appearance in* ACT II, *the classroom looks lived-in, lately abandoned. When the music finishes, the door of the classroom opens and* JARRETT, MEDBOURNE, *and* HERSHEY *enter noisily,* MEDBOURNE *with cane. They begin straightening out the furniture and arranging a little law-court set-up, within which to carry out the inexorable ways of Justice.*

MEDBOURNE: So, how do you like your new position, Jarrett? All two weeks of it.

JARRETT: Well, it's very queer. I feel like an impostor, telling people how to behave. I didn't think I'd feel that.

HERSHEY: Oh, I felt that way too; you get used to it.

JARRETT: I do get treated with a lot more respect—by masters too.

HERSHEY: That's one of the good parts. You're exempt in everything, save by the Head or your own housemaster. Nobody can touch us—we're the bloody elite.

MEDBOURNE: Just don't abuse it, Jarrett.

JARRETT: That's my problem, Medbourne—I'm sure I do. It's all right for you, or Taverner, or Asbury—

MEDBOURNE: [*Hatefully*] Oh, *A*sbury! No, he's not bad, really.

JARRETT: No—he does his job admirably! Especially when he's on your side. That's what I mean, good responsible chaps. For slackers like me and Hershey, we just glide along, taking advantage of being a prefect.

HERSHEY: It's the best way I know of getting revenge on your enemies.

MEDBOURNE: Hershey!

HERSHEY: Just joking!—Move that form out more, Medbourne, you'd never be able to swing a cane in that little space.

JARRETT: Much less a cat. So all we do is play judges, then?

MEDBOURNE: You mean for Honor Society?

JARRETT: Yes.

MEDBOURNE: Well, the chaps come in and tell their offense... and we do—whatever's necessary.

JARRETT: But do we discuss it, or anything?

HERSHEY: That's seldom necessary.

JARRETT: It will be strange not to be on the receiving end.

HERSHEY: *You* were a frequent visitor to Honor Society.

JARRETT: It's my youthful exuberance. I shall still feel like an impostor.

MEDBOURNE: I think we all do. But you don't let *them* know it.

JARRETT: Heaven forbid. [*Feels in pocket*] Anyone want a sweetie?

[*Door opens again.* TWEED *and* PROCTOR *enter.* JARRETT *and* PROCTOR *hit each other in friendly greeting.*]

TWEED: Hello you chaps. Who's the sacrifice tonight?

MEDBOURNE: Asbury's got the list.

PROCTOR: [*Sourly*] There'd better not be very many. I've got an appointment.

JARRETT: With McGovern?

HERSHEY: That tart.

PROCTOR: Shut up.

TWEED: Been a quiet week, hasn't it?

MEDBOURNE: The Lower School's still too homesick to raise much of a row.

PROCTOR: Yes, but in two more weeks, Tweed, it'll get more lively. Then you'll see the *real* job of the Honor Society, Jarrett. Tonight's just piffle; just a practice run.

JARRETT: Well, you must have a bit to do, Proctor, being Prefect of Games.

PROCTOR: Well, not really, just organizing matches and runs and all.

HERSHEY: Oh, no runs, Proctor. No bloody paper-chases!

PROCTOR: [*Sweetly*] Oh, I love 'em!

JARRETT: Me, too! [*Reaches into blazer-pocket and pulls out a folded lavender envelope. He tears little bits off and drops them on the floor, leaving a trail behind him. Coquettishly, to* HERSHEY] Catch me if you can!

TWEED: [*In the same simpering tone*] Ooh, Jarrett, that's *lovely* stationery you've got there.

JARRETT: [*Stops tearing it; holds it up to display*] Isn't it feminine? The color of cold lips.

HERSHEY: [*Also simpering*] I prefer to call it mauve, thank you.

JARRETT: And take a whiff, Proctor.

[*He thrusts the envelope under* PROCTOR's *nose.* PROCTOR *sniffs and his eyes open wide.*]

PROCTOR: My word, Jarrett, who's been writing letters to you? Chanel?

MEDBOURNE: Let me smell. [PROCTOR *gives* MEDBOURNE *the envelope.* MEDBOURNE *sniffs it.*] Phew, what a stench.

HERSHEY: All right, Jarrett, explain. And don't tell us that it's your mother, because it's not.

JARRETT: No, it's not. It's from a friend of my sister's who stayed with us over the hols. Bloody little nuisance she was, too.

TWEED: Now, Jarrett, is that any way to—

JARRETT: No, it's true. She was convinced I was madly in love with her.

PROCTOR: But you resisted manfully.

JARRETT: Yes. You all would have been so proud of me. Didn't deter her, of course. Listen to this: "Why have you not written me? What about your promise—pet?"

HERSHEY: Let me see that!

[JARRETT *avoids* HERSHEY *neatly. He sits up on a desk, while the others surround him.*]

MEDBOURNE: She sounds a horror.

JARRETT: A *fright*. She plans to visit me, here. Isn't that... plummy? We're to meet in the chapel.

HERSHEY: In the moonlight, I hope.

TWEED: With violins playing.

PROCTOR: Is she pretty?

JARRETT: [*Thinks*] As girls go.

HERSHEY: [*Gossipy*] You know who *is* pretty? That new boy Aisling.

JARRETT: Isn't he, though.

[JARRETT *crumples the letter and the envelope and throws them into the fire. The others look at him silently for a moment after his line, and then break into laughter.* JARRETT *takes a second or two to join them.*]

HERSHEY: I think we ought to call him up.

MEDBOURNE: Don't you wish you may get him.

TWEED: I say, I just wish that beast Lane would be called up. What wouldn't I give to get my hands on him! I'd pulverize him!

JARRETT: I'd help.

PROCTOR: Hear hear!

HERSHEY: Ah, Lane. Lane... is not pretty. [*The others laugh.*] Have you ever seen him at footer? He's all left feet! [*Gives burlesque demonstration. All laugh.*]

JARRETT: No it's this way.

[*Gives demonstration; falls*]

MEDBOURNE: It's terrible—he can't do anything! He's a clumsy oaf, he can barely do First Form Latin—

PROCTOR: What's terrible is that he doesn't even try. He never comes to games—maybe half the time? And every time he gets sent to me for shirking, and *every time* I tell him, "You know, if you'd come more often, you'd get better at it, and you'd *enjoy* coming," but the silly bastard is too stupid to listen.

TWEED: I don't really care if he listens to me—I hate him.

JARRETT: I know that Taverner's always decent with him, and he never listens to him, either. It's just his blasted stubbornness.

MEDBOURNE: [*Having checked watch*] We still *need* Taverner—and Asbury. [*Church bell begins ringing 7:00.*]

JARRETT: Tsk, tsk, late again. [ASBURY *rushes in, bearing list, cane.*]

ASBURY: All here?

MEDBOURNE: Yes, except for Taverner.

ASBURY: Not like him to be late.

JARRETT: Not like you to be late, either.

ASBURY: Look here, you jolly well watch how you speak to the Head Prefect, you cur! [HERSHEY *mocks* ASBURY *in pantomime to* TWEED.] Good news, only two tonight.

PROCTOR: Well, très bien.

HERSHEY: [*Simultaneously*] Oh, piss, I was in such a lovely sadistic mood.

MEDBOURNE: Who are they?

ASBURY: Some youngster—[*Checks list*] Warner and Lane.

Epiphany

[*Surprised laughter*]

HERSHEY: Good.

[*Knock on door. All exchange looks.*]

ASBURY: Come in!

[WARNER *enters. He is terrified.*]

PROCTOR: Hello Warner. Come in.

TWEED: Why couldn't you have been Lane? [WARNER *looks at him blankly.*] Never mind.

ASBURY: Warner, you have been unpardonably insolent to members of the Sixth Form on the following days: last Monday and last Wednesday, when you were on duty as a study-fag.

WARNER: Who, sir?

ASBURY: [*Looks at list*] Who? Don't you know? [WARNER *looks at the floor, squirming nervously.*] Well?

WARNER: Eubanks and Watts!

ASBURY: Mmm, very good. Have you anything to say for yourself?

WARNER: I . . . no.

JARRETT: Oh, come on—say something.

HERSHEY: That's right. Don't be a cowardy custard.

WARNER: I was only larking about, sir.

PROCTOR: Is that any sort of excuse?

WARNER: . . . No, sir.

TWEED: Well, Medbourne, what do you think?

MEDBOURNE: [*Looks questioningly at* ASBURY] I'd say six of the best.

[ASBURY *nods.*]

PROCTOR: Yes, that ought to curb his uncouth tongue.

JARRETT: *We'll* make you couth!

[*Prefects laugh.*]

ASBURY: I think that will do famously, don't you, Warner?

WARNER: . . . Yes, sir.

[*Knock on door*]

ASBURY: Come in! Well, Warner, come—Good evening, Lane. [*All prefects tense up.*] Oh— [ASBURY *takes* WARNER'S *shoulders, turns him around, and pats his behind in the direction of the door.*] Cut along, Warner—and show some respect for your elders in the future.

WARNER: Thank you, sir!

[WARNER *rushes out, slamming the door.*]

HERSHEY: Decent little beggar.

[*Grunts of agreement*]

PROCTOR: Don't be a stranger, Lane. Come here and be sociable.

[LANE *approaches slowly.*]

TWEED: What have you done this time, Dobbin?

[JARRETT *bursts into a snort of laughter at* "Dobbin." LANE *doesn't answer.*]

ASBURY: You'd better answer.

LANE: I—umm—Eubanks caught me out in the passage after lights on Thursday night. [*Looking at the floor, in a steady voice*] I was sleepwalking.

PROCTOR: Oh, come off it! You weren't sleepwalking, you were going off to stroke Perry!

LANE: I wasn't!

PROCTOR: Of course you were!

LANE: He's my *friend*, that's all.

ASBURY: Sir.

LANE: [*Not listening*] He's just my *friend!* I'm not after his body!

JARRETT: You may be his friend, but he isn't yours.

LANE: No one believes anything I say!

ASBURY: *Sir!*

LANE: [*Pause; quietly*] Sir . . . But you don't—

HERSHEY: Oh, shut up! Do you think we're morons? Do you think we jolly well don't know? You've been after Perry since the first time you laid eyes on him. You certainly don't make any secret of it.

MEDBOURNE: [*Almost kindly*] You're such an ass. Perry's been with Taverner ever since Third Form. They're not going to separate now—especially not over you.

TWEED: [*The conversation turns inward now, excluding* LANE.] They haven't been together very much this term.

HERSHEY: I know. It's almost as if Taverner purposely avoids him.

PROCTOR: Maybe Taverner's lost his heart to someone else.

JARRETT: [*Uncomfortably, looking at* LANE] Not lost it. Only—mislain it.

MEDBOURNE: Mislai*d*.

JARRETT: No, mislai*n*! It's a pun!

PROCTOR: It is?

JARRETT: Oh, some day you'll appreciate my humor!

Epiphany

[*No one has understood but* LANE, *who absolutely blanches.*]
TWEED: Does Perry know?
JARRETT: [*Trying to change the subject*] Course not! It's nothing really.
ASBURY: Incidentally, where *is* Taverner?
TWEED: Dunno.
[*Others indicate ignorance.*]
MEDBOURNE: Maybe he's ill.
HERSHEY: Love-sick.
JARRETT: [*Exploding*] Shhh!
LANE: [*In pause*] I wasn't going to see Perry.
JARRETT: We know, you were sleepwalking.
[TAVERNER *bursts into the classroom, looking hurried. He sees that the meeting is in progress and stands confused.*]
PROCTOR: Speak of the devil.
TAVERNER: Oh, golly, I didn't know you'd started. I'm most awfully sorry, Asbury.
ASBURY: See me later.
[TAVERNER *approaches the prefects and leans against the master's desk uncomfortably.*]
TAVERNER: Uh... what have I missed?
TWEED: Lane here is on the carpet.
TAVERNER: Oh dear.
TWEED: Tell the nice man what you've done, Dob.
LANE: I've done nothing.
[*Pause*]
TAVERNER: [*Sensibly*] Well, if he's done nothing, why is he here?
ASBURY: He was taking a tour of the college after lights.
TWEED: [*Oh-so-sarcastic*] In his sleep, you understand.
TAVERNER: Oh, that's naughty.
LANE: *Why* is it naughty if I can't help doing it?! I've got no control over sleepwalking!
TAVERNER: [*Very uncomfortable*] Were you really and truly sleepwalking, Lane? [*Turns*] If he was, you know, we can't punish him.
PROCTOR: Oh, Taverner, of course the putrid ass wasn't sleepwalking! He was going to—
LANE: [*Slightly hysterical*] I wasn't! I wasn't!
MEDBOURNE: Keep your voice down!
LANE: No!

TAVERNER: [*Under the yelling*] You weren't what?

ASBURY: If you don't keep quiet Lane, you won't even have a hearing.

LANE: As if I'm having one now!

[*The prefects are shocked and enraged.* TAVERNER *is surprised but less emotional.*]

PROCTOR: [*In righteous indignation*] How dare you?! How *dare* you say that?!

MEDBOURNE: You're getting a hearing just the same as everyone else, and if you have any complaint with it I suggest you speak to the Head.

JARRETT: Which will get you nowhere.

PROCTOR: I vote we give him six as a warning.

TWEED: Six isn't enough of a warning. I say nine.

MEDBOURNE: I heartily second the motion.

HERSHEY: I third it.

LANE: [*Hysterical*] Just let me alone!!

ASBURY: Lane, shut up before we jolly well kill you. You're having twelve cuts already.

TAVERNER: Calm yourself, Lane.

LANE: [*He detests* TAVERNER] *You* shut up!

[TAVERNER *is extremely taken aback.*]

TWEED: That's it.

ASBURY: Take his coat off. Two of you hold him down.

[ASBURY *canes* LANE *brutally while all the prefects but* TAVERNER *help by taking* LANE's *blazer off, holding him down, etc. At first* LANE *struggles, but then he cries.* TAVERNER *is shocked at the brutality.*]

TAVERNER: I say, that's enough!

PROCTOR: [*Holding* LANE, *snarls*] It is my eye!

[*Agitated,* TAVERNER *moves around, not watching, knowing he cannot leave the group.* ASBURY *stops at twelve, the others let go.* MEDBOURNE *throws* LANE's *blazer at him.* LANE *puts it on. He is crying and ashamed.*]

ASBURY: Come on, then, Lane, put this room back in order. [*The prefects turn and go to the classroom door.* TAVERNER *follows a bit at a distance. The only sound is* LANE's *sobs.*] And stop your blubbing, sissy.

[LANE *begins to hiccup. All the prefects leave but* TAVERNER, *who looks at* LANE, *agitated.*]

TAVERNER: Oh, you bloody idiot, you brought it on yourself.

[TAVERNER *runs out, slamming the door.* LANE *spiritlessly*

Epiphany

moves a form or two with his feet, but soon stops. He sinks down, puts his head on a form, sobbing. Then his anger mounts and he knocks that and many other forms over. He gets very excited, knocking over everything within arm or leg reach. When he calms down a little, he surveys the destruction, pathetically happy. He is about to leave when voices offstage stop him in mid-step.]

JARRETT: Oh, Tweed, we needn't check up on the little beggar. Be reasonable.

TWEED: It's against my better judgment.

JARRETT: Oh, come on up to my study and have a bloody cup of cocoa.

TWEED: I don't mind if I do, you ugly devil.

[*Footsteps die away.*]

LANE: [*Shrinks back into the room. Looks again at his work and cries afresh. He is about to clean up when he is struck with an idea. He goes to the door, stands a moment undecided, then wipes his face and shouts weakly.*] Fag? [*Pause. Louder*] Fag!

[EVANS *and* WARNER *appear from different entrances. They spot each other.*]

EVANS: You can go, Warner.

WARNER: [*Sarcastically*] Oh, thanks very much.

[EVANS *runs off.*]

LANE: Fag!

WARNER: Coming, sir!

[WARNER *enters classroom, sees that it is* LANE.] Oh.

LANE: Could you—ah, please, would you go and find Perry for me? If you don't mind, Warner?

WARNER: [*A ghost of insolence creeps in*] Yes, I could.

LANE: And tell him to come here? Please?

WARNER: Yes, all right.

[*Saunters out.*]

LANE: Thank you.

[*Finds his handkerchief, blows his nose.*]

Scene 2

LANE *freezes as lights dim on classroom. Lights up on* TAVERNER'S *study, where he is seated at his desk, writing. He dips his pen thoughtfully.*

TAVERNER: A Poem to Miss Lane. [*About to write*] Uh—to Miss Georgina Lane, yes. [*About to write*] No. To my Beloved—Darling. Good. [*Writes*] My dear Georgina, you are the sun—no. In your eyes I see the... In *thine* eyes I see the sun—uh—no. That's not sincere enough. [*Doodles on desk-top*] I could never write anything worthy of her. [*Lights dim on* TAVERNER'S *study.*]

Scene 3

Lights up on classroom. LANE *unfreezes as* PERRY *enters briskly.*

PERRY: What's happened, Lane?
LANE: They all... [*Begins to cry*] were bullying me.
PERRY: [*Sighs*] Who was?
LANE: The prefects—they were.
PERRY: [*Incredulous*] They *fought* you?
LANE: No, they licked me.
PERRY: They're entitled. That's why they're prefects. Come now Lane, you know that.
LANE: They wouldn't listen to me! They wouldn't let me talk! [PERRY *looks away exasperated. He realizes the awful state of the room.*]
PERRY: Aren't you supposed to've straightened up? [*Crying,*

Epiphany 203

LANE *nods*.] Well, let's get to it, then. We can't leave the room like this. [*He begins righting forms. As* LANE *reluctantly begins to help,* PERRY *muses*.] Looks as if you gave them quite a battle.

[*This only brings fresh tears from* LANE. *Lights dim on Scene 3 as Scene 4 has already begun.*]

Scene 4

TAVERNER'*s study.* TAVERNER *is in the same position. He unfreezes as the lights come up. He is writing.*

TAVERNER: I can't expression mine—oh—I cannot *ex*press mine elation, oh good! [*Writes*] Nor e'er be cruel to thee. [*Begins writing*] Oh, but I've rhymed "thee" twice. Oh, golly. I cannot *ex*press mine elation... elation... I've got it! Or radiate my—mine ecstasy. Ecstasy... e-x-t-i-s-y. That's wrong. [*Crosses it out*] E-x-t-a-s-y, that's it. I'm awfully bright. Or—what is it? My ra— Mine radiant ecstasy. [*Writes*] The end. No, it's too short... Oh. [*Bites lip, thinking*]
Thou looketh like an angel's form
When I look at thee.
 Oh, that's good. [*Writing*] Thou—looketh—like—an—
 [*Lights dim.*]

Scene 5

Lights up on classroom. PERRY *and* LANE *are just finishing straightening up.*

LANE: Perry... thank you.

PERRY: [*Looking away*] 'Sall right, Lane.

LANE: No, really, Perry, you're the only one who's nice to me at all here.

PERRY: Oh, come off it! Taverner's decent with you, so's McGovern and Jarrett and so's... ever so many others!
[*But it's only a pep talk.* PERRY *doesn't believe it himself. He sits on a form.*]

LANE: They're not. I wish...

PERRY: Cough it up.

LANE: I wish I was in a school with just you and me, and no stupid rules like prefects. I wish I were back at Lawrence Park.

PERRY: [*Uncomfortably*] Well, you're not. And I wouldn't go to any school unless Taverner were along.
[*They freeze, but the lights stay up.*]

Scene 6

TAVERNER's *study is spotlit.*

TAVERNER: [*Writing*] Each corner of my mind is filled with thoughts—no, fantasies—of thee... Each corner of my mind is filled with fantasies of thee. Good.
[*Keeps on writing. The light does not go out on* TAVERNER's *study, but regular lighting comes up gradually, so that by the time* PERRY *knocks at* TAVERNER's *door,* TAVERNER's *study is normally lit.*]

Scene 7

LANE *and* PERRY *unfreeze in the classroom.*

LANE: It doesn't matter.
PERRY: What doesn't matter?
LANE: [*In a tone implying that this is the most obvious thing in the world*] He doesn't need you. He doesn't even like you!
[PERRY *tries to hide the immediate shock by laughing.*]
PERRY: What?!
LANE: I see him being cold to you. You know he is. [*Almost nastily*] Because he's got someone else.
PERRY: [*Stands infuriated*] You're a bloody liar!
LANE: [*Calm*] I'm not. I know who it is.
PERRY: [*Angrier by the second, nearly dancing in his rage*] Damn you, Lane! Shut up— I'll— This is why everyone hates you, you bloody liar!
LANE: [*Singsong*] You can even ask him.
PERRY: You bloody—
[*About to hit* LANE, *but stops just in time. Strides out, slamming door. Immediate blackout on classroom.*]

Scene 8

TAVERNER'*s study, normally lit.* TAVERNER *still at desk, writing.*

TAVERNER: With love ... Richard Taverner ... Silly ass! Spelt my name wrong! [*Crosses it out*] Taverner, twenty-fifth September—

[*Knock on door.*]

PERRY: [*Immediately*] Taverner, it's me.

[*Opens door, enters. Shuts door, observes* TAVERNER *in surprise*]

TAVERNER: [*Frantic*] Wait, get out! [*Covering poem hurriedly with hands, he stuffs things into drawers.*] Who said you could come in here?! [PERRY *approaches*.] No! Don't look!

PERRY: I'm not! I just—

TAVERNER: Get out!

PERRY: I just wanted to—

TAVERNER: I'm a prefect, Perry, and you're not, so get *out!* [PERRY *doesn't move.*] I can report you.

PERRY: You are a bastard. Lane was right.

TAVERNER: I'm not a bastard. I just—I—just drop it. What do you want?

PERRY: To talk.

TAVERNER: I haven't got the time.

PERRY: But I've got to!

TAVERNER: Perry, I said—

PERRY: Well, can I borrow your French dikker, then?

TAVERNER: Oh, all *right!* [*To himself*] Where is it? [*To* PERRY] You stay there.

[*Looks around study for book*]

PERRY: I was just talking to Lane and I've got to—

TAVERNER: Just now? Wasn't the bastard cleaning up? Can't he ever do as he's told? Why were you talking to him?

PERRY: I just was, and shut up. He was telling me things about you—not that I didn't know them already.

[TAVERNER *is jealous.*]

TAVERNER: About me? [*Stops looking for book*] What could he possibly have to say about me?

PERRY: Well...

TAVERNER: And another thing, why are you always off talking to Lane?

PERRY: I'm not.

TAVERNER: More than you talk to me. What's between the two of you?

PERRY: Nothing! Anyhow, we're talking about *you*, not me.

TAVERNER: Seems it was a rather intimate conversation.

PERRY: Stop it! I believe you're jealous of him!

Epiphany

TAVERNER: Of course I'm not! What did the bastard have to say about me?

PERRY: Calm yourself. He said—please don't be angry—he said that you've... well, that you're carrying on behind my back.

[*Shocked pause*]

TAVERNER: Perry!

PERRY: I said no, but—

TAVERNER: [*Attempting joviality*] Well, that's what I'd jolly well expect!

PERRY: But he said—

TAVERNER: [*On guard again*] What?

PERRY: That you don't love me, and everyone knows but me; and you love someone else, and that's why you've been so—well, so *cold* to me this term. Lane says he *knows* him, and—

TAVERNER: Knows who?

PERRY: HIM.

TAVERNER: [*Laughs with relief as the light dawns*] Oh, Perry, I haven't met any fellow I like half as much as you! I swear it!

PERRY: [*Very slightly mollified*] Why are you always so distant, then, and why did you nearly throw me out just now?

TAVERNER: You don't understand! I've not been distant or cold to you. I can't come and see you of course, but that was all decided last term. Being a prefect, I can't risk it, you know.

PERRY: [*Small, indecisive*] Oh... Why did you try to boot me out just now? What were you doing?

TAVERNER: What was I doing? Nothing... Well it was something. I—I didn't want you to see it... yet. I was... [*In a rush*] writing a poem.

PERRY: [*Thinking it is for him, after an emotional pause*] May I see it?

TAVERNER: [*Who has been scanning it*] Here it is.

PERRY: To My Beloved Darling—

In thine eyes are dancing moonbeams
Serener than the stars above.
And in winter, the bright sun of June seems
To emanate from out my love.

Each niche in my imagination

Is brimming full of thoughts of thee.
I cannot express mine elation
Or mine radiant ecstasy.

Thou art belike an angel's form
When on thee humble eyes I cast.
And I pray to be held safe and warm
Inside thy heart, till all time's passed.

> With love,
> Richard Taverner
> 25th September 1912

[PERRY *stands, holding poem, trying not to cry.* TAVERNER, *having witnessed it all, is overcome with terrible guilt. Timidly, he touches* PERRY's *hand.*]

TAVERNER: Nothing's wrong; nothing's changed. It's just the same as it used to be, and just the same as it always will be. Always, Perry. [*Embraces* PERRY *timidly*] Don't listen to him—don't listen to any of them. They're jealous of you. But their words don't mean *anything*. What do anyone's words ever mean? It can only mislead you. Words, Perry, just useless, crippling words. Even saying, "I love you"... that's—meaningless, too. [*They embrace.*] I'm sorry.

PERRY: Yes. Me too.

[*Blackout*]

Scene 9

One month later. The chapel. It looks different from the way it did in Act I in that it is ready for the service which is to take place later that afternoon. Now a choir rehearsal is in progress. The choir is dressed in blue serge suits (as opposed to their weekday grey flannel) and seated in the choir stalls. No one is seated at the organ (or piano). WOOLWEAVER, *the choirmaster, stands in front of the choir, directing them.* TAVERNER *and* PERRY *are seated next to each other.* JARRETT *sits behind* PERRY. PROCTOR *and* McGOVERN *are seated next to each other.*

Epiphany

LANE's *seat is empty. It is immediately after dinner and the rehearsal is half-over. The choir is singing Mozart's* "Ave Verum" *when the lights come up.*)

WOOLWEAVER: [*Cutting them off*] Stop! [*Those not watching carry on. Throughout the rehearsal there is a marked lack of attention, as it is a beautiful crisp fall day outside and the treble and alto sections are extremely fidgety.*] I did cut you off, boys. I do wish you'd attend.

JARRETT: [*So innocent*] *I* was, sir.

WOOLWEAVER: How extraordinarily kind of you, Jarrett. Now, basses, you're singing a wrong note. It's in the thirty-first measure. You sing a G. You boys are only managing an F. The line sounds like this, now *listen* to me. [*Sings line, punches corrected note*]

JARRETT: [*Over* WOOLWEAVER's *singing*] Where's our paragon of equine boyhood?

PERRY: What?

JARRETT: Lane. Where do you suppose he is?

TAVERNER: [*Leaning over*] Shhh!

PERRY: Oh, Taverner, stop being such a pig. [*To* JARRETT] He's probably shirking.

WOOLWEAVER: Boys!

TAVERNER: [*Generally*] Shut up!

WOOLWEAVER: Did you get that, basses? [*Affirmative noises*] Now, do stop talking or we'll never get this done.

PERRY: [*Another innocent*] *I* wasn't talking, sir.

McGOVERN: You liar.

[PERRY *smiles.*]

JARRETT: [*Generally*] Be quiet.

WOOLWEAVER: Enough now, boys. Basses, sing the line back to me. [*They sing measures 30-37.*] Better. Now, trebles and altos, you're not blending. Start from measure thirty. Got it? Pitches. [*Plays their pitches on organ*] Slowly boys. Follow me. [*They sing.*]

TAVERNER: [*Over singing, making obvious effort at enthusiasm*] Perry, come with me when I get my surplice. I've got some ginger beer in my study.

PERRY: With pleasure! Where did you get it?

TAVERNER: Shhh! My cousin, when he was up from Oxford last week. I'm afraid it's rather warm.

PERRY: Last week? If it had been mine, it would have been

gone long ago. [*Pause*] I didn't know he'd brought you any grub.

TAVERNER: I—forgot to tell you.

PERRY: [*Gives* TAVERNER *sidelong, slightly suspicious look. Then dismisses his suspicions and laughs*] You bloody selfish pig.

WOOLWEAVER: All parts.

[*All begin singing at measure thirty. Very soon, the door opens at the end of the aisle.* LANE *and* GEORGINA *enter. All the boys are distracted and they watch.* JARRETT, *after a moment's frozen shock, tries desperately to efface himself behind* PERRY. *By measure forty-eight the singing is dismally discordant.* LANE *leads* GEORGINA *to a far pew.*]

LANE: You stay put. [GEORGINA *sits, looking around interestedly.*]

WOOLWEAVER: Boys! Stop! That was horrendous! Start again, from measure thirty— What's this? [LANE *taps him. He turns.*] Oh, Lane.

LANE: [*Hands him a chit, walks to empty seat*] I was seeing the Head, sir. [STOWE, *next to the empty seat, upon hearing that, whips off blazer and places it on* LANE's *seat.* LANE, *approaching, is annoyed.*] He was *talk*ing to my *moth*er.

STOWE: Oh, *par*don me. [STOWE *puts his blazer back on. Boys are amused.* WOOLWEAVER *missed that exchange, as he was puzzling over the chit.*]

PROCTOR: Shurrup!

WOOLWEAVER: Who scribbled this, Lane?

LANE: The Head.

McGOVERN: Let me see it, sir, I'm an expert on forgery!

WOOLWEAVER: [*Crumpling it*] No one could have forged this. Page four, Lane. And please try to make it on time in the future. Trebles alone, from measure thirty.

[*They sing. The lights dim slowly, with two spots of focus on* TAVERNER *and* GEORGINA, *she trying to evade his ardent stare, while giving* JARRETT *one of her own. Then those spots fade.*]

Scene 10

Lights up on the HEAD's *study. The* HEAD *and* MRS. LANE *are deep in conversation. There is no tea.*

HEAD: I'm terribly sorry, madam, but I cannot allow him to stay on. He's had ample time to settle in, but simply can't, or doesn't. [*Pause*] Some boys are simply unable to live a communal life, especially when they start so late.
MRS. LANE: I had such a difficult time initially getting Horace accepted anywhere. What good school will take him now, having been expelled from Thomas More?
HEAD: Oh, he'll stay the term, of course. He's not expelled, madam. Merely "asked to leave."
[*The lights dim.*]

Scene 11

Lights up again on the choir rehearsal.

WOOLWEAVER: Let's do it again. All parts, page one. Pitches. [*He plays their pitches in measure 3. They all sing, except for* TAVERNER. *Soon,* WOOLWEAVER *notices.*] Taverner, why aren't you singing? [TAVERNER *looks* WOOLWEAVER's *way, puzzled. Then he understands and starts singing quickly. He looks flustered. At* "Natum de Maria," WOOLWEAVER *frantically conducts a crescendo.*] Crescendo . . . I said crescendo, you cretins! Oh, stop! [*Boys are imitating,* "You cretins!"] Shut up. Bottom staff, first measure. That whole phrase builds, believe me, and *then* you diminuendo. But

it doesn't do it by itself. You've got to coax it along. And I shouldn't have to tell you, either. How ought you to know to crescendo there? Stowe?
STOWE: That arrow sort of thing between the staffs?
WOOLWEAVER: Correct.
McGOVERN: Good for you, Crater-Face!
WOOLWEAVER: Quiet; also, it's veer-jin-ay, not verge-in-ay. *Listen* to yourselves. Again. [*They begin at measure 3.*] Taverner! Much better. [*At "natum"*] Go on. [*The lights dim.*]

Scene 12

The HEAD's *study.*

MRS. LANE: That doesn't leave many alternatives, Dr. Mapes. England abounds with second-class academies, it's true, but my son deserves better.
HEAD: Please, Mrs. Lane, I'm fully aware of your predicament. I've considered everything, and I believe the decision I've made is the wisest.
MRS. LANE: Wise? To do a child out of an education?
HEAD: Oh, madam! Our goal is nothing but education! I'm a schoolmaster myself. I want your son to be as fine and manly a chap as he can be! I hold that a little bullying is character-building, but Horace is not as strong as most—ah, some boys, and in his case it seems to be having the opposite effect. He's a bright boy, he *can* learn—no, please let me speak—he *can* learn, but not in this particular situation. He doesn't fit in, he can't conform. He can't set his mind to any sort of study or athletics.
HEAD: If Horace is so bright, I don't see why—
HEAD: Have you seen his marks, madam? They are deplorable! [*Opens folder*] A history essay—twenty-three out of one hundred. An exam in English literature—two out of fifteen. And he shows up for football less than half the time. [*The lights dim.*]

Scene 13

Lights up on the choir rehearsal.

WOOLWEAVER: Do you suppose it's in any way possible that we could do the entire thing, or is that a positively foolhardy supposition?
PERRY: [*Enthusiastically*] Oh, we can do it, sir!
McGOVERN: [*Damply*] No we can't.
JARRETT: You're a beast, McGovern, of course we can, sir.
WARNER: Yes, McGovern, you're a beast.
BOYS: [*Joining in*] You beast. Oh, McGovern, you're such a beast! etc.
PROCTOR: Shut up!
WOOLWEAVER: Shhh. All right then, boys. Watch me. [*He, or whoever the accompanist is, begins on the instrument. Several small boys start immediately.*] Stop! Hardly off the first measure, and you've already fouled it up—Warner.
WARNER: [*Cocky*] I'm frightfully sorry, sir.
[PROCTOR *turns and gives him a very poisonous look.* WARNER *is immediately subdued. General noise*]
WOOLWEAVER: The first bit, the introduction, is instrumental. Boys! McGovern, repeat what I have just said.
McGOVERN: ... Yes, sir. Umm...
[*Pause*]
BOYS: [*Gradually*] Oh, McGovern, you beast, etc. [*This is funny; all laugh.*]
McGOVERN: I'm sorry, sir.
WOOLWEAVER: Yes, I'm sure you are, McGovern. Lane, can you tell me what I just said?
LANE: No, sir.
[*Utter silence*]
WOOLWEAVER: I thought not.
JARRETT: [*Self-righteous*] *Now* will you shut up?
WOOLWEAVER: Boys, you've got to wait for the organ to begin the piece. No singing. Attempt it once more.
[*The music begins, not too loud. The lights dim somewhat. Lights up on the* HEAD'S *study, with the music underneath, the dialogue beginning in Scene 14 after "virgine."*]

Scene 14

HEAD's *study*.

HEAD: Home education seems the best idea. One can hire outstanding tutors, you know. Have you any experience with home education?

MRS. LANE: Well, yes. Since Lawrence Park, my daughter's been educated at home.

HEAD: Well, there's no problem then! What is she studying?

MRS. LANE: Uh... French conversation, the piano. She's learning some maths, reading literature, Shakespeare, that sort of thing; she's just read *Don Juan*. [HEAD *looks shocked and mouths "Don Juan?"*] She has drawing lessons, oh! and history.

HEAD: A very well-rounded curriculum, Mrs. Lane. I should seriously consider having your son educated at home alongside your daughter. He's used to girls, anyway, having attended Lawrence Park.

MRS. LANE: You don't think he could get on well at *any* Public School?

HEAD: I shouldn't expect so, madam.

MRS. LANE: How dreadful to fail at Public School! How demoralizing! Especially when one considers that Horace did well—he excelled at Lawrence Park.

HEAD: Yes, so it said on his reports. But you must have realized the very great change Thomas More is from Lawrence Park.

MRS. LANE: My late husband sent the children there. I was very disappointed when he refused to send Horace to Rugby. [*This is* MRS. LANE's *last, desperate attempt.*] Both my father and brothers attended Rugby. You're a Rugby man yourself, are you not?

HEAD: [*Coolly*] I am, madam.

[*With a ghost of a smile*] Eight years.

MRS. LANE: —And you left in eighty-one?

HEAD: [*Surprised and taken aback*] Yes.

MRS. LANE: That's the year my eldest brother left.

HEAD: [*Thinks he's caught her in a lie*] Madam—there were no Lanes at Rugby in my year.

Epiphany

MRS. LANE: Oh! Lane is my married name.
HEAD: [*Slightly embarrassed*] Of course!
MRS. LANE: My maiden name is Thornton.
HEAD: Thornton? Why, Donald, of course! [*Remembering*] And young Jeremy.
MRS. LANE: Yes, Donald and Jeremy are my brothers.
HEAD: [*To himself*] Young Jeremy... [*Looks at* MRS. LANE, *not seeing her. Puts his hand on the folder containing* LANE's *papers. He flips through them. Nearly in a whisper*] Young... Jeremy. [*He stares at one paper, deep in thought. Then he looks up and shuts the folder with a slap.*] I don't see why we shouldn't give Horace one last chance.
[*Blackout*]

Scene 15

The chapel. When the song ends there is a pause.

WOOLWEAVER: Thank you, boys. [*Slight pause*] Please be back here in half an hour for the service. Lane, that includes you. It's sounding lovely. Dismiss.
[*The boys begin leaving both by the side door and the back door, chattering.*]
JARRETT: [*Amidst the chatter*] I'm off!
[LANE *takes* GEORGINA *out the back door.* PERRY *pulls at* TAVERNER's *sleeve as he hurries after* GEORGINA, *not seeing that she's left.* WOOLWEAVER *exits.*]
PERRY: Where are you dashing?
TAVERNER: [*Frantic*] To—to—
[*Stops*]
PERRY: [*Looks at* TAVERNER *oddly*] You're a very nervous boy these days. I think you ought to go to the sick-house for a lie-down.
TAVERNER: [*Aware that the chapel is emptying rapidly*] No, I've got to do something. Go get your surplice.
PERRY: [*Unruffled*] Do it afterwards.
TAVERNER: No, it can't wait. I've got to do it now. [*Still* PERRY *does not move.*] Don't wait for me. Go on.
[PERRY *doesn't.*] Go *on!*
PERRY: If you need to piss that badly, you can do it just outside. Everybody does, you know.

TAVERNER: I don't need to piss! You couldn't possibly understand. Just go on!

PERRY: All right! I'm sorry, Taverner. See you in chapel.

TAVERNER: Righto. [PERRY *walks all the way up the aisle into the shadows, but before he reaches the door, someone slides into the chapel through the side door.* PERRY *hears, stops, turns, stands watching, eventually going into a pew.* TAVERNER *sees* GEORGINA.]

GEORGINA: [*Happily*] Cli— [*In surprise*] Oh. Richard.

TAVERNER: Georgina! [TAVERNER *takes* GEORGINA's *hand and leads her to a seat.*] You shouldn't have come in. I was just going out to meet you. [*He kisses her lightly. She doesn't respond.*] I can hardly comprehend seeing you. It's been three months. [*He kisses her more seriously. She pushes him away.*]

GEORGINA: Don't!

TAVERNER: [*Stunned*] What is it? [GEORGINA *sidles free of him, not answering.*] Mayn't I kiss you?

GEORGINA: [*Firmly*] No! I'm sorry.

TAVERNER: [*Misunderstands her apology*] Then may I kiss you now?

GEORGINA: Oh, no! Oh, Richard... [*Turning away from him, she looks around the chapel.*] I expect you're wondering why I didn't answer your letters.

TAVERNER: [*Coming up behind her*] As a matter of fact—I was.

GEORGINA: [*Stops procrastinating; turns to face* TAVERNER, *business-like*] Richard—listen. I've got to explain myself. I know that when we met it seemed as if we were absolutely fated for one another—and for a time, I thought we were. But we're not, Richard. I was a very immature girl when we met, and I was bound to go overboard in my emotions. But I think I understand my feelings better now. It was just... infatuation, Richard. I don't... love you.

TAVERNER: [*Confused and plaintive*] Georgina, yes you do.

GEORGINA: [*As forcefully as she can*] I don't. Indeed I don't, Richard.

TAVERNER: [*Moving toward her*] But you *do!* You said—in the garden—

GEORGINA: [*Backing away, up the steps to the altar*] I know, but you'll just have to forget about all that.

TAVERNER: Forget about it?! Georgina, [*Stops*] I can't forget it.

GEORGINA: [*Figuring it's safe to stop, leans back against the*

Epiphany

altar] I didn't know you'd take it this badly.

TAVERNER: Georgina, listen. You don't know what you're really saying.

GEORGINA: [*Shakes her head; softly*] Oh yes I do.

TAVERNER: [*Positively*] No you don't. Come here, Georgina. [*She doesn't move. He goes after her, she darts around to the other side of the altar. They play cat and mouse. He catches her. She is not playing anymore. She struggles free and slaps his face quickly, simply to stop his advance. It works.*]

GEORGINA: Richard, stop. Just let me go. I'm sorry. [TAVERNER *stops stalking her and stands still, startled by the slap. There is a slight pause.*] Good-bye.

[GEORGINA *runs up the aisle, past* PERRY, *whom she does not see. The door slams.*]

TAVERNER: [*Toneless*] Good-bye. [*He stands still. Compulsively he brushes an arm across his eyes and sniffles. But then he changes his mind. Running up the aisle*] Wait!!

[*But the livid* PERRY *blocks his way.* TAVERNER *stops, not really understanding the situation. It takes some seconds. He closes his eyes in defeat.*]

PERRY: I've got to *do* something—but you couldn't possibly understand. I'm not acting different with you; you don't understand.

TAVERNER: [*Softly*] Oh, go away.

PERRY: You see, Perry, it's just my way of saying that I've gone right off you, but I've not got the courage to tell you. You see, Perry, for the past six terms, I've been hopping into bed with anything that struck my fancy. But I didn't want to hurt your feelings, so I didn't tell you.

TAVERNER: Please shut up.

PERRY: [*Erupts*] No, I won't shut up! I'm always shutting up for you, and risking *my* career for you, and bloody doing everything for you, and when you've had a bad time you take it out on me, and I bloody take it and love you for it! I just sit there and take it every single time, because that's what friends are for! Aren't they? [*No answer*] You'll bloody answer me! Aren't they? Aren't they?!

TAVERNER: Yes, Perry. I was—

PERRY: [*Approaching hysteria*] Shut up! Shut up you bastard! All term you've been a bastard! And do you want to know something else? I don't even care! And do you know why? Because I hate you. [*Grabs* TAVERNER'*s shoulders, looks*

him straight in the eye] I hate you. I hate you, you bloody liar! *I never lied to you in my life!!*
TAVERNER: [*Now he is crying too.*] Oh, let me go!
[TAVERNER *fights to break loose.* PERRY *takes this as an offensive and retaliates. An energetic fight ensues;* PERRY *is the aggressor. He is seriously attempting to kill* TAVERNER. *They do not stay in one place for more than a few seconds.* TAVERNER *is still crying.* PERRY, *on the other hand, is yelling.*]
PERRY: [*Fighting*] A girl! That's who you like better than me—a bloody girl!
[*The back door of the chapel opens and in march* WARNER *and* EVANS, *in immaculate white surplices. They resemble angels. Seeing the fight, they get excited and yell encouragement.*]
EVANS: Bash his head in! Oh, ripping!
[LANE *rushes in, also in surplice. He stops dead when he sees the fight.*]
LANE: [*Pleased*] Oh, are they fighting? [LANE *stands on a pew to watch with dark satisfaction. More angel-boys enter the chapel, through both doors. They mount pews and scramble to get the best view. They all shout bloodthirsty encouragement.* LANE *is all alone on his pew when* TAVERNER *and* PERRY *smash their way dangerously close.*]
CHURCHILL: You'll be hit, Lane! Get over here!
[LANE *hurries to stand with* CHURCHILL. JARRETT *enters with* WOOLWEAVER.]
WOOLWEAVER: [*Shocked*] Boys! Stop that! [WOOLWEAVER *and* JARRETT *rush over to pull* PERRY *off* TAVERNER.] Taverner! Stop this now! [JARRETT *tries his best to intervene, while* WOOLWEAVER *points to* WARNER.] Warner, go and get the Head. Tell him there's a fight.
WARNER: Oh, sir, can't I stay?
WOOLWEAVER: [*Severely*] Go!
[*Scared,* WARNER *scampers off. Other masters arrive, also prefects.* TAVERNER *and* PERRY *are separated. They struggle wildly to get back at each other's throats.* PERRY *does break free, and his rush at* TAVERNER *is accompanied by a swelling cheer from the boys. Prefects and masters throw the boys in seats, in a vain attempt to restore order.* PERRY *is soon caught again. The* HEAD *enters. He surveys the situation and is furious. The boys quiet down in deadly fear of the* HEAD. TAVERNER *stops struggling;* PERRY *does not even*

notice the HEAD's *presence. A moment later, however, he sees him. He, too, stops struggling. There is total silence.*]
HEAD: All right, thank you, sirs. [*Takes* TAVERNER] Come along, boys. [*Firmly grabs* PERRY's *collar.* PERRY *is panting and unwilling. The* HEAD *marches* TAVERNER *and* PERRY *out of chapel.*] Come on.

[*As they exit,* WILLARD *mounts the altar with a clipboard.*]
WILLARD: Abbott. [*Chatter has begun. Louder*] Abbott!
BOY: Here, sir!

[*Gradually the boys sit down. Masters and prefects push them, yelling, "Get in your seats!" etc. The boys are quite excited.*]
WILLARD: Adams?
BOY: Here, sir!
WILLARD: Adelbert?
BOY: Here, sir!
WILLARD: Addison major?
BOY: Here, sir.
WILLARD: Let's have it quiet, boys! Addison minor?
BOY: Yes, sir.
WILLARD: Aisling?
BOY: [*Amid wolf-whistles*] Here, sir!
WILLARD: Aldredge?
BOY: Here, sir.
WILLARD: Allen?
BOY: Here, sir.

[*The lights fade to blackout.*]

Scene 16

TAVERNER's *study. The next afternoon. There is an open foot-locker on the bed, also folded clothes, books tied together in bundles, etc.* TAVERNER *is very unhappy. He fondles dear objects as he tosses them into his trunk: his cricket-bat, his school tie, etc. As he packs,* PERRY *runs up the same aisle as he did in Act I, Scene 1, laden with* TAVERNER's *belongings. The lock has been taken off the door, and there is a hole in the door in its place.* PERRY *opens the door and walks in a bit rudely.*

PERRY: [*Dumping objects on bed*] Here's all of your things that I borrowed.
[*Finishes dumping. A book slides to the ground.* PERRY *bends.*]

TAVERNER: Oh—don't bother. I'll pick it up.

PERRY: [*Shortly, as he crosses to the door*] Bloody please yourself.

TAVERNER: Please—stop.

PERRY: Can't. I've got packing to do, too. You're not the only bloody cretin in this school who's got himself expelled.

TAVERNER: Just a moment? Can't we talk?

PERRY: No.
[*But* PERRY *doesn't move.*]

TAVERNER: [*Looking down sadly, sees the book that he has picked up*] Perry, this *Romeo and Juliet*'s yours. I gave it to you.

PERRY: I don't want it.

TAVERNER: But—

PERRY: I don't want any part of it! Or of you! [TAVERNER *sits on the bed, exasperated and upset. He flips through the pages of the book, not looking at it.* PERRY *studies the floor. Softly*] Page twenty-one.

TAVERNER: [*Looks up in surprise, then finds page and reads aloud*]
"Dost thou love me? I know thou . . .
thou wilt say 'Ay,'
and I will take thy word: yet, if thou swear'st,
thou mayst prove false: at lovers' perjuries,
they say, Jove laughs."

PERRY: [*Joining in;* TAVERNER *trails off, listening.*]
"thou wilt say ay
And I will take thy word.
Yet if thou swearest,
Thou mayst prove false.
At lovers' perjuries, they say Jove laughs."

[PERRY *turns to* TAVERNER *and their eyes meet.* PERRY *stays motionless. Quietly but strongly*] Good-bye, Taverner.
[PERRY *walks out, shutting the door quietly, and he walks back up his aisle.* TAVERNER *remains motionless into the blackout. Organ music is heard—William Boyce:* "Voluntary in D Major" *1785, #1; Larghetto.*]

CURTAIN

BLUFFING

by Peter Murphy

CHARACTERS

PETE, about forty
STEW
RICK
BILL
TONY
CHARLIE, in his late thirties

SCENE: *A dark stage except for the lone lamp, suspended over a green felt table. On it are a deck of cards, a box of poker chips, and ashtrays. At stage right,* PETE, *a short, stocky man, forty-ish, casually dressed and shoe-less, is on the phone.*

PETE: Ah, come on Charlie, what else are you gonna do tonight?... You gotta be kiddin'... Tell the anchor to buzz off... Jes' tell her... You've got a right to your own fun, too... Jes' tell the warden you'll be home early... All right then, you'll come then, you'll be here?... What? About eight... The usual group: Bill, Rick, Stew... I know, I know... but if the rest o' the guys can stand him, you can too... Yeah, well whenever he starts talkin' about his kids—go get a beer, or jes' don't listen... I know it's a pain in the butt... Well, he asked me if we were playin' tonight, cripes, what was I gonna do, say no?... Bull—you would've done the same thing... [*Long pause*] So like I said—jes' grab another beer or shut your ears when he starts talkin' 'bout junior's battin' average in little league... Don't worry, jes' do what I said... [*Knock at the door*] Crap, that's him, hope he didn't hear me... gotta go... listen—eight o'clock, right?... See ya!

[PETE *hangs up the phone and strides to the door. He opens it and in walks* STEW, *a tall, gaunt man with long, out-of-date sideburns, and dressed in a style obviously too young for him.*]

STEW: Jeez, that damn dog almost got me again. Why don't you complain about the mutt. You can't keep pets in apartments.

PETE: He don't bother me. Besides, it's all the old guy's got.

STEW: Who cares? The S.O.B. damn near killed me. I think I will complain. That old coot's breakin' the law.

PETE: Who gives a damn?

STEW: Well, it was a thought, anyways. Say, who's comin' tonight?

PETE: The usual group.

STEW: You mean: Charlie, Bill, Tony, and...

PETE: Rick.

STEW: Cripes—not Rick?

PETE: Why? Whatsa matter with Rick?

STEW: Well, he's just such a bad-mouther.

PETE: Bad-mouther?

STEW: Yeah, you know, always complainin' about money an' stuff.

PETE: Oh, that. Jes' natural cheapness, I guess.

STEW: Natural, like hell. If you ask me, he's senile. One of these days I'm gonna pull his plug and do the world a favor. I'll betcha ten bucks, five-to-two, he'll complain right off about the beer or the food, or who's gonna pay for the cards.

PETE: Yeah. I guess you're right. But could you try an' keep your cool tonight? If it don't bother anybody else it shouldn't bother you. Jes' try an' ignore him.

STEW: All right, but it won't be easy.

PETE: Jes' try. We only do this once a week.

STEW: [*Reclining, more relaxed now*] Say did I tell you what Jimmy's hittin' for the Lions? He's leadin' the league. Tuesday he went four for...

[*Loud knock at the door*]

PETE: That'll be Rick. Now remember what I told you.

STEW: Yeah, yeah. [PETE *goes to the door*. STEW *lights up a cigarette. In walks* RICK, *rather short with poor posture and huge horn-rimmed glasses. He has the weasely look of a chronic complainer.*]

RICK: Hi guys.

STEW: [*Nonchalantly*] Yo.

PETE: Hava seat. You guys wanna beer?

[*Goes backstage to the kitchen.* STEW *offers* RICK *a cigarette.* RICK *takes it but puts it in his shirt pocket.*]

RICK: Later.

[*He smiles.* STEW *shrugs his shoulders.*]

PETE: [*Coming in from offstage*] Here.

[*Lobs a can of beer to each of them.* RICK *puts the beer beside him without opening it.*]

RICK: Say, who else is gonna' be here tonight?

Bluffing

STEW: The usuals.

PETE: You know, Charlie, Tony, Bill...

RICK: Bill? Crap, who invited him? If I hear how tough it is down at "the office" one more time I'm gonna heave "the executive" out the window.

STEW: Affirmative. He oughta try dumpin' that crap on his wife instead of us.

PETE: You kiddin'? She got sick of it years ago. She don't listen no more. That leaves only us.

RICK: He better put a sock in it tonight. I'm in no mood for any of his crap.

PETE: Nobody is.

RICK: Nobody is any night or any day.

[*Agreeing chuckle from the trio*]

PETE: Listen, let's not have any brawls tonight.

RICK: I just wish he could talk about something else for once. Just once!

STEW: He's so boring!

PETE: Cool it you guys—he'll be here any sec'.

RICK: That's too soon. Say how much does each...

[*Knock on the door*]

PETE: Cripes, that's him. Kill it you guys.

RICK: Stew, go let Milton Berle in.

[STEW *goes to the door and greets* BILL, *an average-size man with an ill-fitting business suit, collar open and tie askew. His hair is graying and an unlit cigar is stuck in his mouth.*]

BILL: Excuse me, is this Monte Carlo?

[*Forced chuckle from the others*]

STEW: Come on in, the draft is puttin' out my cigarette.

BILL: Anyone got a light?

[*Flicks the cigar in his mouth*]

STEW: Yeah... here.

[*Throws* BILL *a pack of matches, who lights his cigar and then hands them back. He walks over to the table and fondles the chips.*]

BILL: Well, here's four of us. Who's the fifth?

PETE: There's six tonight.

BILL: Oh? Who?

PETE: Charlie and Tony. I had to grab Charlie by the teeth to get him...

BILL: Aw, not Tony?

PETE: Cripes! What's wrong with him?
RICK: Jeez. You haven't noticed?
STEW: No one's told you?
PETE: Told me what?
STEW: I guess not.
PETE: Told me what?
RICK: Well... you know...
PETE: Know what?
STEW: He's... you know.
PETE: WHAT!
BILL: For cripes sake, he's a damn fairy!
PETE: What?
BILL: You heard me.
PETE: You don't mean... [*Displays a limp wrist*] No... not Tony?... But, he's always braggin' about...
STEW: Probably a cover-up.
PETE: No crap.
BILL: If he lays a hand on me... I'll rip his eyes out... just like Oedipus...
PETE: That was incest.
BILL: Oh... anyways... we had a guy down in accounting that was one. I heard that...
[*Knock on door*]
PETE: That's him! Everybody stay cool... Jes'... Jes'... Stew, open the door!
RICK: I'll get it. Maybe Tinkerbell will give me some flying lessons.
PETE: Hey—don't say anything about this.
RICK: Yeah.
[*He opens the door and* TONY *comes in. None of the other men give any indication of the subject they were just discussing.*]
TONY: Como estás?
RICK: Yeah, and your mother too... no wait... sorry...
PETE: [*To* RICK] Maintain.
TONY: What?
PETE: Forget it.
STEW: Let's start, Charlie'll be late... He always is.
BILL: No, he'll get ticked off.
STEW: He's got some nerve... Always bein' late... Expectin' us to cater to him... If he's more 'an an hour late—forget it. He won't play.

Bluffing 227

RICK: It's only a poker game.

PETE: Yeah, well don't make too much of it.

BILL: How can ya make too much of it? He'd be late on a date with Bo Derek if it meant he could stuff his face with another twinkie.

TONY: Right on. He's really grandé.

RICK: Will you cut the Iranian shit?... I thought you were a Wop anyways.

TONY: Sicilian. And that wasn't Iranian—it's Spanish. I'm takin' it up.

RICK: [*Mockingly*] It's really suave.

PETE: Hey—go easy.

RICK: Hey, why should we pay for the food? He eats it all.

STEW: What, you gonna save the three bucks for grandma's operation?

RICK: Kiss...

PETE: Hey! Enough!

BILL: Say Pete, you got another beer?

PETE: Yeah, we could all use one.

[*Goes backstage into the kitchen again*]

RICK: I wouldn't mind it if he'd just stop talking with his mouth full of hostess pop-'n-crud.

STEW: In a couple of months he's gonna need two chairs.

[*Knock on the door*]

BILL: Hey, Dumbo's outside. Tony go get the door.

TONY: Hey, gotta tell you about this chick I met. She's really...

BILL: Later, jes' get the door.

[TONY *gets the door and lets in* CHARLIE, *an overweight, sweaty-looking man in his late thirties, with an upbeat sense of humor.*]

TONY: Buenas Noches!

CHARLIE: Never on the first date. How's everybody? Sorry for bein' late. I couldn't get away from Madame Defarge.

BILL: No prob... who?

STEW: Now that everybody's here... let's play.

RICK: What's your hurry?

STEW: I gotta be home by one or my wife'll lock me out.

TONY: You're kiddin'.

STEW: Nope. Came home at three last week, said she'd do it next time, and I believe her.

RICK: Hey, Pete, you hear this... Stew's gotta be home at one or the tigress has him for breakfast... hey... Pete?

TONY: Where the hell is he?
CHARLIE: Hey, Pete... Pete?
BILL: Since when do beers take so long to brew?
RICK: I'll— [*Goes backstage*] Pete— [*Comes back*] He ain't in the kitchen... where do ya suppose he could be?
CHARLIE: Maybe he committed suicide by swallowing a microwave.
RICK: Christ, I better look again. [*Goes backstage*] Pete... Pete?
PETE: [*Loud voice from offstage*] What the hell is it? Can't I even have some peace and quiet in the john?
RICK: Well, who's bright idea was that?
CHARLIE: Agatha Christie over there.
  [*Tilts his head to* BILL]
BILL: Just bein' careful.
CHARLIE: Who made you Robert Young?
BILL: Huh?
CHARLIE: *Father Knows Best?*
BILL: What?
CHARLIE: What'd you do as a kid, read?
STEW: Come on, let's start the game.
TONY: Okay you guys, let's play.
  [STEW *and* BILL *grab a knowing glance at each other.*]
PETE: [*Returning*] Grab a seat.
  [*Everybody moves over to the table and grabs a chair.*]
BILL: I think this is gonna be my lucky night. I can feel it.
CHARLIE: You always say that.
RICK: And you're always wrong.
BILL: I know but tonight—
RICK: Tonight'll be just like the others. You'll go home with no sleep and an empty wallet.
BILL: Yeah, well, you'll go with me.
RICK: Why don't you—
TONY: How much to play?
CHARLIE: Anyone wanna switch chairs? Any chow on the premises?
RICK: I don't think I have enough.
PETE: Do you ever? Twenty bucks each, all cash in.
RICK: That mean you'll cover if we're short?
BILL: Jesus Christ.
RICK: Jes' makin' sure.
PETE: Yeh, Yeh. Don't worry about it.

CHARLIE: [*Flips twenty dollars*] Here's mine.
STEW: [*Flips twenty dollars*] Here's mine.
TONY: Uno, dos, tres—
   [BILL *snatches money from* TONY *and throws it on the table.*]
BILL: He wants twenty and so do I.
   [PETE *collects money and counts bills and passes out chips to players. While doing this,* RICK *is carefully counting money. Eventually everyone is looking at him.*]
RICK: I only have eighteen—
BILL: Shit, every damn week—
PETE: That's fine.
   [*He grabs money from* RICK *and gives him a pile of chips.*] I'll take twenty, too.
CHARLIE: Okay you guys, first jack deals. [*Starts flipping a card to each player*] Hey, Stew, how's that terrific kid of yours hittin' the ball this year?
STEW: Good, real good. So Tony, old stallion, what's the scoop on this new chick?
PETE: [*Looking around, toasting with his beer.*] Here's to good friends!

[*Curtain falls.*]

IN THE WAY

by Stephen Gutwillig

CHARACTERS

FATHER, mid-to-late forties
SON, fifteen to sixteen

Scene 1

As the house lights dim, a soft song (the "Mother's Theme"), played on a piano, begins. It is sad but pretty. The curtain rises to reveal the FATHER, *a man in his mid-to-late forties, seated at the piano. The setting is a living room. No lights are on and all of the curtains are drawn. Early-morning sunshine filters in, nevertheless, creating a dim haze.*

There is a couch, center, to the left of the piano. The dinner table is far right next to a swinging door leading into a kitchen offstage. Several chairs of different types and smaller tables are also arranged tastefully about the room. The front door is far left near the hall closet. At the back of the stage is a staircase leading to the second floor.

The FATHER *is dressed in a white shirt and dark pants. Seated facing the audience, one cannot tell that he is not actually playing. Yet, it appears as if he is. The* FATHER *soon rises, as the "Mother's Theme" continues, and begins the task of closing up the piano. The* SON *quietly descends the stairs unnoticed. About fifteen or sixteen, he is dressed in a bathrobe over pajama bottoms. Remaining silent on the landing, he observes the activity below. The "Mother's Theme" lingers a moment more then fades out as the* FATHER, *now finished, looks up and notices him.*

FATHER: Oh, you up already? [*The* SON *says nothing. The* FATHER *checks his watch.*] What am I saying? It's past eight... Good morning. How did you sleep?
SON: It's very dark down here. Has the paper come yet?
FATHER: I don't know. I haven't checked.

[*Before he can finish, the* SON *is on his way to the door. He opens it and finds nothing on the stoop. He is disturbed by its absence.*]

SON: Not there. Should I make some coffee?

FATHER: It *is* dark down here.

[*He moves toward the curtains but is stopped by the* SON'S *voice.*]

SON: I'm going to make some coffee. Do you want some?

FATHER: When did you start drinking coffee? Well, you'd better let me make it.

SON: Dad, I know how to boil water.

FATHER: Oh, instant! No, I meant real coffee. You'd better take your shot anyway, I suppose. You do that in the morning, right?

SON: Sometimes.

FATHER: Oh.

[*He goes through the swinging door into the kitchen. The* SON *lifts the cover of the piano and fools with the keys. He obviously does not know how to play. The* FATHER *reenters. The* SON *is startled.*]

FATHER: I decided on instant after all. Who needs the hassle?

SON: Right.

FATHER: There's a hell of a lot of fruit in there. You should eat some of it before it goes bad.

[*A pause*]

SON: No, I guess I didn't sleep too well at that.

FATHER: Can't say I did either. [*Walking over to the piano*] She ever tell you about this? [*No answer*] We were on our honeymoon in London. She saw it in some posh music store and fell in love with it on the spot. Something special about it—I never really understood. No matter how great the trip was, she kept saying that the piano was the high-point and she had to have it. Well, Christ, the damn thing was more expensive than the whole two-week package itself. I don't know how I did it, but I got her mind on something else. Anyway, a couple of weeks after we got back, I saw what I thought was the same piano in Fredrick's. You know, that place on Cove Road. It was a dead ringer—except for the price. I took a chance that she wouldn't catch on and I gave it to her for her birthday. She's always been so proud of it too. [*Chuckling*] I never had the heart to tell her. [*The* SON *remains silent.*] Well, I thought it was a cute story. You know, the "old days." Jesus, I hope you're not going to react this way—

SON: [*Almost to himself*] Shut up.

FATHER: C'mon, son. There's no point— [*He is interrupted by the kettle, whistling offstage.*] Excuse me. [*The FATHER exits through the swinging door. The SON seems almost relieved, but he starts a little as his FATHER's voice continues, after a pause, from offstage.*] Christ, it's such a mess in here. [*Pause*] Please don't think I don't understand. It's tough all around. So much seems to have changed... [*Quietly*] The rooms all seem bigger somehow. [*Pause*] But, it's not the end of the world. Please, if anything...

SON: [*To himself*] Christ, here he goes again.

FATHER: ...if anything, I want you to remember that. I hope you want it black because... yep, there's no milk in here. [*The FATHER reenters with two coffee mugs which he places on the dinner table.*] I'm sorry if I seem to lecture too much. It's just that... I don't know if you are... uh... You know that everything you feel is perfectly natural, so don't think—

SON: Please stop trying to make this easier. It's shit. It's supposed to be shit. Don't even try to change that, you can't.

FATHER: I'm not trying to do anything.

SON: The hell you're not! All you want to do is make everything easy. Pretend that, within a matter of time, things will get better. They won't.

FATHER: C'mon now, son. I really don't think that utter despair is the solution.

SON: Fine. But I don't want fifty pep-talks a day about how I shouldn't let this get to me. Who are you kidding?

FATHER: All right, you've made your point. Now go take your shot. You might as well get dressed, too. Wait, don't you want your coffee?

[*The SON goes up the stairs. The FATHER looks around the room and goes over to the piano. He stares at it for a moment then slams down the cover. The SON, not having changed, comes down the stairs.*]

FATHER: That was quick.

SON: [*Gravely*] What are you going to do with the house now?

FATHER: Not now. Not today, please.

SON: I see.

FATHER: I didn't mean anything by that. We'll talk about it later.

SON: You gonna leave?
FATHER: Maybe.
SON: [*Going into the kitchen*] And like magic, all the memories will disappear.
FATHER: Christ.

[*The FATHER goes over to the windows and opens the curtains. Light rushes into the room. He walks to the front door, once again, to check for the paper. This time it is there. As he closes the door, the SON enters from the kitchen. He has an apple.*]

SON: [*Looking around the room*] What did you do with all of those flowers?
FATHER: I thought they were a bit... too depressing. Besides, I didn't throw away any of the daffodils—
SON: Oh great, the paper came!

[*He takes it from his father, who seems dazed. The SON sits on the couch and begins flipping through it. The FATHER stares at him.*]

FATHER: You remember? Daffodils, they were her favorites.
[*The SON says nothing.*] Should I make some more coffee? [*When there is, again, no response, the FATHER goes and sits on the opposite end of the couch. He speaks more to himself than to his son.*] That's right. Daffodils.
SON: No sports section again.
FATHER: So beautiful.

SON:
[*Flipping through newspaper*] I swear, there is always some part of this damn thing missing. Last week, it was the television section. Had to go out and buy a goddamn T.V. Guide. Now it's the sports section. IT'S NOT HERE! [*The SON's last line pierces the air.*]

FATHER:
God, that woman loved flowers. I had no idea that daffodils were her favorites. But, by some fluke, I gave them to her on our first date. She took it as some kind of an omen, I guess. So beautiful.

SON: [*Putting down the paper and heading for the stairs*] I should get dressed.
FATHER: Do you hate being in this house? [*The SON stops dead in his tracks with his back to the audience. The FATHER speaks directly out without looking at him.*] I suppose you

In The Way

do. I would too. Losing your mother and then... well, there's me. You know, nobody's forcing you to stay here. There are a couple of good boarding schools nearby if you don't want to go too far away. [*The* SON *turns around.*] You've still got two more years of high school left. We can look into it this summer.

SON: [*After a pause*] Yeah.

[*The* SON *goes up the stairs. The* FATHER, *having heard him go, walks over to the phone and dials a number he finds in an address-book on the hall table.*]

FATHER: Good morning, I'm glad you're open. I'd like to confirm the pick-up of a baby-grand at 43 Fenimore Road... that's right, this morning. Yes, and it's very important that you come no later than 12:30. No, there won't be anyone here. The key is in the flowerpot just to the left of the front door. And, uh, it's really necessary that you do it this morning. No, no... I just wanted to make sure you understood that. Great, well, thanks... very much.

[*He hangs up and stares around the room. His gaze finally fixes upon the piano. He hears the* SON *coming down the stairs and walks downstage toward the couch. The* SON *has put on dark shoes, pants, and a white shirt. He carries a matching jacket which he drapes at the base of the bannister. He is now dressed similarly to his father. The* FATHER *now turns around and briefly inspects his son's appearance.*]

FATHER: Thank you.

SON: Do we really have to see all of those people before the ceremony?

FATHER: "Those people?" Why, most of them are relatives and close friends. They've come to be with us... because they care. You must know that.

SON: Sure, but... Oh, Christ, you know how it's going to be.

FATHER: What are you talking about?

SON: You remember how it was two years ago when Uncle Bill died, and all three of us had to go to Salt Lake for the funeral. I—I'd never been to a funeral before... it was so uncomfortable. I barely knew the guy. I asked mom what I should say to Aunt Claire. Well, you know mom, she said I'd know what to say when the time came. So much for that advice. When the time came, all I could do was stare at her like an idiot. Finally, I just had to say something... and I asked her how she was. I couldn't believe it. Her husband was about to be buried and I asked her—well, she just looked at me for a minute and said she was as well as could be expected. I felt so goddamn stupid... I don't want all those people not knowing what to say to me, and telling me how sorry they are, or asking me how I am.

FATHER: We have to thank everyone who sent us flowers or all that fruit. I'm sorry but there's no way around it. Did you take your shot?

SON: Will Aunt Claire be there?

FATHER: For God sakes! How about the shot?!

SON: Jesus Christ! Will you leave me the hell alone about it. I can take care of it myself. I always have.

FATHER: Come on! Your mother had to hound you about it all the time, who are you kidding?

SON: That doesn't mean you have to do it now. Do you really think you could handle it, anyway?

FATHER: Just as long as it gets done. I suppose, by now, you know what you're doing. [*The* FATHER *turns and goes to the closet upstage to get his jacket and tie. Yet, he stops, just having opened the door. He remains facing into the closet with his hand on the doorknob through the next line.*] You know, this is the first time I've ever felt glad that we couldn't have any more children. This would really be hell. [*Chuckling*] Shit, I was sure I'd be the first to go, anyway. [*The* FATHER *shakes his head and then gets the jacket and tie. The former he places on the couch, the latter he puts on.*] There are some things... some things about today that I haven't talked to you about yet. Some details about the ceremony.

SON: Were you really expecting to die first?

FATHER: The casket will be closed.

SON: Closed?

FATHER: Well... yes... It is best... under the circumstances.

SON: Oh, I get it. She looked pretty gruesome at the end, didn't she? I guess no one's going to want to look at that today.

FATHER: C'mon, son. Don't say things like that. It's true she... changed. She lost a lot of weight.

SON: Yeah! She lost a lot of hair too. [*Pause*] Sorry. But, just don't mince words with me. You don't have to try to spare me.

FATHER: Sorry.

SON: I used to come home from school and, when the day nurse had left, I'd go up and watch her sleep. Standing there in the doorway, I'd wonder how much pain she was really in. Sure, she was pumped full of drugs but, I wasn't ever sure. I don't think she would even have told me.

FATHER: Well, now, son...

SON: No, it's true. She always acted so damn brave...even when it was me giving her the pain-killers, even when it was me helping her to the bathroom at 4:30 in the morning—cleaning up after her, changing her sheets—

FATHER: Yes, you're right! She acted brave in front of you, but she had to. Your mother knew how children like to think of their parents as being invincible. It makes them feel secure. It was bad enough that she was going to lose—she didn't want you to have to see it...*She* had to try to spare you.

SON: But I just wanted to be with her. She didn't have to pretend—I knew it all anyway.

FATHER: I guess that was it. She didn't want you to know.

SON: But all the years when she took care of me...all the insulin. She didn't let me take care of her—until she had no choice.

FATHER: None of it was too fair, was it? [*Pause*] But, at least we were prepared for her...to be taken away from us. I mean, we didn't just get a phone call one day saying she got hit by a truck or something. At least we knew it was coming.

SON: Yeah, lucky us. [*A pause*] What time do we have to leave?

FATHER: Not for a little while. [*The* FATHER *sits on the couch. He looks out and remembers.*] But you're right. Your mother sure was brave. It's impossible to imagine what she must've had to go through...and with absolutely no chance—

SON: [*Moving to the piano*] I really don't think I can stay in here much longer. I'm suffocating.

FATHER: [*Defeated*] All right. We'll look at schools this summer.

SON: [*Quickly*] No. I meant just now, today. [*They stare at each other. A pause*] Okay. We'll look this summer.

FATHER: Whatever you want, son. You need some room to yourself. I can understand that.

SON: [*Bitterly*] Yeah, I guess you do.

FATHER: We should get moving. Would you grab my coat,

please. Wait. Where's your tie?

[*The* SON *grabs his own coat off the bannister and reaches inside the pocket. He yanks out a tie, dangles it apathetically before his father's face and heads for the door. He exits, leaving the door open behind him. The* FATHER *waits a moment watching him leave. He looks briefly around the room then heads out, stroking the piano as he passes it. The door closes and the lights dim.*]

Scene 2

The same. It is several hours later, about mid-afternoon. The piano is gone. In its place lie three glass castors on which it rested, still arranged in the formation of the wheels.

The FATHER *and* SON *enter. They stand for a moment in the doorway. The* FATHER *then moves across the room and into the kitchen. The* SON *watches him and then goes upstairs, without closing the front door. The* FATHER *reenters with a drink. He notices the open door, places his drink on the coffee table and goes to shut it. He then sits on the couch, takes off his jacket and loosens his tie.*

The SON *descends the stairs. He has removed his jacket and tie. He remains on the landing staring at the back of his father's head. The* SON *then goes and stands in the spot once occupied by the piano. He faces his father.*

FATHER: There was no right time to tell you. You were upset enough as it was. [*The* SON *continues to stare at him almost in disbelief. The* FATHER's *voice becomes increasingly desperate.*] Well, who was going to play it? It couldn't just sit there. I wouldn't have been able to stand it and neither would you. Daffodils are one thing, but... [*The* SON *turns away and starts heading for the kitchen.*] C'mon. Don't do that. You'll understand. Please, don't walk out on me. Hey!

In The Way

SON: [*Quickly turning around*] You're accusing me of walking out? You— You're trying to wipe out every memory of her just because it hurts to remember. What're you going to do next? Burn your wedding pictures?

[*The* SON *storms into the kitchen. The* FATHER *gulps down his drink and puts it down on the coffee table. Suddenly, there is a loud sound of breaking glass from the kitchen. The* FATHER *jumps up and the* SON *reenters.*]

FATHER: What did you do?

[*The* SON *tries to get by him to the stairs but the* FATHER *grabs him by the arm, pulls him back, and holds him tightly.*] What did you do?

SON: [*Glancing at the glass on the table*] I see you've returned to some old habits, dad. I thought you might have a little more self-control. I guess it's understandable, though. There's nobody left to scold you when you screw up, is there? I'm sorry, but I seem to have broken a bottle of gin in there. You should be more careful where you hide your booze... dad.

FATHER: Put a lid on it.

SON: Oh yeah. I guess drunks are a bit touchy on that subject. [*The* FATHER *raises his hand to slap him across the face. He quickly stops himself. A pause*]

SON: Oh now, that would be familiar, too.

FATHER: Son, I'm sorry. But, Jesus Christ, why did you have to say all that? Okay, I'm drinking again. I've just come from my wife's funeral... I've just buried twenty years of my life. I need—I deserve a drink. [*The* SON *turns to go.*] C'mon, you can't act like this... even if you don't want to stay here. [*A pause*] But, I can't say I blame you.

SON: I'll bet.

FATHER: I suppose we should discuss the house.

SON: What does it matter? I won't really be around, will I? Do whatever you like.

FATHER: What is with you? You're so goddamn snide. I'm only trying to make this whole nightmare easier for you.

SON: For *me?* Bullshit.

FATHER: My God! Didn't I practically break my back today to keep all those people you're so afraid of away from you? What more proof do you need? I mean, I didn't know what to say to half of them. They sure as hell didn't understand why you refused to see them. I realize that this is a hard time for you, but do you have to be so selfish?

SON: Don't you call me selfish. [*As the* FATHER *moves toward him*] No! You're the one who's selling the house and dumping her piano and sending me to God-knows-where just so you won't be bothered with memories. You're the one who paid so little attention to her while she was dying that, when she *was* rational, she didn't know what to think anymore. You're the one who's never really realized how much she had to put up with from you. And when she needed you... what happened? She took so much of your bullshit— She knew that piano wasn't the one you saw in London! She just didn't want to hurt your goddamn pride. [*The* FATHER *turns away.*] I promised her that I'd never tell you that. But, now that you've had it carted away, what does it matter? [*They are now both facing out, staring blankly. During the following section, they do not address one another directly. They are speaking more to themselves.*] I knew she was going to die for such a long time. Even after she finally told me, it was so long. Shit, it sort of became another phase in our lives: I would go to school, you to work and she'd stay home with that damn nurse. Sure it still hurt, but it seemed so far off. Christ, it was such a shock when it finally happened. I'd always known that it would eventually, but that didn't make any difference. It hadn't become final until then—I didn't really have to believe it until then.

FATHER: I sure as hell didn't turn out to be as strong as I always thought I was. You spend more than half your life with one person, it's damn hard giving her up. I guess I didn't do it too well. I wish to God I understood why you could deal with what was happening to her and I couldn't. It just made me so sick to watch her fall apart. That wasn't my wife, whatever it was she turned into, and I couldn't look at her. Didn't seem to matter to you, though.

SON: I couldn't believe how easy it was today. I've been dreading this day for so long, trying not to think about putting her underground. I suppose, though, after everything else, it could only get easier. This is the first real calm.

FATHER: It wasn't that I didn't appreciate everything she had done for me, you know. I just couldn't watch her die. I never had a chance to thank her for putting up with me. [*There is a pause as the* SON *turns and stares at him. The* FATHER *rises abruptly.*] Neither of us really had anything to eat this morning. Want anything now?

SON: [*Frustrated*] No, not now. [*The* FATHER *turns to go. He is stopped by the* SON'*s next line.*] You're the one who can't stand to be in this house, you know. Not me.

FATHER: Please, don't start this again.

SON: I'm right, aren't I? You're running away because you're scared...of me. What, you don't think you can handle your sick kid by yourself? The diabetic needs too much care, is that it? Well, I don't need your pity. Sure mom pampered me...she had to. But, I don't need it now. I can take care of myself.

FATHER: Which is exactly what I'm letting you do.

SON: Bullshit! That's not what you're doing. You're running away and you know it.

FATHER: For what I've been through in the past year, I deserve to run away. This house is a goddamn torture chamber and I can't live in it. I'm getting old and I'm running out of choices. I might as well get out of here while I still can.

SON: *You* are not old.

FATHER: I'm pushing fifty.

SON: That's not old.

FATHER: I've got hair starting to grow out of my ears. Don't you tell me that's not old.

SON: But you're still trying to bury everything along with her. I can understand you not wanting me around, but do you have to ruin everything you had with her?

FATHER: In the car on the way home, I realized that next month is our anniversary. Shit, it hadn't occurred to me before: What's it going to be like dreading that day for the rest of time...and her birthday and Christmas—every day has some goddamn thing to make it special, some story attached to it...every piece of clothing, every stick of furniture. It's going to take forever to get used to it.

SON: I always remember the smallest things—they're so stupid—so long ago. When I was about five or six and I began taking shots regularly, mom sat me down and tried to explain exactly what was happening to me. She said that she wasn't really hurting me but the medicine would help me to be normal. She said that someday I would have to learn how to give them to myself. I got really scared, but she told me that I didn't have to worry about it because she would always be there to help me. [*The* SON *is, by now, speaking more to himself. He chuckles nervously.*] Now I haven't got anyone to help me.

FATHER: Well, that's by your own choice, of course.

SON: What?

FATHER: You're by yourself because that's the way you want it. No nosy relatives and you certainly don't want me to help you.

SON: I can tell that's very high on your list of priorities, along with selling the house. Don't give me all that bullshit, dad.

FATHER: What are you talking about? Getting the hell out of here seems to be just what you want.

SON: Well, that's because I don't exactly feel wanted here. But that shouldn't be any surprise.

FATHER: Your mother spoiled you. I didn't think you would be able to handle losing her.

SON: [*Becoming increasingly upset*] My mother has nothing to do with this. And if anyone can't handle it... [*Referring to the glass*]... it's you.

FATHER: Oh, I guess I lost her a long time ago.

SON: You mean when I came along? What, did I ruin your life then, too. That's a real sad story you got there, dad.

FATHER: Will you shut up. You still don't really understand about your mother, do you? You know the doctors said we couldn't have any more kids after you. Christ, you were going to be the only one she'd ever have. A family had meant so much to her. [*Quickly*] Sure, we were real happy before, but... she needed something more.

SON: I guess a sick little diabetic wasn't exactly what she had in mind.

FATHER: No, no that's not it. You were perfect... everything she could ask for. She could dote on you all she wanted and still not feel guilty for spoiling you. After a while, it didn't matter that there weren't going to be any others. And you got so close, the two of you. I think that's when I started to drink.

SON: Jesus.

FATHER: So, I understand how hard it is to lose her... especially for you.

SON: Christ, she was your wife. You're entitled to a little grief, too. Why should it be any harder on me?

FATHER: You're so young. Kids aren't supposed to see death

happen... in front of them. I know it doesn't seem too fair. You have every reason to feel bitter. I guess I'd feel pretty much the same way. [*A pause*] But you can't expect me to pretend I don't know what you'll always be wishing... that it'd been me instead of her. Christ, I sure as hell can't blame you for feeling that way, but do you really expect me to live with it?

[*There is a pause as the* SON *lets this sink in. He shakes his head and semi-chuckles in disbelief.*]

What is with you?

SON: Whenever we used to talk about you, mom always said that there's usually something hidden. She'd laugh about how she would finally get things out of you. Christ, you never seemed that deep to me.

FATHER: Will you give me a break? [*Rising*] I'm going to go make a sandwich. I'm tired of listening to you go on about things you don't understand.

SON: Well, I think you should listen to this, asshole. You obviously don't have the whole picture yet.

FATHER: Hey, I don't care where the hell you're living, but you don't call your father that. Oh, what's the use.

SON: [*Moving to him*] I'm sorry, but you don't get it at all. Sure, I was really close to mom and I'll never be able to handle losing her, but there's more to it. Of course, I'm angry and bitter and really scared, but am I supposed to hate you for it?

FATHER: C'mon, calm down.

SON: No. I won't be like you. I'm going to say what I feel. And I feel bitter sure, but I feel lucky, too. Lucky that I had fifteen full years with her. Fifteen years of memories that can never be taken away from me. But, if it had been you—what would I have? I don't know who you are. I don't even know my own father. I would have no memories, nothing. How am I supposed to live with that?

FATHER: I guess I know what you mean. I'm sorry, I should never have gotten rid of the old piano.

SON: No, that's okay. It would only be in the way, anyhow.

[*The* FATHER *agrees. Both the* FATHER *and the* SON *face out as the curtain falls.*]

HALF FARE

by Shoshana Marchand

CHARACTERS

CLAUDIA, sixteen
EVAN, nineteen to twenty
GEORGE, thirty-seven

A run-down New York City apartment. Lots of lights burning; it is night. Up right, a single bed draped with an Indian-fabric spread. Next to the bed, a wooden chest-of-drawers. On it are a portable radio/tape player, some makeup, scattered papers, etc. Up left, a wall of kitchen appliances, a large and rather expensive liquor supply on top of the refrigerator. Over the sink, a peg-board with neatly hung cooking utensils. Between bed and kitchen is an open doorway covered with another piece of Indian fabric. This door leads offstage to the only other room, a bedroom. At the foot of the bed, that is, down right, is the entrance/exit of the apartment. A few posters, perhaps World War Two propaganda and some late sixties leftist slogans, but the walls are mostly filled with shelves of scholarly books and journals. Over the bed, the decor is noticeably different: an alienated James Dean and a snarling Sid Vicious or some-such. Downstage and left of center, a battered but good-looking wooden table and four matching chairs. The table is covered in half-eaten containers of food. As the lights come up CLAUDIA, *a girl of sixteen, is seated at the table. She wears a button-down shirt, much too large, and underpants. Bare leg propped on the table, she is meditatively licking ice cream off a spoon. After a few beats of silence,* EVAN, *three or four years older, enters from the bedroom. He is buttoning up a pair of army pants, which are all he's got on.*

CLAUDIA: Do you want some ice cream?
EVAN: No. I should go.
CLAUDIA: [*Stretches seductively*] Mmmmnnn.
EVAN: Tired?
CLAUDIA: No, I could stay awake all night. I love staying up all night.

EVAN: Well, I'm tired.
CLAUDIA: Boys always do that. It wakes me up. You know what I mean?
EVAN: Sure.
CLAUDIA: Like, I always want to run outside and play. [*Deliberately crude*] Or do it again.
[*Leans forward and kisses him on the neck*]
EVAN: What time is it?
CLAUDIA: Jesus, it's almost three o'clock.
EVAN: I should go.
CLAUDIA: No, don't, you can stay a little longer.
EVAN: Look, I think we should at least get dressed.
CLAUDIA: Will you stop worrying so much. There's no rush. Have some ice cream.
EVAN: I don't want any.
CLAUDIA: C'mon.
[*Tries to put a spoonful in his mouth*]
EVAN: Stop it! I don't want any. Just give me my shirt, okay?
CLAUDIA: Do you want some olives? You can spit the pits at me.
EVAN: No.
CLAUDIA: Olives [*Strikes a pose, holding jar of olives aloft*] are the fruit of Athena, gray-eyed goddess of wisdom. [*Collapses onto Evan's lap*] Supplicate yourself, mortal.
EVAN: Claudia, c'mon.
CLAUDIA: Abase thyself. [*Snaps fingers in the air*] Waiter! Sackcloth and ashes for this man.
EVAN: [*Joining in a little*] You're getting your religions mixed.
CLAUDIA: Not a word, mortal! On your knees.
EVAN: Oh goddess, gray-eyed goddess . . .
[*He does a very ornate salaam, and is all the way down to the floor when we hear a key in the lock and the door opens.* GEORGE *enters, a thirty-seven-year-old man dressed in jeans, a tucked-in shirt, rather expensive, and an old pair of hiking boots. He pauses at the scene before him, and delicately finishes off the bottle of imported beer he's holding.* EVAN *scrambles up and looks nervously at* CLAUDIA, *who, standing between the two, is paying no attention whatsoever to* EVAN. GEORGE *pockets his keys, and puts up a brave front, larger than life.*]
GEORGE: Claudia, hi.
CLAUDIA: This is Evan, George. George: Evan. Evan: George.

Half Fare

GEORGE: My, we're formal. How are you, Evan.

EVAN: I'm good, how are you?

GEORGE: Fine, just fine. Having a late dinner, I see. Very late dinner. Or is it just an early breakfast?

CLAUDIA: Where were you?

GEORGE: At Liz and Gary's downstairs.

CLAUDIA: All night?

GEORGE: Yes.

CLAUDIA: Was it a party?

GEORGE: Not really. We made Chinese food. You know that huge wok they have? Well, we all kind of danced around it throwing things in. Until Betsy dropped the soy-sauce bottle and it broke. I mean, it broke in the food. In the wok.

CLAUDIA: [*Nodding mockingly*] Oh, yuk.

GEORGE: Yeah. Glass everywhere. So we ordered out from the Szechuan place on ninety-sixth.

EVAN: That's a nice place.

GEORGE: [*Notices Evan*] Overpriced. Anyway...

CLAUDIA: Well, we just stayed here. [*Still sexing it up*]

GEORGE: Ah. Yes.

CLAUDIA: How's Betsy?

GEORGE: She's fine.

CLAUDIA: I haven't seen her in a while, George. [*Catty*] Everything okay with you two?

GEORGE: Fine, fine. Just fine. [*Goes offstage, singing "Bess, you is my woman now," from* Porgy and Bess, *saying "Betsy" instead*]

EVAN: Will you give me my stupid shirt back already?

CLAUDIA: As soon as he clears out of the bedroom.

[*Silence.* GEORGE *back on with a film canister and rolling-paper*]

GEORGE: Anybody have any matches?

EVAN: Yes, here.

GEORGE: Thanks. [*Leans on the wall and rolls a joint as he speaks*] What are you doing tomorrow night, Claude?

CLAUDIA: I don't know. Why?

GEORGE: Well, Betsy's coming over and I'd kind of like to have some time alone with her.

CLAUDIA: Oh. [EVAN *looks at her sharply*.] Well, I'll probably be going out anyway. *Last Tango in Paris* is at the Thalia; maybe I'll go there, I guess. Want to go with me, Evan?

EVAN: Maybe. How about I call you tomorrow?

CLAUDIA: Could I maybe sleep over?
EVAN: [*Looks at* GEORGE] I guess so.
GEORGE: Well then, that's good.
   [*He turns on the radio, passes several stations, listens to a born-again sermon for a moment, then tunes it to Beethoven's "Archduke Trio." Lights the joint, passes it to* EVAN, *who looks confused, but takes some anyway.* EVAN *offers it to* CLAUDIA, *who shakes her head "no," and gets up to brush her hair furiously.* EVAN *gives the joint back to* GEORGE, *who starts conducting Beethoven, joint in hand. This is a long silent scene.*]
CLAUDIA: [*Angrily looking at* GEORGE] Evan, let's go out for a walk.
EVAN: Now?
CLAUDIA: Yeah, let's go for a walk.
EVAN: Well, okay.
CLAUDIA: Here, I'll go give you your shirt back, Evan.
   [*She looks at* GEORGE *for reaction, but he's busy conducting. She goes off to bedroom.*]
EVAN: Ah... Excuse me... We're going for a walk... Is that all right?
GEORGE: What? Oh, fine. [*Back to conducting. Yells to Claudia*] Oh, Claudia...
CLAUDIA: [*Offstage*] What?
GEORGE: I want to speak to you before you go out.
CLAUDIA: [*Still offstage*] About what?
GEORGE: Just come out for a minute, please.
   [CLAUDIA *comes on, wearing a pullover sweater and zipping up a pair of black pants.*]
CLAUDIA: Evan, here's your shirt back. George, what is it?
GEORGE: I just want to talk to you.
EVAN: My shoes are in the—ah—in there.
   [EVAN *goes off to bedroom. Silence.* GEORGE *looks at* CLAUDIA; *she looks anywhere but at him. Straightens sleeves of her sweater, sits on floor to pull on her shoes, anything*]
GEORGE: Claude, you want to stay here with me?
CLAUDIA: I'm going for a walk. You heard me.
GEORGE: Why don't you stay here?
CLAUDIA: No thanks.
GEORGE: We could talk. The night is young, right?
CLAUDIA: Sorry, George.
GEORGE: C'mon, Claudia. I never see you anymore.

CLAUDIA: You're too busy making Egg Foo Glass. Can I help it? Just one long party, kid.

GEORGE: [*Gets up; turns off radio*] I'm serious. I don't feel like we're connecting much anymore.

CLAUDIA: Oh really, George?

GEORGE: No, be serious. Talk to me.

CLAUDIA: About what?

GEORGE: The time is fast approaching when I won't have much to say about your life. I just don't want that to come any sooner than it has to. You should tell me things, confide in me. You should— Claudia, stop looking at me like I'm dumb, okay? As a matter of fact, that's the other thing.

CLAUDIA: Oh, there are other things.

GEORGE: Yes there are. I shouldn't always have to ask you to talk to me and—

EVAN: [*Back on, unaware that he's interrupting*] Ready to go, Claudia?

GEORGE: Just a second, Evan. Claudia and I are having a little discussion. Perhaps you could—

CLAUDIA: I'm ready, Evan. Come on. [*Pulling on a jacket, and grabbing her handbag*]

GEORGE: You're not going anywhere, Claudia.

CLAUDIA: Come on, Evan. Let's go.

GEORGE: [*Quietly and fiercely, his voice has a quality that simply demands and expects obedience.*] Claudia, come back here. Claudia, come back here right now. Claudia...
[EVAN *is standing by the door, helpless.* CLAUDIA *turns around, stalks back in, slumps down in a chair and sulks.*]

CLAUDIA: Jesus Christ.

EVAN: Look, I think maybe it's me who should go.

GEORGE: Good idea.

EVAN: Good night, Claudia. [*No answer*] Good night.
[*He exits and there's a sudden stillness.*]

GEORGE: We're going to talk this thing through.

CLAUDIA: I don't believe the heavy-handed father garbage.

GEORGE: I *am* your father.

CLAUDIA: When you feel like it.

GEORGE: Claudia, stop it, cut it out now. [*Pause*] What's wrong?

CLAUDIA: Oh, nothing's wrong, don't worry yourself too much. [*Picks up film-canister; rolls a joint, silence the whole time. She lights it.*]

GEORGE: Put that out.

CLAUDIA: Why?
GEORGE: Because I didn't tell you you could.
CLAUDIA: You just offered me some two-minutes ago.
GEORGE: I don't care. Put it out now.
CLAUDIA: Jesus Christ. You're so damned ridiculous.
[*She stubs out joint in ice cream.*]
GEORGE: Oh, and you're not. Good, now that that's settled. [*Silence*] Claudia, why are you so angry?
CLAUDIA: I'm not.
GEORGE: Yes you are.
CLAUDIA: No, I'm not.
GEORGE: Yes, you are.
CLAUDIA: No.
GEORGE: Well then what?
CLAUDIA: [*Over to bed*] I want you to leave me alone. That's all I want.
GEORGE: You wouldn't like that.
CLAUDIA: How do you know what I'd like. Just leave me alone.
GEORGE: No.
[*Sits next to her*]
CLAUDIA: Well, you have to decide what you're going to be.
GEORGE: What does that mean?
CLAUDIA: [*Moves over, away from him, and leans on the wall*] Do I have to simplify everything. Listen, either you leave me alone, and we just live here, and we both do our own stuff and you don't bug me.
GEORGE: Or else what?
CLAUDIA: Or else you play father all the time.
GEORGE: Claudia, it's not a matter of playing father. I *am* your father.
CLAUDIA: Then leave me alone, or else really do the number.
GEORGE: Would you stop putting me in such neat little packages.
CLAUDIA: Well, I can't stand this not knowing.
GEORGE: Maybe you have to.
CLAUDIA: Why? Just because you don't know what you are?
GEORGE: That's not how it is.
CLAUDIA: Not for you, you mean.
GEORGE: No, for everybody. People are just not neat little packages. The world is not a neat little package. It just isn't.
CLAUDIA: Don't give me people and the world.

Half Fare

GEORGE: [*As if she hadn't spoken*] And the world is not my fault.

CLAUDIA: I need to know how to act. You don't give me any clues at all— You can't switch back and forth all the time. You're always making me guess everything. It's not fair.

GEORGE: You can't always know what's going to happen.

CLAUDIA: You live with nothing constant, with nothing! But I won't live like that.

GEORGE: It's my life.

CLAUDIA: Life! You call this life? Look around, George. This place is a rat-hole. You don't make any money. That's one thing you've really fucked up. You haven't had a serious girl friend since my mother—let's face it, Betsy is a joke! And you're one hell of a lousy father. So that's the three most important things—work, love, and children, and you've blown them all. But, hey, who's counting, right? Not you, uh-uh, not George, the middle-aged adolescent, the thirty-seven-year-old burnout failure, the... Well, it's true, isn't it? Isn't it?

GEORGE: Betsy is not a joke. She is a perfectly nice woman and I like her just fine, thank you. I don't need your advice on how to conduct my love-life. As to your intelligently stated observation that I don't make much money, that is the direct result of a choice I made on how I wanted to live my life. I'm sorry if I'm not living up to your ideal of a father, but I think you've got one hell of a nerve complaining. You're just wrong about me. And I might add you're being a wee bit nasty. It hurts, you know?

CLAUDIA: Don't try to put that one over on me, daddykins. You're not hitting me with that old guilt number. I get enough of that from my mother. I'm not taking it in stereo. Forget it.

GEORGE: Don't bring your mother into this. This has nothing to do with her. You just leave her out.

CLAUDIA: [*Sprawls on her back on bed. In sobs*] Nothing to do with this! How can she have nothing to do with this? It's all I get from you guys. I wish both of you would damn well get your own lives together because I'm not doing it for you.

GEORGE: [*Looks at her, and hesitates. Then slowly, sincerely; he's genuinely moved by her.*] I have not been the epitome of responsibility. But, Claudia, plum, you are one hell of a challenge. I have problems dealing with you. I admit it. I'm the first to admit it. [*Gets a drink, scotch, straight-up, and holds on to bottle as he speaks*] I get scared. Think about it. How do I handle this child—no, this woman, almost—who is suddenly just here? You grew up, and I never got to watch. [*Sits on bed, pulls her feet onto his lap. Intensely*] How do I do it? Tell me. [*Pause*] Face it, there's no formula.

CLAUDIA: Then make one up. Your contribution to the human race.

GEORGE: Claudia, I can't.

CLAUDIA: Can't what?

GEORGE: Can't cooperate in this scheme of yours to make me something I'm not.

CLAUDIA: I'm not asking you to be something you're not. Just someone who has a plan about what to do.

GEORGE: Having a plan does not guarantee it can be followed through. It is an illusion of order.

CLAUDIA: Oh, I am sick of trying to understand you. Just let it go.

GEORGE: [*Intensely, holding on to her feet; facing her*] No, I don't want to.

CLAUDIA: You walk around spouting liberal platitudes, calling your lovers your "women-friends," being oh-so-casual. No plans. No order. Mr. Socially Conscious. Mr. Enlightened Politico. I bet you want me to go join a draft-dodger soybean commune in Canada.

GEORGE: You can't grow soy beans in Canada. It's too cold.

CLAUDIA: [*Sitting up and pulling away*] Consider how your enlightened approach was for me, George. Negotiating visits all the time over the phone. You know, I still can't walk into the Port Authority without feeling alienated. It's one big existential joke. They're rebuilding the place now and I feel like someone's moving the furniture around in my bedroom. I've got a permanent public-transportation complex.

GEORGE: You think I don't feel bad? You think it's easy leaving your kid with an ex-wife you don't even like yourself?

CLAUDIA: At least you had a choice. I didn't get to choose, did I? I could hardly even talk... and you're gone. My first word was probably "ticket please."

GEORGE: I bought you commuter books of half-fare tickets. You

Half Fare

did not have to buy them yourself. And I came out to Connecticut on that damn bus every weekend to pick you up until you were nine.

CLAUDIA: Oh, cute, cute, a nine-year-old commuter. Why didn't you just get me a big sign saying "Half Fare" to wear around my neck and an attaché case to put my underwear, toothbrush and homework in?

GEORGE: What did you want me to do, have a custody fight over you? I was trying, Claudia. After years of being what my parents or your mother or some asshole professor wanted me to be, I was finally on my own. I had never had any time before—the city and living alone—I was twenty-three years old, I had a two-year-old child, and I had never spent more than a couple of days on my own! Do you realize what that means?

CLAUDIA: *Yes, I do.* But how am I supposed to get my life together if you haven't even done it yet? All I see around me is messed-up people who are messing up *my* life.

GEORGE: Nobody is messing up your life but you. You're perfectly old enough to mess it up all by yourself.

CLAUDIA: You've been working on it since I was born.

GEORGE: [*Intensely*] That's not true! If there's anything I ever tried to do it's give you a good life. Not just materially. I bought you good books, tried to draw you into discussions with my friends, even when you were tiny, I—

CLAUDIA: Your friends—your friends are as screwed up as you are—cracking rotten jokes, talking politics oh-so-seriously. And not any of you ever really doing anything.

GEORGE: [*Goes to fridge; gets a carrot; eats it as he speaks*] Where do you get off telling me what to do? Who do you think you are? I'm doing just fine as I am. I do just what I want to do. I like my life the way it is. I have no desire to make any changes [*Mouth full*] and as a matter of fact I particularly dislike them. What do you want from me?

CLAUDIA: I want you to make some real decisions.

GEORGE: I do! I make too many decisions every minute of my fucking life.

CLAUDIA: [*Takes his carrot and chomps*] What about me? How about me? You ever make any decisions about anyone besides yourself, George? No. Except maybe whether I should take the 4:50 or the 5:20 from my mother's house.

GEORGE: You really think that would make a difference?

CLAUDIA: You don't understand. There are no rules given to us. We have to start from nothing.

GEORGE: But if you set given rules, you exclude possibilities. You close off options.

CLAUDIA: [*Crusading*] But wouldn't it be just as good to pick one given thing to do... and take it somewhere. It doesn't matter how absurd your choice is, if you have it as a given, you can *do* something.

GEORGE: Claudia, I don't want your "givens"! I don't need your "givens." Now would you get off my back and leave my personal life alone!

CLAUDIA: Oh, great, great, I have nothing to do with you and I suppose you don't care what I do either, huh? I could just walk out of here and you wouldn't stop me, would you? That's really great, just what I need. Some father.

GEORGE: You want to hear what I think of what you do? All right. Here's what I think of what you do. I do not like to walk in here at three o'clock in the fucking morning and find my daughter half-naked with some stud I've never even met before!

CLAUDIA: What should I do, ask you to spend the night out the way you ask me? *I* have a little more class than that. *I* would never do that to anybody.

GEORGE: What was he doing here undressed? Why does he have to be sitting in my kitchen when it's almost light out?

CLAUDIA: It's my kitchen too.

GEORGE: I don't care whose kitchen it is, you may not have boys here till all hours of the morning.

CLAUDIA: Where else am I supposed to go?

GEORGE: [*Pause*] Where *did* you go?

CLAUDIA: [*Slowly and cruelly*] I was on your bed.

GEORGE: You were on my bed! I don't even get to be on my bed half the time because I'm so busy trying not to hurt your feelings!

CLAUDIA: I figure your room is better than just my stupid bed. [*Gestures at twin bed on set*] At least that way you can't literally walk in on me.

GEORGE: This is a thoroughly disgusting conversation.

CLAUDIA: Good. Then let's drop it.

[GEORGE *gets up, goes to the refrigerator, looks aimlessly, but doesn't find anything.* CLAUDIA *breathes deeply, does some kind of balletic or yoga-ish stretch and starts cleaning*

Half Fare

up the table, or really just nervously moving things around.]
GEORGE: [*Turns around, pauses*] You all right?
CLAUDIA: Hunky dory.
GEORGE: [*Another beat*] So, how long have you known Evan?
CLAUDIA: A couple weeks.
GEORGE: You like him?
CLAUDIA: [*Evasive*] I don't know.
GEORGE: Where do you know him from?
CLAUDIA: I met him at a friend's house last week.
GEORGE: [*Softly; he means it*] Claudia, did he treat you badly? He was acting rather strangely when I came in.
CLAUDIA: [*Still looks down*] No, it's not his fault.
GEORGE: What isn't?
CLAUDIA: Oh, I'm just stupid, I wreck everything.
GEORGE: [*He pulls her onto his lap, perhaps playing with her hair*] Well, what did you expect? You're much too young to make love to someone you don't know and expect to feel happy about it.
CLAUDIA: [*Pulls away, hard and fast*] Not right or wrong. Just too young. Is that all?
GEORGE: Look—if you know this is wrong for you then why do you go and do it?
[*For the remainder,* CLAUDIA *must be played with defensive energy; no whining*]
CLAUDIA: I just thought it would make you—I don't know.
GEORGE: What does this have to do with me? This is your sex life.
CLAUDIA: George, everything has to do with you.
GEORGE: What?
CLAUDIA: I don't know.
[*Tries to get away, but he pulls her back strongly. She's still tensed.*]
GEORGE: Yes you do. Now what?
CLAUDIA: Evan wanted to go for a while before you came home.
GEORGE: So why didn't he?
CLAUDIA: I kept teasing him and not letting go and—
GEORGE: Why? You wanted him to stay? If you'd told me, we could have worked it out.
CLAUDIA: No, not that. I kept thinking you'd be home soon and I wanted you to know he was here.
GEORGE: What are you saying?
CLAUDIA: [*In sobs, but no whining*] I didn't want to work it

out! I wanted you to catch me here with him. What do I have to do? What if I get pregnant? Are you going to hand me the abortion money and tell me to take the subway home? What if I'm with *two* naked men next time you walk in? What if one of them is seventy-three years old? What if I'm making it with a goddamned thoroughbred horse? What are you going to do, George? George, you have to do something.

GEORGE: Just calm down a minute so we can discuss this like rational people.

CLAUDIA: George, I told you everything. Now you know what's wrong, you can change it. You can stop me. You can be my father, George.

GEORGE: You're repeating yourself.

CLAUDIA: Please, George, you're supposed to fix it and make it better, you can do that now. I'll listen, I promise. George.

GEORGE: Claudia, I'm tired. You're tired. You're overwrought. Go to bed.

CLAUDIA: What are you? What kind of father are you, what kind of man are you? What kind of person? George, you're not, you're nothing.

GEORGE: I am thirty-seven years old, and I am quite happy with my personal life. Get that? You better get that, once and for all. Whether or not you believe it, I am perfectly happy the way I am. So you can just cut out telling me to change. I'm not interested. Change yourself.

CLAUDIA: No. It's not my job alone. Either you do something or I'll do it. And I can't *do* anything around you, George. I'll leave.

GEORGE: Just calm down for Chrissake.

CLAUDIA: I'll leave, George, I swear I will. You don't want to let me go. I'll leave. George [*Chokes*], do something! Please! [*No response. He stares in disgust and passivity. She sobs, runs to the bureau by the bed, jams clothes in a small backpack, and her sobs quiet down.* GEORGE *does not look at her now. She gets on her knees and reaches under him to grab her shoes from under the table. She gets up slowly and heavily.*]

George, I'm going now. George? [*They stare at each other for a long moment, both sure that neither will go through with it. Then* CLAUDIA *walks quickly and quietly to the door, very controlled. She turns to face him. Very plainly*] George, I love you.

BIOGRAPHIES OF CONTRIBUTING AUTHORS

ADAM L. BERGER *(It's Time for a Change)* wrote his first play at age five. It was cast, produced and performed in his kindergarten classroom. He is now in the fourth grade at the Collegiate School and plans to be a writer, actor, director or producer. Adam lives in New York City with his parents and his brother Douglas. *It's Time for a Change* was written when he was eight years old.

JULIET GARSON *(So What Are We Gonna Do Now?)* was born in San Francisco and grew up in New York City. She attends the High School of Music and Art. Juliet wishes to become a television newscaster. *So What Are We Gonna Do Now?*, her first play, was written when she was thirteen.

STEPHEN GUTWILLIG *(In the Way)* graduated from the Collegiate School and is now at Harvard University. A native New Yorker, Stephen has acted since the third grade and was an apprentice for two summers at the Hampton Playhouse Theatre Arts Workshop in Hampton, New Hampshire. *In the Way*, Stephen's first play, was written when he was seventeen.

JENNIFER A. LITT *(Epiphany)* was born in New Jersey and grew up in Cleveland, Ohio. She is now a freshman at Harvard. *Epiphany* was conceived in 1978, when Jennifer was fourteen, and completed in 1980. It won honorable mention in the 1981 Marilyn Bianchi Kids' Playwriting Festival.

KENNETH LONERGAN *(The Rennings Children)* has been a writer since the age of nine when he wrote his first science-fiction story. He turned to playwriting in the ninth grade and has since written six plays. A native New Yorker, Kenneth attended the Walden School and will continue his college education at New York University this fall. *The Rennings Children* was written when Kenneth was eighteen.

SHOSHANA MARCHAND *(Half Fare)* moved to New York from New Jersey in the eleventh grade and finished high school at St. Ann's in Brooklyn. She is presently a sophomore at Yale. *Half Fare* was written when she was sixteen and seventeen.

JOHN McNAMARA *(Present Tense)* began writing at thirteen. He started a theatre-production company in his hometown of Grand Rapids, Michigan, and produced three of his own works. *Present Tense* was written at the University of Michigan when he was eighteen. There he studied playwriting under Milan Stitt and Steve Reynolds before transferring to New York University where he is currently a junior. Last fall he wrote a one-hour daytime special for CBS.

PETER MURPHY *(Bluffing)* was born in Columbus, Ohio, attended public schools in Massachusetts and Connecticut, and is now a freshman at Columbia University. He has been sports reporter for his local newspaper, editor-in-chief of his high school paper, and a member of the varsity track and soccer teams. An avid poker-player and film-buff, Peter based *Bluffing* on real people with whom he regularly played poker. He wrote the play when he was sixteen.

LYNNETTE M. SERRANO *(The Bronx Zoo)* began writing poetry at the age of eight and had an unpublished book of poems by the time she was ten. Upon graduation from a Catholic high school, she was asked to join the Puerto Rican Traveling Theatre's playwriting division, making her the group's youngest playwright. She is currently writing a play for Periwinkle Productions in Monticello, New York. Lynnette lives with her parents and her older sister in the South Bronx. *The Bronx Zoo* was written when she was seventeen years old.

ANNE PIERSON WIESE *(Coleman, S.D.)* was born in the Midwest, but has lived in New York City for seventeen of her eighteen years. She attended St. Ann's School in Brooklyn Heights for twelve years and is presently a sophomore at Am-